THE UNIX™
SYSTEM V
ENVIRONMENT

INTERNATIONAL COMPUTER SCIENCE SERIES

Consulting editors   **A D McGettrick**   University of Strathclyde
                        J van Leeuwen   University of Utrecht

OTHER TITLES IN THE SERIES

UNIX^{TM} is a trademark of AT & T Bell Laboratories.

THE UNIX™ SYSTEM V ENVIRONMENT

Stephen R. Bourne

(formerly at Bell Telephone Laboratories)

ADDISON-WESLEY
PUBLISHING
COMPANY

Wokingham, England · Reading, Massachusetts · Menlo Park, California
Don Mills, Ontario · Amsterdam · Sydney · Singapore · Tokyo
Madrid · Bogota · Santiago · San Juan

This book was set by the author in Times Roman and Helvetica on a Linotronic 300 phototypesetter using output generated by the troff text-processing system.

Cover illustration by Marshall Henrichs.

Library of Congress Cataloging in Publication Data

Bourne, S.R., 1944–
 The UNIX system V environment.

 (International computer science series)
 Bibliography: p.
 Includes index.
 1. UNIX (Computer operating system) 2. C(Computer program language) I. Title. II. Series.
 QA76.76.063B68 1987   005.4'46   85–28642
 ISBN 0–201–18484–2 (pbk.)

British Library Cataloguing in Publication Data

Bourne, S.R.
 The UNIX system V environment.—(International computer science series)
 1. UNIX (Computer operating system)
 I. Title   II. Series
 005.4'3   QA76.76.063

 ISBN 0–201–18484–2

ABCDEFGHIJKLM8932109876

To Jane, Peter, Mark, and Sarah

Preface

This book is a practical guide to UNIX System V and all users from the novice to the expert should find it useful. Many examples are used throughout the text to illustrate techniques that make the system attractive to use. By giving examples of the interactions between commands, the user is able to take full advantage of the power of the UNIX system.

The introduction reviews the historical background that led to early UNIX systems and presents the components of UNIX systems, including files and processes. The body of the book covers the major elements of the UNIX system including file management, process management, system calls, the editor, the shell, C language, troff and nroff, and the data management tools.

Chapter 2 introduces the user to the system along with some commonly used commands. The logging in procedure is explained and the available documentation is described. The two major topics introduced are the shell and the file system. All later chapters assume that this chapter has been read.

Two editors are introduced in chapter 3, ed and vi. Both programs are intended for use at a terminal and are used to create and modify files. During chapters 2 and 3 it is a good idea to have a terminal close by and to try some of the commands. If you cannot make progress ask a colleague for help. This is often the quickest way to learn how to use a system.

The shell provides the interface to the UNIX system both for interactive users and for scripts used to tailor the environment for an individual or project. Interactive use of the shell is first introduced in chapter 2. Writing shell scripts, or programs, is covered in depth in chapter 4.

The C language is introduced in chapter 5 in sufficient detail to allow reasonably sized programs to be written. Familiarity with another programming language is an advantage when reading this chapter. Managing the source for programs using make and debugging using adb are also covered here.

The next chapter describes the UNIX system interface as seen by C programmers. The emphasis is on writing programs that use the facilities provided directly by the operating system. This chapter is intended for users who write commands in C. The more advanced aspects of the file system, not described in chapter 2, are also presented.

One of the major uses of the UNIX system is text processing and document preparation. The set of programs nroff, troff, eqn, and tbl is described in chapter 7 and, together with the text editor, allow documents to be drafted and corrected with considerable ease. The tools and methods used to produce this book are described along with a description of the formatting package used for this book.

The last chapter covers the data processing 'toolkit' consisting of programs such as awk, grep, sort, and join that provide a flexible way to manage small data bases or manipulate small quantities of data. Examples are presented of complete systems built from these parts. Each example is described in detail and the construction of new tools, not provided with the standard UNIX system, is also presented. The material from all the earlier chapters is required when reading chapter 8.

The appendices summarize the various commands used throughout the book. Not all commands or system calls released with System V have been covered in this text. The subset described here is common to other UNIX system variants, including the Seventh Edition system and the University of California, Berkeley 4.2 BSD system. Commands and system calls only available to the super-user have also been omitted.

This book covers many aspects of the UNIX system from the user's point of view. It assumes that the reader is familiar with modern computing terminology.

Acknowledgements

Many people have contributed to this book.

Peter Bourne prepared the text for publication, making sure that the examples worked on System V and ensuring consistency and accuracy of the text. Carolyn Wilson did the pagination and the final editing needed for the production of the camera ready text. I am grateful to them both for the energy they put into the production and for the quality of the resulting product.

I would like to thank Jeff Schriebman and his staff at UNISOFT for their assistance in understanding System V. The programs in this book were run on UNISOFT System V Release 2.

The production system used for this book consisted of an Apple LaserWriter running PostScript from Adobe Systems Incorporated and the final production runs used a Linotronic 300 also running Adobe software. I am grateful to Adobe Systems for the use of their facilities and to Andy Shore for his help tuning their implementation of the ditroff to PostScript translator.

Peter Frank at the Wokingham office of Addison-Wesley did an excellent job of proof reading the text. Marc Compton reviewed the introductory chapters and provided valuable detailed comments to improve their readability.

I would also like to thank Bob Morris, Dennis Ritchie and many other former colleagues in the AT&T Bell Laboratories Computing Science Research Center for many discussions on the finer points of the UNIX system. I am grateful to AT&T Bell Laboratories for permission to quote much of the material in the appendices.

Contents

Chapter 1 **Introduction**

UNIX describes a family of computer operating systems developed at AT&T Bell Laboratories. The UNIX system includes both the operating system and its associated commands. The operating system manages the resources of the computing environment by providing a hierarchical file system, process management and other housekeeping functions. The commands provided include basic file and data management, editors, assemblers, compilers and text formatters. A powerful command interpreter is available that allows individual users or projects to tailor the environment to suit their own style by defining their own commands.

The background leading up to the first UNIX system is worth exploring. During the sixties the major issues being addressed by the computing science community included programming language and operating system design. In the former area such languages as PL/I, APL, SIMULA 67, ALGOL 68 and COBOL were designed and were the subject of debate, often fierce, over their relative merits. In the United Kingdom the Combined Programming Language project (CPL) was undertaken jointly by London and Cambridge Universities but failed to produce any direct results. However, it did form the basis for BCPL (Basic CPL), an ingredient of the UNIX system story.

The operating systems of this period were designed for medium and large scale computers as a means of sharing the resources among users in a cost effective way. Time-sharing and interactive (as opposed to batch) use was introduced. Such questions as paging strategies, protection, activity scheduling and file system design were explored. Systems like CTSS (Crisman, 1965), Multics (Feiertag, 1969) and, in Europe, the Cambridge Multiple Access System (Hartley, 1968) were being designed and provided many of the key ideas found in the UNIX system. For example, file systems and device independent input-output, processes and command languages were all available in one form or another in these systems.

1.1 History

The story begins with Ken Thompson in 1968. Thompson had recently returned from Berkeley where Butler Lampson was working on the SDS930 operating system (Deutsch and Lampson, 1965). Dennis Ritchie joined Bell Laboratories in 1967 from Harvard where his interest was applied mathematics.

Thompson shared space with a talented group many of whom had recently abandoned Multics; a joint project between Bell Laboratories, General Electric, and The Massachusetts Institute of Technology. Following the withdrawal of Bell Laboratories from Multics and the removal of the GE 645 system in March 1969, the computer science research group began looking for a replacement computing environment. Proposals for new equipment were submitted and rejected as too expensive. Also, operating system development was not a popular research direction after the Multics debacle.

Thompson's own interests were to build a file system rather than an operating system. During discussions between Rudd Canaday, Thompson and Ritchie the design was sketched out and Thompson wrote simulations of early versions of this file system on the GECOS system.

Another thread of the story is the 'space travel' program written on the GECOS machine by Thompson and Ritchie. This program performed poorly on the time-shared computer and better response was needed. A cast-off PDP 7 with a 340 display was available but the PDP 7 provided only an assembler and link editor. One user at a time could use the computer, each user having exclusive use of the machine. This environment was crude and parts of a single user UNIX system were soon forthcoming. The space travel program was rewritten for the PDP 7 and an assembler and rudimentary operating system kernel were written and cross assembled for the PDP 7 on the GECOS system. This early system did not provide time-sharing. Indeed, much like the modern personal computers, the PDP 7 hardware was simple and provided no support for such activities. An assembler and a command interpreter were soon available. This file system provided a name structure that was a directed graph. A single directory was used for all subdirectories and links made through this directory.

Cross assembling meant using two computer systems and carrying paper tapes of programs from one to the other each time a change was made. The system was soon bootstrapped onto the PDP 7. The process creation primitive, fork, and process images were added to the system during this rewrite. Essential utilities, such as file copy, edit, remove, and print were soon available. This system supported two people working at the same time and the term UNIX was coined by Brian Kernighan in 1970.

The computing research group still had no computer of its own. Following a series of unsuccessful attempts a proposal was made by Joe Ossanna to purchase a PDP 11/20 for a text preparation project. In late 1970 the PDP 11 arrived and work started to transfer the UNIX system to this more powerful machine.

The text processing project was successful and the Patent department became the first user of UNIX, sharing the facility with the research group. This First Edition system was documented in a manual authored by Thompson and Ritchie dated November 1971. All the important ideas found in modern UNIX systems except pipes, but including the file system, process management, system interface, and major command utilities, were provided with this edition.

The Second Edition appeared in June 1972 incorporating pipes at Doug McIlroy's urging. The system and utilities were still written in assembler. Thompson had also been working on the language B and the assembler for this system was written in B. B was a direct descendant of BCPL, but programs were compiled in one pass to produce interpretive code.

Both B and BCPL were typeless languages, providing a single data object called the machine word making access to the PDP 11 byte handling instructions difficult. Types were therefore added to B to produce NB and an attempt to rewrite the system in NB was unsuccessful. Ritchie started work on a code generator for NB to make execution of programs faster. This language was called C (Kernighan and Ritchie, 1978) although there were no structures or global variables. The language was sufficiently attractive, however, that new utilities were being written directly in C.

The year 1973 saw major progress. The system was still written in assembler but following the addition of structures to C the UNIX system was successfully rewritten in C. Thompson wrote the process management and Ritchie the input-output system.

The Sixth Edition UNIX system that became the first widely available version was issued in May 1975, and was distributed for a nominal fee.

Work continued to improve the system. A new file system allowing for larger files was written and the shell was modernized to provide better support for the many programs written in this language. This shell is the one described in this book and was designed and written during late 1975 and early 1976.

During 1977 Thompson and Ritchie began rewriting the system so that it could be transported from one computer to another. The pilot project used an Interdata 8/32, a 32-bit computer similar to the IBM 370 series, that was sufficiently different from the PDP 11 to unearth most machine dependencies. This project also generated some additions to the C language, including unions, casts, and type definitions. This work resulted in the production of the Seventh Edition UNIX system released for general use in 1979. Although the Seventh Edition is still in use in some installations it has been generally superseded by either UNIX System V or 4.2 BSD from U. C. Berkeley.

The UNIX system is now regarded as a standard operating system and has been implemented on many different computers ranging from micros to main-frames. The Seventh Edition system was made available for the PDP 11 16-bit computers. The first VAX 11/780 system, UNIX 32V, was bootstrapped by John Reiser and Tom London, also at Bell Laboratories. This system was further developed under a DARPA contract, and is now distributed by the University of California at Berkeley. AT&T has also continued to develop the UNIX system; UNIX System V Release 2 is the version currently available for license from AT&T.

Some differences exist between these versions both in the operating system and in the commands although these should cause the reader little difficulty. This text is applicable to each of these systems and features found in only one system have been avoided. The programs in this book have been compiled and run on UNIX System V from AT&T, and on the University of California, Berkeley Release 4.1.

Many commands were initially written for the PDP 11 where address space was limited to 64K bytes. This constraint had a generally beneficial effect on the software. Systems are designed as a set of loosely coupled commands. Lack of address space did prevent such languages as LISP from effective implementation until the arrival of 32-bit machines.

The UNIX system is well engineered and has set a standard of simplicity for

time-shared operating systems. It was one of the first operating systems to be
widely available on a mini-computer, namely the PDP 11. This combination was
affordable by university departments and a generation of computer scientists has
been educated on UNIX systems.

The initial interface has aged well and is essentially unchanged since its original design. This stability provided the basis for the development of the user level
commands. The UNIX documentation has a conciseness that is appealing although
some consider it to be too brief.

The UNIX system is very successful. At the time of writing there are over
3000 UNIX systems in active use throughout the world. These can be found in
universities, government laboratories, commercial organizations and many other
areas of industry. At Bell Laboratories it is used by staff members both for interactive program development and as a communications and word processing system.
The system is portable, easily grasped by both users and maintainers, and provides
facilities not available in other, sometimes larger, systems.

1.2 The programming environment

The UNIX system is simple and elegant and provides an attractive programming
environment. The facilities available include the following:

- a C compiler and debugger;
- a variety of other language processors, including APL, Basic, Fortran 77,
  Pascal, and Snobol;
- the text editors ed, vi, and emacs;
- text processing facilities and document preparation aids including
  mathematical typesetting tbl, eqn, troff, and nroff;
- compiler construction aids yacc, and lex;
- communication among users mail, and write;
- graphics and plotting; and
- applications such as circuit design packages.

These tools are made available to users via a command language that provides
the interface between users and the UNIX operating system. This program is
called the *shell* and programs written in this language are sometimes referred to as
shell scripts.

The shell provides notation for directing input and output from commands and
control flow mechanisms typical of algorithmic languages.

Techniques for effective program development have emerged in this environment and include the following:

- Arrange each program to perform a single function.
- Avoid cluttering the output of a program unnecessarily. Assume that the
  output from any program will be the input to another.
- Use or modify an existing tool if possible rather than rewrite a new tool
  from scratch.
- Get something small working as soon as possible and then modify it incrementally until it is finished. This requires that the framework of the

design should be in place before significant quantities of program are written.

1.3 UNIX system concepts

1.3.1 The file system

A file system allows users to store information by name. Protection from hardware failures can be provided and security from unauthorized access is also available. The UNIX file system is simple; there are no control blocks, devices are hidden, and there is a uniform interface for all input-output. Within the file system three types of file are distinguished.

- An ordinary file contains characters of a document or program. Executable programs (binary files) are also stored as ordinary files. No record structure is imposed on files; a file consists of a sequence of characters. A newline character may delimit records as required by applications.
- A directory holds the names of other files or directories. A user may create sub-directories to group files related to a project. Consequently, the file system is a hierarchy. A directory can be read, but not written, as if it were an ordinary file.
- Special files correspond to input or output devices. The same interface as ordinary files is available; however, information is not kept in the file system, it is provided directly by the device. The same access protection is available for special and ordinary files.

1.3.2 Processes

All user work in the UNIX system is carried out by processes. A process is a single sequence of events and consists of some computer memory and files being accessed. A process is created by a copy of the process being made. The two processes are only distinguished by the parent being able to wait for the child to finish. A process may replace itself by another program to be executed. This mechanism is both elegant and effective.

1.3.3 The shell

The shell is a command language that provides a user interface to the UNIX operating system. The shell executes commands that are read either from a terminal or from a file. Files containing commands may be created, allowing users to build their own commands. These newly defined commands have the same status as 'system' commands. In this way a new environment can be established reflecting the requirements or style of an individual or a group.

The standard input and standard output are used by many commands as the default for reading and writing data. Commands that process data in this way are called filters. Pipes allow such processes to be linked together so that the output from one command is the input to the next. The shell provides a notation enabling pipes to be used with a minimum of effort.

Chapter 2 **Getting Started**

2.1 Logging in

Before you can start using the system you will need a *login-name* from your system administrator. If your system uses dial-up lines you will also need the phone number of your system. In addition to your login-name you will be given a password that protects your login-name from unauthorized use.

The UNIX system supports many different terminal types ranging from simple printers to high resolution graphics terminals. Since terminals differ be sure that all the options are set appropriately. Options to check for include terminal speed, parity (even/odd), full duplex (remote), and upper/lower case; phone connections (via modems) usually operate at 300 or 1200 baud, whereas hardwired connections are more likely to operate at 1200 or 9600 baud. (300 baud is approximately 30 characters per second.)

When you first connect to the system it tries to detect the speed of your line from the first character you type, usually a return. If the computer prints some garbage characters try hitting break briefly; in some systems this signals a change of speed.

Eventually you should see

    login:

and you should now type your login-name followed by a return. Until you type return the system will normally do nothing. login will now ask for your password and, if possible, the terminal printing is turned off while you reply. If your login-name and password do not correspond to those known by the system

    login incorrect

is printed and you will again be prompted for your login-name. Some versions of login have a timeout that hangs up the line if you wait too long to type your password.

If you log in successfully a message may be printed, called the 'message-of-the-day'. This will be followed by a prompt character, usually a $ or % from the shell. You can now start typing commands to the system.

If something goes wrong and you are unable to log in then you should get help from a local expert. There are too many potential problems to enumerate here.

2.2 Commands

A command consists of a sequence of words separated by white space (spaces or tabs). The first (and possibly the only) word is the name of the command. To illustrate,

    date

will respond with output of the form

    Wed Sep 1 12:12:19 EDT 1982

The three letters EDT denote Eastern Daylight Time.
    The command

    who

will produce a list of those users currently logged on, in order of terminal number, e.g.

    srb   tty00   May 5   11:30
    jmg   tty01   May 5   21:22
    lca   tty13   May 5   22:29
    cc   tty29   May 5   16:11
    jack   tty41   May 5   08:39

Your own login-name should appear in this list along with the time you logged in and your terminal (tty) number. The abbreviation tty is derived from Teletype, a manufacturer of terminals.
    When more than one word appears in a command the second and subsequent words are available as *arguments* to the executed command. For example, to change your password after you are logged on, type

    passwd srb

replacing srb by your own login-name. The passwd command will then prompt as follows:

    Old password:
    New password:
    Retype new password:

Following each prompt terminal printing is turned off.
    A password of at least six characters is recommended; some systems enforce this minimum but the practice should be observed to make password detection more difficult. Choosing a password that consists of a word with one letter replaced by a digit will make it hard for anyone to find out what your password is. For example,

    elc8mino

    Another example of a command with arguments is the calendar printing command. cal prints a calendar for a particular year or month. With one argument cal prints the calendar for the entire year specified by the argument. The calendar for a particular month is printed by giving the month and year as arguments. For example, cal 2000 prints a calendar for the year 2000 and cal 9 1982 prints

```
        September 1982
  S   M  Tu   W   Th   F   S
                1    2   3   4
  5   6   7   8    9  10  11
 12  13  14  15   16  17  18
 19  20  21  22   23  24  25
 26  27  28  29   30
```

2.3 Terminal characteristics

Mistakes made while typing at the terminal may be corrected by *erasing* characters or by *killing* (deleting) a whole line and retyping. To erase a character a # is used. For example,

```
passq#wd
```

is equivalent to

```
passwd
```

To kill (or delete) a line, @ is used and the system will respond by printing a new-line. These two characters (erase and kill) can be redefined by the user. Early UNIX systems used # and @ for character and line delete respectively and these are still the default; however, for video terminals backspace is a convenient erase character.

Terminals that use the ASCII character code use the character return on input to end a line. On output this character is printed as a return followed by a linefeed and this combination is often referred to as newline.

Terminal options are described to the system using the stty (set tty) command. These options can be expected to differ from terminal to terminal and may be altered by an individual user. For example,

```
stty erase ~
```

alters the erase character to ~, so that, typing

```
whx~o
```

is equivalent to who.

If the erase and kill characters, # or @, are needed as input, a \ is used as an escape character to prevent their interpretation as erase and kill. Then \# is equivalent to # and \@ is equivalent to @.

When a program loops, or when enough has been seen of the output of a program, it may be necessary to interrupt the activity. The del character or a break generates an interrupt signal for this purpose. Normally del and break cause the shell and other interactive programs to resume at the command level with a prompt. The character that generates the interrupt can be altered using the stty command; however, break is a signal transmitted on the serial line, and cannot, therefore, be changed.

Some terminals have a tab mechanism available that may need to be set when the terminal is switched on. The tabs command may be used to set the tabs for output on your terminal. Some older terminals do not interpret tabs on output and some have no tab key for input. On terminals that do not possess a tab key, the tab character can be entered using control-I. If your terminal does not print tabs correctly the command

stty −tabs

can be used to instruct the system to replace tabs by a suitable number of spaces on output. An 8-space tab is assumed. The stty command (appendix 1) has many other options for describing terminal characteristics.

The notation used in this book for control characters such as control-I is ∧I. Two other characters are available to stop and start the flow of output at a terminal. ∧S will stop the flow of output to the terminal and ∧Q will restart the output. Typing any other character will also restart the flow and the character will be passed on to the program. This way of controlling the flow of output is invisible to the executing program.

2.4 Documentation

A user has access to over 200 different system commands. These do not include commands written by users themselves. Complete descriptions of the system commands are available from the *UNIX Programmer's Manual*. Appendix 1 also contains summaries of the more frequently used commands.

CAL(1)   UNIX Programmer's Manual   CAL(1)

NAME
       cal − print calendar

SYNOPSIS
       cal [month] year

DESCRIPTION
       cal prints a calendar for the specified year. If a month is also specified, a calendar just for that month is printed. *year* can be between 1 and 9999. The *month* is a number between 1 and 12. The calendar produced is that for England and her colonies.
       Try September 1752.

BUGS   The year is always considered to start in January even though this is historically naive. Beware that 'cal 78' refers to the early Christian era, not the 20th century.

Figure 2.1 The output from man cal

The documentation is also available on-line using the man command that, given a command name, prints sections of the user manual. For example,

    man cal

will print the manual page for the cal command as shown in figure 2.1.

References to other commands take the form

    command-name (section)

For example, a reference to the stty command would appear as stty (1).

A standard format is used for each of the manual entries; there are at least three sections:

NAME   Gives the name of the command and a short description of its effect.

SYNOPSIS

> This section summarizes the use of the command. Words appearing in bold are literal and are typed as they appear. Other words denote arguments to the command as described in the DESCRIPTION section. An argument beginning with a minus sign often indicates an option applicable to the command. Square brackets indicate arguments that may be omitted. Ellipses (...) indicate the possible repetition of the previous argument. For example,
>
> **stty** [option ...]
>
> is the SYNOPSIS for the stty command; the command name is stty and one or more options may follow.

DESCRIPTION

> Describes the effect of the command and how its arguments are interpreted.

Other sections may also be present. A FILES section indicates files used by the command; a SEE ALSO section refers to related commands; a DIAGNOSTICS section discusses diagnostic information that may be produced; finally, a BUGS section lists known bugs and design errors in the command.

The manual is divided into six major sections. The breakdown for each section is given below:

1   Commands available to users.
2   UNIX/C system call interface.
3   C library routines, including the standard input-output package, stdio, and the mathematical function library.
4   File formats.
5   Miscellaneous facilities.
6   Games.

Appendix 1 contains a brief description of the commands in this book and the Bibliography lists related documents.

2.5 The file system

The file system provides a hierarchical naming structure. Each directory contains
the names of files or further directories. There is no formatting of the file contents;
each file consists simply of a sequence of characters. It is convenient to establish
conventions for formatting files but this is left to individual programs. The UNIX
system knows about the file format used by executable programs (a.out files).

   A complete file name or *pathname* is written as a sequence of component
names separated by /. The pathname

   /usr/srb/mbox

starts with the directory / called the *root* that contains usr. The directory /usr contains the directory srb and within this directory is the file mbox. In this example
there are three directories: /, /usr, and /usr/srb, each of which, except /, is contained
in its predecessor or *parent* directory. Each / separated component of a name is
limited to 14 characters. Component names may not include / and should not start
with characters such as − since this can lead to confusion between command options and file names.

/	− usr	− srb	− ucds	− ...
			− mbox	
		− include	− ...	
		− src	− ...	
		− bin		
		− lib		
		− ...		
	− bin	− cat		
		− date		
		− ...		
	− etc	− passwd		
		− group		
		− motd		
		− ...		
	− lib	− c0		
		− libc.a		
		− ...		
	− dev	− tty		
		− null		
		− ...		

Figure 2.2 Part of the directory hierarchy

Directories are used to group together files related by ownership or by the purpose
for which they are to be used.

   Initially, each user will have a *home* directory created by the system administrator; user rhm will typically have a directory such as /usr/rhm.

Each logged in user has a *working* directory. The command

   pwd

will print the complete pathname of the current (or working) directory. Immediately after logging in, the working directory is the user's home directory. (See also $HOME in the shell.)

To specify a new working directory the cd command (for change directory) is used. File names may be specified relative to the working directory. For example, after executing

   cd /usr/srb/unix

the current directory will be /usr/srb/unix and the file /usr/srb/unix/ch1 can be referred to as ch1.

A user may create further sub-directories to hold files related to different projects as illustrated in figure 2.2. The directory /usr contains system and user directories. /etc contains control files including the password file. /bin contains executable system commands and /lib contains essential libraries including the C compiler and library.

2.5.1 Simple file manipulation

The cat (catenate) command is one of the primitive file copying commands and copies a list of files to its standard output. The standard output is, initially, attached to the terminal although this may be changed (see below). cat is normally used to print a file at the terminal, as in,

   cat /etc/motd

that prints the file /etc/motd. (This file contains the message-of-the-day printed by login.) If no file names are given as arguments then cat reads input from the standard input. By default the standard input is also connected to the terminal.

The cat command may be used to create files by typing the contents from the terminal. For example,

   cat >newfile
   text of file
   ^D

creates the file newfile. Input is terminated by an end-of-file indication from the terminal, signaled by return followed by ^D (control-D).

This technique is of limited value. When a typing error is made only the erase and kill characters can be used. It is more convenient to use a text editor to create a file and then mistakes can be corrected as they are made. Editing files is discussed in chapter 3.

To copy the contents of one file to another the copy command, cp, is usually used. The form of use of cp is

   cp from to

where both the file names from and to are required. The two commands

    cat file

and

    cp file /dev/tty

are equivalent, since /dev/tty is the file name corresponding to the terminal.

If necessary cp and cat create files. Files can also be renamed and removed. The rm command completely removes both a file name and its contents. For example,

    rm junk

will remove the file named junk in the current directory. If a file is removed by mistake it can sometimes be recovered by a system administrator.

The mv command moves (or renames) a file. To illustrate,

    mv oldname newname

renames the file oldname as newname. The name of the file is changed, but the contents are unaltered. If the destination file, newname, exists then it is replaced by mv. If the file cannot be written the user is prompted to verify that the file should be removed. If the response is a y then the file is removed. Both rm and mv should be used carefully since they may destroy information.

2.5.2 Manipulating directories

Files can be created, deleted, or renamed. The same operations can be applied to directories. However, for directories these operations are privileged and can be performed only using the commands:

    mkdir   Create (or make) a directory.
    rmdir   Remove an empty directory.
    mv   Rename a directory.

If the current directory is /usr/mdm,

    mkdir tmg

creates the directory /usr/mdm/tmg and

    rmdir tmg

removes it. rmdir only removes empty directories that are not in use as a current directory.

When a directory is created two standard entries . and .. are automatically created as a convenience. The name . is synonymous with the directory itself and the name .. refers to the immediate parent directory. The file names ./mbox and mbox are therefore equivalent. If /usr/mdm/tmg is the current directory,

```
cd ..
```

will return to the parent directory, /usr/mdm, as the new current directory.

Files may be moved or copied as a group into a directory using the mv or cp command. Both

```
mv file₁ file₂ ... directory
```

and

```
cp file₁ file₂ ... directory
```

achieve this effect, the files having their original names in the new directory. The first moves or renames; the latter copies, leaving the original files unchanged.

When moving or copying files to a directory, particular care should be taken to ensure that the destination is a directory since the mv command also removes files. For example,

```
mv x d
mv y d
mv z d
```

will rename the files x, y, and z as d/x, d/y, and d/z respectively, if d is a directory. If not, x is renamed as d, then y is renamed as d overwriting the previous file. Finally, the file z will be renamed as d.

2.6 The shell

Simple commands are written as sequences of *words* separated by spaces. The first word is the name of the command to be executed. Any remaining words are passed as arguments to the invoked command. For example, the command

```
ls −l
```

prints a list of file names in the current directory. The argument −l (l for long) tells ls to print the date of last use, the size, and status information for each file. The output is sorted alphabetically by file name.

To execute a command, the shell normally creates a new process and waits for it to finish. Both of these operations are primitives available in the operating system. A command may be run without waiting for it to finish using the postfix operator &. For example,

```
print file &
```

calls the print command with argument file and runs it in the background. The & is a metacharacter interpreted by the shell and is not passed as an argument to print. To help keep track of such a process the shell reports its process number following its creation. A list of currently active processes may be obtained using the ps command.

Associated with each process, the system maintains a set of file descriptors numbered 0,1,... that are used in all input-output transactions between processes and the operating system. File descriptor 0 is termed the *standard input* and file descriptor 1 the *standard output*. Most commands produce their output on the standard output that is initially (following login) connected to a terminal. The *standard error output* (file descriptor 2) is also provided and is conventionally used for error messages. The standard output may be redirected for the duration of a command, as in

```
ls −l >file
```

The notation >file is interpreted by the shell and is not passed as an argument to ls. If the file does not exist, the shell creates it; otherwise, the contents of the file are replaced with the output from the command and the original file contents are lost. To append to the end of a file, the notation ≫ is provided, as in

```
ls −l ≫file
```

Similarly, the standard input may be taken from a file instead of the terminal, by writing

```
wc <file
```

The wc command prints the number of characters, words, and lines contained in the standard input.

2.6.1 Pipes and filters

The standard output of one command may be connected to the standard input of another with the *pipe* operator, indicated by | , as in,

```
ls −l | wc
```

Two commands connected in this way constitute a *pipeline,* and the effect is similar to

```
ls −l >file
wc <file
```

except that no file is used. Instead, the two processes are connected by a pipe that is created by an operating system call. Pipes are uni-directional; synchronization is achieved by halting wc when there is nothing to read and halting ls when the pipe is full. The synchronization is provided by the operating system, not the shell.

A *filter* is a command that reads its input, transforms it in some way, and prints the result as output. One such filter, grep, selects from its input those lines that contain some specified string. For example,

```
ls | grep old
```

prints those lines, if any, from the output of ls that contain the string old. Another useful filter is sort. For example,

```
who | sort
```

will print an alphabetically sorted list of logged in users.

A pipeline may consist of more than two commands, for example,

    ls | grep old | wc -l

prints the number of file names in the current directory containing the string old.

2.6.2 File name generation

Many commands accept arguments that are file names. For example,

    ls -l main.c

prints information relating to the file main.c.

The shell provides a mechanism for generating a list of file names that match a pattern. For example,

    ls -l *.c

generates, as arguments to ls, all file names in the current directory that end in .c. The character * is a pattern that will match any string including the null string.

Shell patterns are specified using the following notation.

*	Match any string of characters including the null string.
?	Match any single character.
[...]	Match any of the characters enclosed. A pair of characters separated by a minus will match any character lexically between the pair.

For example,

    [a-z]*

matches all names in the current directory beginning with one letter from a through z.

    /usr/fred/epns/?*

matches all names in the directory /usr/fred/epns that consist of at least one character. If no file name is found that matches the pattern then the pattern is passed, unchanged, as an argument.

This mechanism is useful both to save typing and to select names according to some pattern. It may also be used for finding files. For example,

    echo /usr/fred/*/core

finds and prints the names of all core files in first-level directories of /usr/fred. (echo is a standard command that prints its arguments, separated by spaces.) This last feature can be expensive, requiring a scan of all sub-directories of /usr/fred.

There is one exception to the general rules given for patterns. The character . at the start of a file name must be explicitly matched.

    echo *

will therefore echo all file names not beginning with . in the current directory.

    echo .*

will echo all those file names that begin with . in the current directory. This
avoids inadvertent matching of the names . and .. meaning 'the current directory'
and 'the parent directory' respectively. (ls suppresses information for . and ...)

Care should be taken when using the rm command with generated patterns.
More files could easily be removed than intended. One way to reduce the chance
of error is first to echo the pattern. For example,

    echo tmp*

followed by

    rm tmp*

taking care not to introduce a space between tmp and *.

2.6.3 Quoting

Characters that have a special meaning to the shell, such as <, >, *, ?, |, and &, are
called metacharacters. Any character preceded by a \ is *quoted* and loses its special meaning, if any. The \ is elided so that

    echo \?

will echo a single ?, and

    echo \\

will echo a single \. To allow long strings to be continued over more than one line
a \ followed by a newline is ignored. This is sometimes called a hidden newline.

A \ is convenient for quoting single characters. When more than one character needs quoting the above mechanism is clumsy and error prone. A string of
characters may be quoted by enclosing the string between single quotes. For example,

    echo ´*?[´

will echo

    *?[

The quoted string may not contain a single quote but may contain newlines, that are
preserved. This quoting mechanism is the most simple and is recommended for
casual use.

A third quoting mechanism using double quotes is also available preventing
interpretation of some but not all metacharacters. Discussion of the details is deferred to section 4.2.4.

Shell comments begin with # and are terminated by a newline.

2.6.4 Prompts

When the shell is used from a terminal it will issue a prompt before reading a command. By default this prompt is $. It may be changed by setting the prompt
string, for example,

```
PS1=yesdear
```

that sets the prompt to be the string yesdear. If a newline is typed and further input
is needed then the shell will issue the prompt > . Sometimes this can be caused by
mistyping a quote mark. If the prompt is unexpected then an interrupt will return
the shell to read another command. This prompt may be changed by saying, for
example,

```
PS2=more
```

2.6.5 The shell and login

Following login the shell is called to read and execute commands typed at the terminal. If the user's home directory contains a file named .profile then it is executed
by the shell before reading any commands from the terminal.

```
date
calendar

MAIL=/usr/spool/mail/srb
HOME=/usr/srb
PATH=.:./bin:/bin:/usr/bin:$HOME/bin
TERM=...
export MAIL HOME PATH TERM
```

Figure 2.3 A typical .profile

The profile in figure 2.3 contains typical settings of shell variables described
further in section 4.1.4. This profile also prints the date and checks the calendar
reminder service. The export command is described in section 4.2.1. If you always
use the same terminal the TERM variable can be usefully set in the profile.

2.6.6 Review

ls	Print the names of files in the current directory.
ls >file	Put the output from ls into file.
ls | wc –l	Print the number of files in the current directory.
ls | grep old	Print those file names containing the string old.
ls | grep old | wc –l	
	Print the number of files whose name contains the string old.
cc pgm.c &	Run the cc command in the background.

2.7 Useful commands

2.7.1 Communication

The UNIX system is friendly, in part because it allows easy communication among
users and between users and the system. The commands described in this section
allow users on the same or different machines to send mail, or to write to another

user. The mail command sends messages or letters to other users, whereas the write command is used to communicate interactively with a user at another terminal.

The mail command

The mail command allows messages to be received from, and sent to, other users on the system. These messages are stored in a file until the recipient reads them and removes them.

When you log on you will be informed if there is any mail waiting for you. The shell will also let you know, before prompting, if any new mail has arrived. (See the $MAIL variable in the shell.)

There are different versions of the mail system depending on which version of the UNIX system you have. The general behavior of these mail systems is similar although they differ in the details. The version described here is the mail command originally distributed with the Seventh Edition UNIX system.

    mail

will print the first item of mail, preceded by its postmark. It will then prompt with a ?. This item of mail can be deleted (d), printed again (p), or the next item printed by typing a return. To save the item of mail the request

    s file

is used. The request s with no file name will save the mail item in the file mbox in the home directory. If an item is saved or deleted it is removed from the mail file on exit from mail. The q request will exit from the mail command. To exit without making any changes to the mail file the x request should be used. This is useful when mail items have been deleted in error.

When mail is being read, typing del causes the current action (usually printing) to be terminated and a prompt is issued for the next request.

To send mail to one or more users

    mail jhc ken
    . . .
    .

will send the text including the sender's name and a postmark. The text is terminated by an end-of-file or by a . on a line by itself. An interrupt while composing a mail message will leave the partially constructed mail in the file dead.letter in the home directory and exit from the mail command.

Mail systems provide communication between users on a single machine. Communication between users on different machines is achieved via an *ad hoc* network that uses the phone system to establish connections. This network originated, and is still used, to provide a machine-to-machine file copying service. Each machine in the network is named and a list is maintained on each machine of the names of other machines and their phone numbers. The mail system uses this network to deliver inter-machine mail. The mail address consists of the machine name, followed by !, followed by the user's login-name on that machine. For example, mail research!!llc

followed by the message is sufficient to send mail to llc on the research machine. Some machines are also prepared to forward mail so that

    mail allegra!ucbvax!wnj

will send the message to allegra and then forward it to ucbvax!wnj. This forwarding service should be used only after agreement with the intermediate installation.

The uucp command

The uucp (UNIX to UNIX copy) command copies files from one machine to another. Connections between computers are either made via the phone system or, in some cases, direct high-speed links are utilized. On your system the command uuname will print the names of the systems that are directly accessible. This informal network of computers is in constant use.

    The synopsis is similar to the cp command. For example,

    uucp file research!/usr/srb/ufile

will copy file from the local machine to research, the file name on that machine being /usr/srb/ufile.

    In its original form uucp could be used to copy files from one machine to another, the only security checks applied are those provided by the file system on each machine.

    The ability to copy files into and out of a computer by knowing its phone number and a relatively simple protocol presents some installations with an unacceptable security risk. Therefore uucp imposes additional restrictions over those imposed by the file system. On System V there is a single directory used to copy files into and out of the machine called /usr/spool/uucppublic. Normally this directory is open to all users of the machine and each user will create a (sub) directory for personal use. The system administrator may also enable files to be accessed by uucp from specific directories elsewhere in the system.

The write command

In addition to mail, users can communicate directly from one terminal to another using the write command.

    write bill

will look to see whether user bill is logged in and if so will write a message of the form

    Message from srb on tty20 at 13:36

at his terminal. If bill is logged in more than once, write prints a message and chooses one terminal to write to. The normal protocol is for bill to reply by saying

    write srb

that will produce a similar message at the initiator's terminal. srb would then send the first message

> Hi, are you ready to eat lunch (o)

where (o) means over. Conversation can then continue until one or other party decides to finish. An end-of-file, ^D, will terminate the conversation on one side and print EOF on the other terminal.

Occasionally, when a terminal is being used as a printer or when in use by a visual editor (see vi) having a message appear at random is inconvenient. Some users simply prefer not to be interrupted.

> mesg n

denies other users write access to your terminal.

> mesg y

will restore message permission and mesg without an argument informs you of the current state (y or n).

2.7.2 System inquiries

The ps *command*

A list of the active processes within the system can be obtained using the ps command (ps for process status). The options and output format for this command vary from one UNIX system to another. The −a argument requests a list of all processes; otherwise, only processes for the logged in user are listed. The output from the command

> ps −a

is shown in figure 2.4 where the fields signify the following.

PID	The process identification number.
TTY	The terminal (or tty) number.
TIME	How much processor time the command has used in minutes and seconds.
COMMAND	The command being executed (including arguments).

PID	TTY	TIME	COMMAND
22932	00	0:03	ed ama.temp
22864	16	0:07	vi t2
22963	16	0:00	sh −i
22968	16	0:00	ps −a
22967	40	0:00	sleep 15
27786	40	6:28	/bin/sh /usr/haw/bin/prints

Figure 2.4 Output from the ps command

The du command

This command determines how much disk space is being used by files in a directory and (recursively) all its sub-directories. The output from du is a list of file or directory names and the associated number of 512-character blocks used. Without an argument du lists the current directory. If arguments are specified then those files or directories are listed.

The df command

Files are stored in a *file system* that corresponds to an area of disk. The number of blocks of space available and allocated to each file system is printed by the df command. Disk space is allocated in units called blocks; a block is typically 512 or 1024 characters depending on your system. On some systems disk space is always in short supply. This command is useful if you are planning to create large files as a check to ensure that the space is available.

2.7.3 Process management

The nice, nohup, and kill commands

Whenever a command is run it competes with all other active processes in the system for processor time. The nice command informs the system that an activity is not urgent and that a lower scheduling priority is appropriate. For example,

    nice cp largefile newfile

runs the command

    cp largefile newfile

at a lower priority. This allows other, more urgent, work to proceed.

Work is often performed by issuing commands from a terminal and waiting for them to finish. This is particularly true of file management and editing activities. If a command or set of commands is expected to take some time to finish it is convenient to relegate the work to the background and continue working at the terminal. The shell provides the & notation for this purpose.

    cp largefile newfile &

instructs the shell to run the command but not wait for it to finish. nice may also be used with & so that,

    nice cp largefile newfile &

will run the copy in the background at low priority.

If you log out and leave your terminal before the background activity finishes the nohup (no hang up) command should also be used. This prevents disconnecting (hanging up) the terminal from aborting the job. nohup and nice are used in a similar way, so that,

    nohup cp largefile newfile &

is typical.

When a process has been started but is no longer required it may be killed using the kill command. kill requires a process number to be specified, such as that produced by the ps command. Usually, kill is used for processes that have been started in the background. However, processes that have been started using nohup are immune to the default kill. Such processes may be killed by specifying

kill −9 *process-id*

This form is not usually used since it does not give the receiving commands an opportunity to clean up.

The at *command*

The at command enables a user to queue a set of activities to be executed at some future time. Each user community adopts its own rules governing the use of the computer resources. On heavily loaded machines, for example, it may be unacceptable to run more than one job in the background. at may be used to defer an unimportant job until a later time when the computer is not so busy.

All commands described so far have been executed when they were issued. To schedule an activity for a future time at is used. For example, in

at 1600 fri runcmd

runcmd is scheduled to be executed at 4 p.m. next Friday. The command runcmd is run exactly as if it were typed now, except that the terminal is not available for input and output. Other arrangements must be made for the standard input, standard output and error output.

No direct means is provided for killing an at job. The scripts are kept in the directory /usr/spool/at and can be removed using the rm command by the file owner.

2.7.4 Other commands

The calendar *command*

The calendar command provides a reminder service for individual users. To use the service create a file called calendar in your home directory containing lines such as

jun 27 9 a.m. visit the dentist

Each day the system will look at the file and send, via mail, those lines that contain today's or the next day's date. The calendar file is left unchanged, providing a record of events.

The cpio *command*

The tar command and cpio copy groups of files to or from tape. They can also be used to move complete hierarchies from one part of the file system to another.

cpio −o (copy out) reads the standard input to obtain a list of pathnames and copies those files onto the standard output together with pathname and status information.

cpio −i (copy in) extracts files from the standard input, which is assumed to be the product of a previous cpio −o. Patterns are specified using the name-generating notation of sh. In patterns, metacharacters ?, @, and [...] match the slash (/) character. Multiple patterns may be specified and if no patterns are specified, the default for patterns is @ (i.e. select all files). The extracted files are conditionally created and copied into the current directory tree.

cpio −p (pass) reads the standard input to obtain a list of pathnames of files that are conditionally created and copied into the destination directory tree.

For example,

    ls | cpio −o >/dev/mt/0m

copies the contents of the current directory to tape.

The file command

The file command classifies its argument file names according to the information stored in the file. It is not foolproof, and sometimes confuses shell scripts and C programs. Try, for example,

    file /usr/lib/*

for a representative sample of output.

The find command

The find command scans a directory hierarchy (i.e. a directory and its sub-directories recursively) for files with a specified property. Among others, the name, age, owner, and mode of a file can be tested. When a suitable file is found a command can be executed or the file name printed. find is useful if, for example, you cannot remember the directory a file is stored in but can remember its name.

    find . −name precious −print

will look in the current directory hierarchy and, if a file named precious is found, its complete pathname is printed starting at the current directory.

    find . −name precious −exec ls −l {} \;

is similar, and will also execute the command ls −l .... The argument to ls, represented as {}, will be replaced by the complete pathname of the file each time ls is executed. The \; terminates the command to be executed and is quoted to prevent interpretation by the shell. The following examples illustrate other uses.

    find / −user mark−b −print
            Look everywhere in the file system (i.e. starting at the root) for files
            owned by mark−b.

    find . −size 0 −print
            Print the names of files with zero length in the current directory
            tree.

The grep *command*

grep has already been introduced in earlier examples, and selects lines containing a string from a list of files. If no files are specified the standard input is searched. The lines found are copied to the standard output. For example,

    grep Unix *

will print the lines from files in the current directory containing the string Unix. If more than one file is searched, grep will prefix each output line with the file name.

The general form for invoking grep is

    grep pattern [file ...]

The pattern is reminiscent of that used by the shell for file name generation. In the simplest case pattern is a literal string. The description of the general form of patterns is deferred until section 8.1.

Some of the frequently used grep options are as follows:

−h	Suppress printing of file name prefix on each line.
−n	Each line output is preceded by its line number in the file.
−v	Only lines not containing the string are printed.

The ls *command*

The ls command lists status information for files and directory contents. Without arguments ls lists the names in the current directory sorted alphabetically. The entries . and .. are not normally listed. The more frequently used options are listed below.

−C	Print multi-column output with entries sorted down the columns.
−d	For a directory list only the name, not the names contained.
−g	Suppress the owner field. Only the group name is printed.
−l	List (long) the mode, number of links, owner, size, and modification time.
−r	Reverse the order of sorting.
−t	Sort by the file modified time instead of by name.
−u	Use time of last access instead of last modification.

The od *command*

Files that contain strange characters can be printed using the 'octal dump' command od. For example,

    od −b file

prints each byte of file as an integer to base 8 (octal). Other options for od include:

−c	Print ASCII with non-graphic characters escaped using a \.
−x	Print 16-bit hexadecimal.

Files containing more complicated formats may be printed using the adb command.

The pr *command*

Listings of one or more files are produced using the pr command. For example,

    pr *.c

will print all files with names ending in .c in the current directory. The output is separated into 66-line pages each headed by the file name, date and time, and page number. The final page is padded with blank lines to complete the 66-line page. Useful options include:

−t   Suppress the additional lines at the top and bottom of each page.
−n   Produce *n*-column output.
−h *text*   Use *text* as the heading of each page.
−m   Merge. Print files simultaneously, one in each column.

The stty *command*

Terminals have widely differing characteristics that are communicated to the system via the stty (set tty) command. When called without arguments, stty reports the current settings of the most important options, such as terminal speed, parity and the erase and kill characters. If your terminal behaves strangely you should check that its configuration corresponds to the stty options. Terminal input and output are discussed further in chapter 6.

The tar *command*

Files may be copied to and from magnetic tape using cat or cp. However, copying single files in this way is not particularly convenient. The tar (tape archive) command copies a directory hierarchy, usually from tape to disk or from disk to disk. For example,

    tar rc .

reads all files and (recursively) directories from the current directory, ., and writes them onto tape. The r option reads the directory and c creates a new tape archive. The tape is a special file, like /dev/tty, whose name depends on your system. tar uses /dev/mt/0m as the default tape drive. The name of the special file need not be specified since it is built into the tar command.

To list the names of files on a tape the command

    tar t

is used. The t option stands for titles. Files are extracted from the tape and written to disk by the command

    tar x

The disk files written have the same names as those listed by tar t.

The names given to tar should be expressed relative to the current directory so that files can be extracted conveniently in other parts of the file system. Saying, for example,

    tar rc /usr/srb

should be avoided in favor of

```
cd /usr/srb
tar rc .
```

2.7.5 Review

The following commands allow a user to log in to the computer and get started using the terminal.

login	Read the login-name and password.
mail	Send and receive mail between users.
man	Print a section from the user manual.
stty	Set terminal options.
who	List users who are logged in.

The following important file manipulation commands have also been introduced.

cat	Catenate and print files.
cp	Copy files.
ls	List the entries in a directory.
mkdir	Make a directory.
mv	Move (or rename) a file or directory.
rmdir	Remove a directory.
rm	Remove (or delete) a file.
pr	Format and print a file.

Chapter 3 **Editing Files**

Files such as programs or text for inclusion in a document may be created and modified from a terminal using a text editor. The editors are interactive allowing a dialogue to take place between the user and the system.

There are two commonly available editors: ed and vi. Of these, ed is the more widely available and uses only the basic facilities available on any terminal. Another editor, vi, is a screen editor that takes full advantage of video terminals. This chapter describes the features of both editors.

3.1 The editor ed

The editor ed is invoked by the command

    ed

No prompt will appear and the editor will wait for an editing *request* to be typed. The term *request* is used for the instructions given to commands to distinguish them from the commands themselves.

ed keeps text in a storage area called a *buffer* and provides requests to append to, delete, or modify this text. All requests are introduced by a single letter and requests may not, except where noted, be on the same line. If something goes wrong, ed will print a ? and wait for another request to be typed.

3.1.1 Creating files

Initially, the ed buffer is empty. To place information in the buffer, the append request, abbreviated to a is used:

    a
    text to be placed in the buffer

    .

While text is being appended, the editor is in *append mode*. To get out of append mode and to terminate the text a . is required at the start of a line, followed by a return.

The contents of the buffer are written to the file draft.ch1 using the write request

    w draft.ch1

The character w is separated from the file name by a space. The editor responds with the number of the characters placed in the file and the contents of the buffer

are unaltered by the request. After writing the buffer to the file, the quit, q, request
may be used to exit from the editor. An end-of-file, ^D, will also exit from the editor. If the buffer has been changed and not written back to a file the editor will
respond to e or q with a ?. This is the only message normally received from ed and
can be unhelpful to the new user. Typical ed errors include:

- An unknown ed request.
- An error in the form of the request.
- A file does not exist, or cannot be read or written.

Although the process described above illustrates how to create a file, it does
not indicate how to edit the contents of a file that already exists. Just as

    w draft.ch1

writes the contents of the buffer to a file

    e draft.ch1

reads the contents of draft.ch1 into the buffer and destroys any information that was
already in the buffer. One way to invoke ed is as follows:

    ed
    e filename
    [editing requests to alter buffer contents]
    w filename
    q

An equivalent effect is achieved by

    ed filename
    [editing requests to alter buffer contents]
    w
    q

When ed is given a file name as an argument the e request is not needed. Further,
there is no need to remember the file name for later use by the w request, as in the
second example above. The remembered file name can be printed using the f request and is set by the e and w requests.

3.1.2 Line editing

The text in the buffer is divided into lines and some requests operate with entire
lines of text. The general form of requests is

    starting-line, finishing-line request

The request is then applied to each line of the buffer from the starting-line to the
finishing-line inclusive. Lines may be addressed numerically, starting with line 1. If
the starting-line and finishing-line are the same line the general form may be
abbreviated as:

    particular-line request

The following examples introduce some commonly used requests.

1,4p	Print lines numbered 1 to 4 inclusive.
1,4n	Print lines 1 to 4 inclusive; each line is prefixed by its number.
10,15d	Delete lines 10 through 15 inclusive.
4,14w part1	Write out lines 4 to 14 inclusive to a file called part1. If no starting and finishing lines are given the entire buffer is written.
4r new.part	Read the contents of the file new.part and insert it immediately after line 4; when no line number is specified the contents are appended to the end of the current buffer.
4,14m 21	Move lines 4 to 14 inclusive and place them after line 21 (and before line 22).
1t2	Place a copy of line 1 after line 2. The r, m, and t requests place information *after* a particular line.

The last line of the buffer is represented by a $. Thus,

    1,$d

deletes from the buffer everything from line 1 to the end, inclusive. This should only be used if it is intended to remove all the lines from the buffer. Similarly,

    1,$p

prints the entire contents of the buffer.

Current line

The current line is the particular line under scrutiny and is like a finger pointing into the buffer. It is referred to as *dot* and is usually the last line edited. After an a request it is the last line appended, and after m it is the last line moved. The d request is exceptional since the last line edited no longer exists; the current line is the first line that has not been deleted. When in doubt the current line can be printed using the p request. Further, the current line number can be found by typing

    .=

To change *dot* to a particular line, without doing any editing, type the line number. Thus

    4

prints line 4 and sets *dot* to 4. Generally, whenever a new current line is established and a new request is needed, the current line is printed.

Line addressing

Lines may be addressed in ed using a numeric line index, the current line *dot,* or as the last line of the document $. Addresses may also be formed by adding or subtracting a number from one of the above, although adding to the last line of the document will always be an error. An address that begins with + or − is taken relative to the current line. A + or − on its own is used to step forwards or backwards a line at a time.

The following editing requests illustrate some typical line addresses.

+	Advance to the next line and print it.
−	Go back one line and print it.
. , $d	Delete everything from the current line to the end of the buffer.
.−1 , .+1p	Print the previous line, the current line and the next line.
.+2,$−1p	Print everything from two lines beyond the current line up to but excluding the last line of the buffer.

In all cases *dot,* the current line, is changed.

Adding and removing material

The append request is the general facility for adding information to a buffer. The request

```
10a
text to be included between lines 10 and 11

.
```

will append information immediately after line 10 of the buffer.

Two other requests are similar to the a request. Lines may be changed using the c request that combines the effect of deleting and inserting material. For example,

```
4,27c
text to replace lines removed

.
```

replaces lines 4 to 27 inclusive with the specified text. As might be supposed

```
4c
text to be added

.
```

replaces line 4. In both cases a . on a line by itself terminates the input.

The insert request, i, is similar in form to the a request except that information is inserted before, rather than after, the stated line. Thus

```
1i
.ce 2
Chapter One
.sp 2
Fundamentals
.sp 2

.
```

adds information at the start of a buffer and is equivalent to

```
0a
. . .

.
```

If no line numbers are specified, the a, c, d, i, and p requests use the current line number as default so that

>   a
>   *text to be included*
>   .

is equivalent to

>   .a
>   *text to be included*
>   .

Furthermore,

>   d

deletes the current line and a subsequent

>   p

request prints the new current line, i.e., the next line in the buffer. This can be written on a single line as

>   dp

After each of the a, c, i, and m requests the current line becomes the last line appended, changed, inserted or moved respectively.

3.1.3 Context searching

Referring to lines only by number is inconvenient unless a listing is available. Simple insertions or deletions cause line numbers to alter. It is more convenient to look for a string of characters using the editor and decide if it is right, then edit it, then look again.

The request

>   /Fotran/

for example, will look through the contents of the buffer for the *next* line containing the characters delimited by / and /. The line of text found is displayed so that it can be checked to see if the intended line has been reached. In performing the search, the editor looks through successive lines of text starting at the line after the current line. If it reaches the end of the buffer without finding the line, the editor will then proceed from the start of the buffer until the entire contents have been searched back to the current line. If the line is not present, perhaps because of a mistake in the request, a ? is printed.

A search, such as /Fotran/, is another way of addressing a particular line. Just as line numbers were used earlier, search patterns of the kind described here can also be used. A request such as

>   /switch/,/case/d

deletes everything between the next line containing switch and the next line containing case. It is assumed that the line containing case is the same as, or follows, the line containing switch.

If the last line of the buffer is reached without finding the search pattern, ed wraps around, starting again at the first line. Searching stops when the current line is reached or when the pattern is found.

A search pattern may be used as part of an address. For example,

/main/−1

will position the current line one line before the next line containing /main/.

Use of semicolon

The request

/begin/,/end/d

begins the search for end at the same point as it begins the search for begin, namely the current line. To start the search for end after begin has been found, a ; rather than a , is used as separator, as in,

/begin/;/end/d

Backward searching

Context searches using /.../ scan forward through the text. Backward scans are also possible using ?...?. When performing the backward search wrap around occurs; on reaching line 1 of the buffer the editor will jump to the end of the buffer and search backwards from there until the entire buffer has been searched.

3.1.4 Context editing

Editing a document line-by-line is slow and can be error prone. Making changes within a line is known as context editing.

Part of a line may be modified using the substitute request, s. The effect of

s/Fotran/Fortran/

is to replace, on the current line, the first occurrence of Fotran by Fortran. Examples illustrate some of the possibilities.

s/Fotran// Replace Fotran by the empty string, i.e. delete it.
s/Fotran/Fortran/p
        Replace the first occurrence of Fotran by Fortran and print the edited line for review.
., .+1s/Fotran/Fortran/
        Replace the first occurrence of Fotran by Fortran on the current line and the next line.

The substitute request has the same general format as the requests previously encountered, allowing

starting-line , finishing-line s/old text/new text/

or

particular-line s/old text/new text/

When line numbers are omitted the current line is assumed.

In context searches the string searched for is often the subject of the substitute request. This can happen with spelling or typing errors. The request

/Fotran/

followed by

s/Fotran/Fortran/

can be abbreviated to

/Fotran/
editor responds with the line found
s//Fortran/

The editor remembers the previous search or substitute pattern. When used after an s request,

//

searches again for the next occurrence of the previous pattern. If the wrong line appears, // may be used again to find the next line with the same pattern.

Global substitution

A simple application of the substitute request, such as

s/Fotran/Fortran/

will replace only the first occurrence of Fotran by Fortran on the current line.

s/Fotran/Fortran/g

replaces all occurrences in the current line. The g modifier indicates global replacement throughout the line.

The p modifier may also be used.

s/Fotran/Fortran/gp

causes global replacement and prints the edited line;

1,$s/Fotran/Fortran/g

causes every occurrence of Fotran in the buffer to be replaced by Fortran. When looking for strings it sometimes helps to be able to specify that a particular string occurs at the start or end of a line. The start and end of line are denoted within patterns by ∧ and $, respectively. To illustrate:

/∧At/	Find the next line that starts with At.
/};$/	Find the next line that ends with };.
/∧$/	Find the next empty line.
/∧Unix$/	Find a line that contains only Unix.

These same patterns may be used in the first substitute string.

s/∧/The /p   Place The before the first character of the current line and print the line.

4s/$/;/   Add a ; to the end of line 4.

/^UNIX$/s//Unix/

        Find the next line containing only UNIX and replace these four characters by Unix.

The undo request

If a substitute request is executed in error the undo request,

   u

will restore the line to its original form. This request only applies to the most recently executed substitution.

3.1.5 Pattern matching

Within a search or substitution string certain characters have a special meaning as described below.

The dot character

A . matches any character, so that,

   /x.y/

will find the first line that contains strings like x+y, x−y, x=y.

The asterisk character

An * denotes repetition and finds zero or more occurrences of a character. The pattern

   /.*;/

matches everything on one line up to and including the last ; . The longest possible match is used so that if a ; appears more than once on the line, all will be matched. For example,

   s/.*;//

removes everything up to and including the last ; on the line. The request

   s/(.*)//

removes from the first (to the last) and everything between them. The parentheses matched are not necessarily balanced.

    This use of the * character should be distinguished from its use in the shell. In the shell * is similar to .* in the editor.

    As another example,

   /a.*b/

will search for a line containing both a and b in that order, possibly separated by other characters.

The bracket *characters*

Square brackets denote character classes as illustrated in the following examples. As in the shell, one character from the specified class is matched.

[;:,]	Match any of the characters ;, : or ,.
[a–z]	Match any lower case character a through z.
[A–H]	Match any upper case character between A and H inclusive.
[0–9]	Match any digit.
[^0–9]	^ denotes the complement when it appears as the first character after [. This example matches any character except a digit.
[.\$*^[]	Match any of the special characters. Only the characters ^ and] are treated specially in character classes. To include] itself in a character class it should be listed as the first character. A ^ is included when listed as anything other than the first character in the class.

The following examples illustrate the use of patterns within a substitute request.

1,$s/^[0–9]*//	Remove all digits from the start of each line.
1,$s/[0–9]*$//	Remove all trailing digits from the end of each line.
s/[.\$*^[ ]//	Remove the first occurrence of any special character from the current line.
s/, e\.g\. .*/./	Replace everything from the string , e.g. to the end of the line with a . .

Naming

Part of a pattern matched by a search or substitute request may be named by enclosing the pattern between \(and \). For example,

    /\(.*\) ⓣ \(.*\)/

will search for a line containing a tab (represented here by ⓣ). The two strings enclosed between \(...\) may be used in the replacement string of a substitute request, as in,

    s/\2 ⓣ \1/

\1 and \2 refer to the first and second parenthesized patterns. In this example, the two fields are interchanged. If more than one tab occurs within the line the rightmost one is matched.

Quoting

Within a search string the following characters are treated specially:

    ^   . $ [*   \   /

To be used in their own right, as normal characters, it is necessary to *escape* them with a \. Thus

    /\./

looks for the next line containing a ., whereas

/./

looks for the next line that contains any character (i.e. the next non-empty line).

Recall that the same quoting convention is used for the erase and kill characters, # and @. Even within the editor these characters have a special meaning when input from a terminal and must be typed as \# or \@, respectively.

To look for a line containing a / a \ is also required. Thus

s/\//*/p

will replace / with an * on the current line and then print out the modified line.

3.1.6 Global editing

The *global request* selects lines that match a pattern and executes another request for each line found. This may be used, for example, if a word is consistently spelled wrongly or whenever a change to the whole file is required. The g request takes the form

g/pattern/requests

For example,

g/^{/.-1p

finds all lines starting with a { and prints the preceding line.

As with other requests the g request may be limited to a range of lines. Thus

1,20 g/^chapter/s/c/C/

executes the request s/c/C/ on all lines starting with chapter in the first 20 lines of the buffer. When several requests are to be executed then each newline must be *escaped* with a \. For example,

g/^chapter/s/c/C/\
i\
.ul1\
.

changes every occurrence of chapter at the start of a line to Chapter and a line containing only .ul1 is inserted immediately before it. All lines except the last must end with a \. The requests executed by a g request may not include another g request.

The v request is similar to the g request except that it finds lines that do not match the pattern. For example,

v/^\./d

deletes all lines that do not begin with a ..

3.1.7 Miscellaneous

Interrupt and hangup

An interrupt, generated by typing del or break, will cause the editor to abandon its current activity and return to read the next request. This is useful for interrupting a print request such as

   g/.../p

   If the terminal hangs up while a file is being edited, the buffer is saved in the file called ed.hup in the current directory. The diff command may be used to compare ed.hup with the original file being edited and either the cp or mv command may be used to restore the partially edited ed.hup to its original name.

Delimiters

A context search is specified using /.../. A / is frequently used for delimiting the string in a substitute request. However, any other character, such as a :, can be used provided that all occurrences within the one request are consistent, as in,

   s:Fotran:Fortran:

The delimiter may be quoted using \ if it is needed as part of the pattern.

Executing a command

To execute a command from within the editor the ! request is used. For example,

   !mail djb
   please call me on the phone
   .

will send a message to user djb and return to ed. No changes are made to the buffer or the file being edited.

Abbreviations

Certain abbreviations are permitted in line addresses.

- + can be omitted so that, for example, .+4 and .4 have identical meanings. +4 is also an abbreviation for .+4.
- − by itself moves back a line; −−− moves back three lines and is equivalent to .−3.
- /.../− is equivalent to /.../−1.

Use of ampersand

Having performed a search for a string in a substitute request, as in

   s/abc/.../

an & can be used in the replacement string to denote the first string that is found. Thus

   s/x+y/(&)/

inserts parentheses around x+y.

Non-printing characters

The I request is similar to the p request except that non-printing characters, such as tab and backspace, are replaced by printing characters as shown below.

tab	->
backspace	<-
backslash	\
bell	\07
formfeed	\14

Early versions of ed printed spaces at the end of the line followed by \n, as in,

   ... \n

System V does not provide this facility.

Joining and breaking lines

Consider a line of text such as

   ...abc...

To insert a newline between a and b, the substitute request is used with an escaped newline. For example,

   s/ab/a\
   b/

inserts a newline between the characters a and b. The single request is typed on two lines. Conversely, two lines such as

   if x==y
    && y==z

can be formed into a single line. With the first of these lines as the current line

   j

will join them together leaving the result as the current line. In general a range of lines can be joined, as in

   1,4jp

that joins together lines 1 through 4 inclusive and prints the result.

Marking lines

The request

   line-number kx

marks the addressed line (by default the current line) with the name x. Any lower case letter may be used to mark lines. Such lines may be addressed using a single quote followed by x, as in,

   ´x

E, Q, *and* W *requests*

The requests e and q will print ? to warn that the results of editing have not been written to a file and will not complete the requested action. These safeguards are suppressed if E or Q is used. These requests should be used with care since an entire editing session may be lost.

The w request writes the buffer to a file, destroying any previous file contents. Information may be appended to a file using the W request.

3.2 The editor vi

Once ed has been learned its limitations soon become apparent. It was designed in the days of slow mechanical terminals such as the Teletype model 33 and model 37 teleprinters. Video terminals have space on the screen for at least 24 lines of 80 characters each and vi is an editor developed to take advantage of such devices. For best effect these terminals should be operated at 9600 baud but can also be used reasonably at 1200 baud. Below 1200 baud ed is the best choice.

vi needs to know the terminal type before it can be used. The terminal type is specified by setting the environment variable TERM. In the shell this is written, for example,

TERM=vt100 export TERM

The string assigned to TERM depends on the terminal, in this example a Digital Equipment Corporation vt100.

If the correct name for the terminal is unknown, the TERM variable can be set to dumb and vi will work on any terminal although it will not use the visual features that make it attractive.

The command

vi pgm.c

will display the first few lines of pgm.c on the screen and editing requests may be issued to vi. If there are unexpected characters on the screen, then the terminal type (TERM) is probably incorrect or has not been exported from the shell. The request

:q

terminated by a return will exit from the editor. The request

:q!

corresponds to the Q request of ed and forces vi to exit even if the current buffer has not been written to a file.

Requests to vi consist of one or more characters, another difference from ed, and some requests require a terminating return or esc.

Once the terminal type is set correctly immediate differences from ed can be seen. Some requests take effect immediately and are not printed on the screen. Others are printed on the screen and appear on a line near the bottom. Error messages from vi are explicit, as opposed to the ? from ed and also appear on the line near the bottom of the screen.

3.2.1 Window control

The philosophy of this editor is that what you see on the screen is part of the buffer. The screen acts as a *window* on the buffer. To move this window forward through the buffer the following requests are available:

 ^F

to move a full screen and

 ^D

to scroll half a screen. The notation ^F means control-F and is explained in chapter 2.

  To move backwards through the buffer

 ^B

is used for a full page and

 ^U

scrolls half a page backwards. When the end of the buffer is reached vi will display non-existent lines as a ~.

  You will now be able to observe the *cursor;* on some terminals it blinks; on others it is displayed as inverse video. The cursor marks the current position within the buffer.

3.2.2 Cursor control

The cursor can be positioned on the screen in preparation for editing requests. The line containing the cursor is the current line and the cursor position is also used by vi requests. The requests providing fine cursor control are:

space	Move one character to the right.
backspace	Move one character to the left.
return	Move to the start of the next line.
+	The same as a return.
−	Move to the start of the previous line.
$	Move to the end of this line.

Other requests are available to move the cursor. If necessary these requests will also move the window on the buffer.

 /pattern/

will search forward and leave the cursor pointing at the next occurrence of pattern in the buffer. Like ed, ?...? searches backwards.

  Coarse cursor movement is available using the G request that moves to a specified line of the buffer. A number followed by the G request will position the cursor at that line within the buffer. By default the last line of the buffer is used, so that,

 G

will position the cursor at the end of the buffer.

The cursor can also be moved forwards or backwards a whole word at a time; if there are no words remaining on the current line the cursor will be moved to the next or previous line respectively.

w   Move the cursor forward to the beginning of the next word.
b   Move the cursor back to the start of the previous word.
e   Move the cursor forward to the end of the current word.

In these requests a word is considered to consist of alphanumeric characters and _. The capital letter versions W, B, and E treat any non-blank character as part of the word allowing the cursor to be moved over punctuation and other non-alphanumeric characters. (A non-blank character is any character other than a space or a tab.) These requests may be preceded by a count, so that,

    3w

moves forwards 3 words.

3.2.3 Additions and deletions

Characters can be inserted or removed at the position marked by the cursor. To re-move a single character type

    x

and to remove the next 3 characters at the cursor type

    3x

Characters are inserted using the i or a request. For example, an insert request, i, is written

    i...esc

where ... represents inserted material and esc is the escape key on your terminal. Inserted material is placed immediately before the cursor and may contain as many lines as needed. Insertion continues until the esc is typed. The append request starts inserting after the cursor rather than before it and has the form

    a...esc

Before describing further vi requests it is worth noting that any ed request can be used from within vi by typing a : followed by the ed request. For example, to quit from vi type

    :q

and to write the buffer back to the file and quit type

    :wq

Once changes have been made you cannot exit from vi using :q unless you have written the buffer to the file.

If a file does not have write permission vi will display a message and refuse to write the file.

3.2.4 Line editing

Material may be appended within a line using the i or a requests. Line by line additions are more readily achieved using the open request

    o
    ...
    esc

that takes the material ... and appends it, line by line, after the current line. The O request has a similar effect but inserts material before the current line.

To remove material from a document, various requests are provided:

x	Delete the current character.
dd	Delete the line containing the cursor.
dw	Delete the current word.
D	Delete the remainder of the current line.
r c	Replace the current character with c.

Most requests may be preceded by a repetition count.

    3dd

will delete 3 lines starting with the current line.

3.2.5 Moving material

Material may be moved from one place to another using a delete request followed by the p request that puts the deleted material after the cursor position. If whole lines have been removed then whole lines will be inserted; whereas, if characters within a line were removed then characters will be inserted after the cursor. A typical sequence would be as follows:

/main/	Look for the string main.
4dd	Delete 4 lines.
3+	Move forward 3 lines.
p	Put the 4 deleted lines after this line.

When characters have been deleted using the x request, the p request will put them back after the cursor, so that for example,

    xp

will exchange the cursor character with the one following it. Deleted material may be put back before the current line or before the cursor using P.

When mistakes are made they can be undone using the u request that reverses the last change. All changes made to the current line may be undone using the U request. However, this does not work if you move to another line and move back even though no editing occurs.

Material that has been deleted can be recovered using the p or P request. Up to the last 9 items deleted may also be recovered. For example,

    "5p

will put back the 5th most recently deleted item.

The . request repeats the last editing change.

dd . . .

will, therefore, remove 4 lines.

Lines may be copied using the yank request Y. For example,

Yp

will yank (copy) the current line into a hidden buffer, and p will place the copy after the current line.

3.2.6 Review

To summarize, the following requests are sufficient to get started with vi, allowing material to be added and removed, the result to be written to a file and to quit. These should be mastered before moving on to the next section.

^D	Scroll the window forwards.
^U	Scroll the window backwards.
^F	Move forward a page.
^B	Move backward a page.
return	Move the cursor down.
—	Move the cursor up.
space	Move the cursor right.
backspace	Move the cursor left.
dd	Delete the current line.
i	Insert text before the current character.
o	Insert text after the current line.
p	Put back deleted or yanked text.
x	Delete the current character.
Y	Yank lines into a buffer.
:w *file*	Write out the changes to *file*.
:q	Quit. :q! bypasses checking.
del	Abandon the current request.

3.2.7 More advanced features

The requests described so far can be learned with a few sessions at a terminal. This section describes features that are useful if the editor is used frequently.

Screen and cursor control

H	Move cursor to the home (first) line of the screen.
L	Move cursor to the last line of the screen.
M	Move cursor to the middle of the screen.
hjkl	Move the cursor left, down, up or right respectively.
wbe	Move the cursor forward, back, or to the end of a word.
/.../	Search forwards for the pattern . . . .
?...?	Search backwards for the pattern . . . .

z.	Center the screen at the current line.
z cr	Redraw the screen at the current line; cr denotes return.
z n.	Use an n line window centered on the screen.
%	Move to the next or previous balanced (,), {, or }.
^E	Display one more line at the bottom of the screen.
^L	Redraw the screen.
^Y	Display one more line at the top of the screen.
0	Move the cursor to the start of the line.

Editing requests

A...	Append to the end of the current line (ends with esc).
C...	Change the rest of the line (ends with esc).
D	Delete the rest of the line.
I...	Insert at the beginning of the current line (ends with esc).
J	Join the current line and the next line.
X	Delete the character before the cursor.
cw...	Change the current word (ends with esc).
rx	Replace the current character with x.
~	Change the case (upper/lower) of the current character.
&	Repeat the last :s request.

Using ed requests

ed requests may be used from vi by preceding them with a :. The following are the commonly used requests.

:sh	Execute a shell.
:!cmd	Execute cmd and return to vi.
:r file	Read file.
:s...	Substitute one string for another.
:g...	Globally search for a string.

Objects

Some requests, such as d take as an argument an *object* specifying what to delete. When the request letter is doubled, as in dd, the request applies to the current line.

Examples of object specifications have already been used, as in dw and cw, where w denotes a word. Objects are specified as follows:

c	A single character.
w	The next alphanumeric word.
W	The next non-blank word.
H	The home line (top) of the screen. 3H is 3 lines from the top of the screen.
L	The last line on the screen. 3L is 3 lines from the bottom of the screen.
/.../	The next line containing the pattern ....

)   The end of the current sentence. A sentence ends with a blank line, or one of the characters . ! ? followed by a blank line or two spaces.

(The start of the current sentence.

}   The end of the current paragraph. A paragraph is defined as ending with a blank line or one of the nroff requests .bp, .IP, .LP, .PP, .QP, .LI, or .P.

{   The start of the current paragraph.

]]   The end of the current section; defined as ending with one of the nroff macros .NH, .SH, .HU, or .H

[[The start of the current section.

The following requests take one of the objects listed above:

cx...   Change up to and including *x* with material terminated by an esc.
dx   Delete up to and including *x*.
yx   Yank the object *x* for use by a subsequent p or P request.
>x   Indent by 8 spaces up to and including the line containing *x*.
<x   Remove an indent of 8 spaces up to and including the line contain-ing *x*.
!x cmd   The text of the object specified is passed as the standard input to cmd. The command is executed and its standard output replaces the object text.

For example,

   !!date

replaces the current line with the output from the date command.

   !}sort

will call sort with its standard input as the next paragraph and replace the para-graph with the sorted output.

Counts

A number preceding a request is a repeat count with the following exceptions.

new window size   [[   ]]   :   /   ?
scroll amount   ^D   ^U
line or column number   z   G |

Editing multiple files

vi can be used to edit a list of files. When invoked as

   vi file₁ file₂ ...

the first file in the list, file₁, is displayed for editing. When the first file has been edited the :n request will read the next file, file₂, into the buffer. If the buffer has not been written back to the file, an error message is printed and no action taken. Also, the quit request, :q, will display a message and refuse to exit unless all files in the list have been edited. The autowrite option of :set (see below) can be used to change this behavior.

If a directory contains many files and only the subset containing a string needs editing the command substitution notation of the shell can be used. For example,

```
vi `grep −l string *`
```

Crash recovery

A system crash happens when the hardware or the system fails and has to be re-started. Although this should be infrequent, vi protects the user from loss of editing time by saving a copy of the buffer in a file. This saved copy is also available if your terminal line hangs up. In either case vi will try to leave mail for you, giving the name of the file being edited and how it can be recovered. The file can be recovered using the −r option when vi is invoked. For example, if the file being edited was named precious, then

```
vi −r precious
```

will restart the editor from where you left off using the saved copy of the buffer. The last editing operation may have been lost depending on the time of the crash.

Setting options

vi has many options for controlling its behavior. To print the current settings the request

```
:set all
```

is used. Each option has a name and is set by one of the forms

```
:set option-name
:set option-name= value
```

and is unset by

```
:set no option-name
```

The options are described below with the abbreviations, if any, in parentheses.

autoindent(ai)	Supply program indentation automatically.
autowrite(aw)	Automatic write before :n and !.
ignorecase(ic)	Ignore upper/lower case when searching.
list	Tabs print as ^I.
number(nu)	Lines are displayed prefixed by numbers.
paragraphs(para)	The names of nroff macros that start paragraphs for the } and { requests. Initially set to IPLPPPQPbpP LI.
redraw(re)	Simulate a smart terminal.
sections(sect)	The name of macros that start sections for the [[and]] requests. Initially set to NHSHH HU.
term	The name of the terminal type being used.

These options may also be set in the environment variable EXINIT. For example,

```
EXINIT=´set ai aw´
export EXINIT
```

arranges for autoindent and autowrite to be set, by default, on entry to vi.

Defining new requests

A definition mechanism is provided in vi allowing a single character to replace a sequence of requests. For example,

> :map = :.=^V CR

defines = to be equivalent to :.= where the ^V escapes the return (CR) at the end of the request. In this request two return characters are required, one for the definition itself and one to terminate the :map request.

As another example,

> :map ; eas^V esc

defines ; to add the letter s at the end of the current word. Again, ^V escapes the character esc in the definition.

The following characters have no associated action in vi and are candidates for definition using the map request.

> K   V   g   q   v   ,   ;   _   *   =

Chapter 4 **The Shell**

The shell is both a programming language and a command language and is often referred to as the command interpreter of the UNIX system. Similarities exist with the command interpreters of the Cambridge Multiple Access System and of CTSS. The notation for simple commands and for parameter passing and substitution is similar in these languages.

As a command language the shell provides a user interface to the UNIX operating system. The shell executes commands that are read either from a terminal or from a file. Files containing commands may be created, allowing users to build their own commands. These newly defined commands may be parameterized and have the same status as the system commands defined in /bin and /usr/bin. In this way a new environment can be established reflecting the requirements or style of an individual or a group.

The design of the shell, therefore, takes into account both interactive and non-interactive use. Except in some minor respects, the behavior of the shell is independent of its input source.

As a programming language the shell provides string-valued variables and control flow primitives including branching and iteration. Functions may be defined using a notation similar to that provided by C. The notation is oriented towards ease of use at a terminal so that strings are not normally quoted. The output from an arbitrary command may be used as a string, enabling arithmetic and other facilities not provided by the shell to be accessed as commands.

Commands are similar to function calls in a language such as C. The notation is different in two respects. First, although the arguments are arbitrary strings, in most cases they need not be enclosed in quotes. Second, there are no parentheses enclosing the list of arguments nor commas separating them. Command languages tend not to have the extensive expression syntax found in algorithmic languages like C. Their primary purpose is to issue commands; it is therefore important that the notation be free from superfluous characters.

4.1 Shell procedures

Interactive use of the shell was introduced in chapter 2. This chapter introduces the shell as a programming language and describes how new commands can be created. The version of the shell described is distributed with System V Release 2.

The shell may be used to read and execute commands contained in a file. For example,

```
sh file [ args ... ]
```

calls the shell to read commands from file. Such a file is called a *command* or *shell* procedure. Arguments may be supplied with the call and are referred to in file using the positional parameters $1, $2, ... For example, if the file wg contains

```
who | grep $1
```

then

```
sh wg fred
```

is equivalent to

```
who | grep fred
```

Files have three independent attributes: *read, write* and *execute*. The command chmod may be used to make a file executable. (See section 6.3.2 for details.) For example,

```
chmod +x wg
```

will ensure that the file wg has execute status. Following this, the command

```
wg fred
```

is equivalent to

```
sh wg fred
```

This allows shell procedures and programs to be used interchangeably. In either case a new process is created to run the command.

As well as providing names for the positional parameters, the number of positional parameters in the call is available as $#. The name of the file being executed is available as $0.

A special shell parameter $* is replaced by all positional parameters except $0. A typical use of this is to provide some default arguments, as in,

```
nroff −T450 −mm $*
```

that simply prepends some arguments to those already given.

Shell procedures can be used to tailor the environment to the tastes and needs of a group or an individual. Since procedures are text files requiring no compilation, they are easy to create and maintain.

4.1.1 Control flow – for

A frequent form for shell procedures is to loop through the arguments ($1, $2, ...) executing commands once for each argument. An example of such a procedure is tel that searches the file /usr/lib/telnos containing lines of the form

```
...
fred mh0123
bert mh0789
...
```

The text of tel is

```
for i do
          grep $i /usr/lib/telnos
done
```

The command

```
tel fred
```

prints those lines in /usr/lib/telnos that contain the string fred.

```
tel fred bert
```

prints those lines containing fred followed by those for bert.

The for loop notation is recognized by the shell and has the general form

```
for name in w1 w2 ...
do command-list
done
```

A command-list is a sequence of one or more simple commands separated or terminated by a newline or ;. Furthermore, reserved words like do and done are normally preceded by a newline or ;. A list of reserved words is given in appendix 6.
name is a shell variable that is set to the words w1 w2 ... in turn each time the
command-list following do is executed. If **in** w1 w2 ... is omitted then the loop is
executed once for each positional parameter; that is, **in** $* is assumed.

Another example of the use of the for loop is the create command whose text
is

```
for i do >$i; done
```

The command

```
create alpha beta
```

ensures that two empty files alpha and beta exist and are empty. The notation >file
may be used on its own to create or clear the contents of a file. Also note the ; (or
newline) required before done. The notation <file may also be used to test for the
existence of a file.

4.1.2 Control flow – case

A multi-way branch is provided for by the case notation. For example,

```
case $# in
        1)        cat »$1 ;;
        2)        cat »$2 <$1 ;;
        *)        echo "usage: append [ from ] to" ;;
esac
```

is an append command. When called with one argument as

```
append file
```

$# is the string 1 and the standard input is copied onto the end of file using the cat
command.

```
append file1 file2
```

appends the contents of file1 onto file2. If the number of arguments supplied to append is other than 1 or 2 then a message is printed indicating proper usage.

The general form of the case command is

```
case word in
         pattern) command-list ;;
             . . .

esac
```

each branch being terminated by ;;. The ;; preceding esac is optional.

The shell attempts to match word with each pattern in the order in which the
patterns appear. If a match is found the associated command-list is executed and
execution of the case is complete. Since * is the pattern that matches any string it
can be used for the default case.

A word of caution: no check is made to ensure that only one pattern matches
the case word. The first match found defines the set of commands to be executed.
In the example below the commands following the second * will never be executed.

```
case $# in
         *) ... ;;
         *) ... ;;
esac
```

Another use of the case construction is to distinguish between different forms
of an argument. The following example is a fragment of a cc command.

```
for i
do       case $i in
         -[ocs])    ... ;;
         -*)        echo "unknown flag $i" ;;
         *.c)       /lib/c0 $i ... ;;
         *)         echo "unexpected argument $i" ;;
         esac
done
```

To allow the same commands to be associated with more than one pattern the
case command provides for alternative patterns separated by a |. For example,

```
case $i in
         -x | -y)   ...
esac
```

is equivalent to

```
case $i in
         -[xy])     ...
esac
```

The usual quoting conventions apply so that

```
case $i in
            \?)        . . .
esac
```

will match the character ? .

4.1.3 Here documents

The shell procedure tel in section 4.1.1 uses the file /usr/lib/telnos to supply the data for grep. An alternative is to include the data within the shell procedure as a *here* document, as in,

```
for i
do        grep $i «!
          . . .
          fred mh0123
          bert mh0789
          . . .
!
done
```

In this example the shell takes the lines between «! and ! as the standard input for grep. The string ! is arbitrary, the document being terminated by a line that consists of the string following « .

```
ed $3 «%
g/$1/s//$2/g
w
%
```

Figure 4.1 The procedure edg

Parameters are substituted in a here document before it is made available to the grep command, as illustrated by the procedure edg in figure 4.1. The call

```
edg string1 string2 file
```

is then equivalent to the command

```
ed file «%
g/string1/s//string2/g
w
%
```

and changes all occurrences of string1 in file to string2. No quit command is needed in ed if the buffer has been written to the file; an end-of-file is sufficient.

Substitution can be prevented using a \ to quote the special character $, as in,

```
ed $3 «+
1,\$s/$1/$2/g
w
+
```

This version of edg is equivalent to the first except that ed will print a ? if there are no occurrences of the string $1. Substitution within a here document may be prevented entirely by quoting the terminating string, for example,

```
grep $i «\:
        . . .
:
```

The document is presented without modification to grep. If parameter substitution is not required in a here document this latter form is more efficient.

4.1.4 Shell variables

The shell provides string-valued variables. Variable names begin with a letter and consist of letters, digits and underscores. Variables may be given values by writing, for example,

```
user=fred box=m000 acct=mh0000
```

that assigns values to the variables user, box and acct. No space should appear around the = character. A variable may be set to the null string by saying, for example,

```
TERM=
```

The value of a variable is substituted by preceding its name with $; for example,

```
echo $user
```

will echo fred.

Variables may be used interactively to provide abbreviations for frequently used strings. For example,

```
b=/usr/fred/bin
mv pgm $b
```

will move the file pgm from the current directory to the directory /usr/fred/bin. A more general notation is available for parameter (or variable) substitution, as in,

```
echo ${user}
```

that is equivalent to

```
echo $user
```

and is used when the parameter name is followed by a letter or digit. For example,

```
tmp=/tmp/ps
ps −a >${tmp}a
```

will direct the output of ps to the file /tmp/psa, whereas,

```
ps −a >$tmpa
```

would cause the value of the variable tmpa to be substituted.

Special variables

Except for $? the following are set initially by the shell. $? is set after executing each command.

$?   The exit status (return code) of the last command executed as a decimal string. Most commands return a zero exit status if they complete successfully, and a non-zero exit status otherwise. Testing the value of return codes is deferred until the section on if and while commands.

$0   The name of the command procedure being executed. This variable can be used to distinguish cases when a command has more than one name. For example, the following script is called ttyhp and a link to the same file exists called ttyblit. If the file is called any other name, and executed by that name then the default case applies. The command sets terminal options using the stty command.

```
case $0 in
        ttyblit)        stty erase ^H kill @ ff0 tabs ;;
        ttytek)         stty erase ^H kill @ tek −tabs ;;
        *)              stty erase ^H kill @ ;;
esac
```

$#   The number of positional parameters (in decimal). Used, for example, in the append command (section 4.1.2) to check the number of parameters. $# is also updated by the set command.

$$ The process number of this shell (in decimal). Since process numbers are unique among all existing processes, this string is frequently used to generate temporary file names. For example,

```
ps −a >/tmp/ps$$
    . . .
rm  /tmp/ps$$
```

$!   The process number of the last process run in the background (in decimal).

$−   The current shell flags, such as −x and −v.

Some variables have a special meaning to the shell and should be avoided for general use. These variables are typically set in the file .profile, in the user's home directory.

$MAIL   When used interactively the shell looks at the file specified by this variable before it issues a prompt. If the specified file has been modified since it was last looked at, the shell prints the message you have mail before prompting for the next command. For example, for user fred this variable is set as

MAIL=/usr/spool/mail/fred

$MAILCHECK This variable specifies how often (in seconds) the shell will check for the arrival of mail in the files specified by the

$MAIL or $MAILPATH variables. The default value is 600. If set to 0, the shell will check before each prompt.

$MAILPATH   A : separated list of file names. If this parameter is set, the shell informs the user of the arrival of mail in any of the specified files. Each file name can be followed by % and a message that will be printed when the modification time changes.

$HOME   The default argument for the cd command. The current directory is used to resolve file name references that do not begin with a /, and is changed using the cd command. For example,

    cd /usr/fred/bin

makes the current directory /usr/fred/bin. The command cd with no argument is equivalent to

    cd $HOME

$CDPATH   The list of directories that is searched by the cd command. Each directory name is separated by :. A typical setting of this variable is

    CDPATH=:...:$HOME/desk

that specifies that cd should search the current directory, the parent directory, .., and lastly, $HOME/desk. For example, if the directory ../src exists and there is no src directory in the current directory,

    cd src

will change directory to ../src and print this string as confirmation.

$PATH   A list of directories that contain commands (the *search path*). A command is either built into the shell, a defined function, or is assumed to exist in the search path. Each time a command is executed by the shell a list of directories is searched for an executable file. If $PATH is not set, then the current directory, /bin, and /usr/bin are searched by default. $PATH consists of directory names separated by :. For example,

    PATH=.:./bin:$HOME/bin:/bin:/usr/bin

specifies that the current directory (the . before the first :), ./bin, $HOME/bin, /bin, and /usr/bin are to be searched in that order. In this way individual users can have their own commands in $HOME/bin that are accessible independently of the current directory. The directory ./bin is included to allow access to any directory named bin from the current directory. This separates commands from data files within a directory associated with some project or activity.

If the command name contains a / then the directory search is not used; a single attempt is made to execute the command. The form ./cmd may be used to bypass the search path for cmd in the current directory.

$PS1	The primary shell prompt string, by default, $.
$PS2	The shell prompts with $PS2 when further input is needed, by default, the value is > .
$IFS	The set of characters used for blank interpretation (see section 4.2.4).
$SHACCT	If this variable is set to the name of a file writable by the user, the shell will write an accounting record in the file for each shell procedure executed.
$SHELL	When the shell is invoked, it scans the environment for this name. If it is found and there is an r in the file name part of its value the shell becomes a restricted shell. The restricted shell provides execution environments whose capabilities are limited. The following are not allowed in a restricted shell: change directory (cd), setting the PATH variable, specifying command names containing /, and redirecting output.

4.1.5 The test command

The test command is intended for use by shell programs. In some versions of the shell test is built-in for efficiency reasons. For example,

    test −f file

returns zero exit status if file exists and non-zero exit status otherwise. In general, test evaluates a predicate and returns the result as its exit status. Some of the more frequently used test arguments are given here.

test s	True if the argument s is not the null string.
test −f file	True if file exists and is not a directory.
test −r file	True if file is readable.
test −w file	True if file is writable.
test −d file	True if file is a directory.

Arithmetic is not provided by the shell but is available indirectly using the expr command.

4.1.6 Control flow – while and until

The actions of the for loop and the case branch are determined by data available to the shell. A while or until loop and an if then else branch are also provided and their actions are determined by the exit status returned by commands. A while loop has the general form

```
while command-list₁
do command-list₂
done
```

The value tested by the while command is the exit status of the last simple command following while. Each time round the loop command-list₁ is executed; if a zero exit status is returned then command-list₂ is executed; otherwise, the loop terminates. For example,

```
while test $1
do        ...
          shift
done
```

is equivalent to

```
for i
do ...
done
```

shift is a shell command that renames the positional parameters $2, $3, ... as $1, $2, ... and loses $1.

When until is used in place of while, the loop termination condition is reversed. The following example waits until the file exists.

```
until test −f file
do sleep 300; done
commands
```

The until test succeeds if the file exists. Each time the loop is executed it waits for 5 minutes (300 seconds) before trying again. (Presumably another process will eventually create the file.)

4.1.7 Control flow – if

Also available is a general conditional branch of the form,

```
if        command-list
then      command-list
else      command-list
fi
```

that tests the value returned by the last simple command following if. The else part is optional. Since this construction is bracketed by if ... fi it may be used unambiguously anywhere that a simple command may be used. Furthermore, there is no dangling else to hinder interactive use.

The if command may be used with the test command to test for the existence of a file as in

```
if test −f file
then      # process file
else      # do something else
fi
```

A complete example of the use of if, case and for constructions is given in section 4.1.10.

A nested if command of the form

```
if ...
then      ...
else      if ...
          ...
          fi
fi
```

may be written using an extension of the if notation as,

```
if ...
then      ...
elif      ...
          ...
fi
```

The example in figure 4.2 is the dw command that recursively scans a directory tree and lists files found. The PATH variable is set to ensure that the right commands are executed. Often the command search path includes ., the current directory. By setting the path explicitly this command has guarded against the possibility of finding a command, also called dw, or test, in a sub-directory.

The for loop checks each name in the current directory. If it exists and is a file, no action is taken; if it is a directory dw is called (recursively) to list the contents in the same way.

```
PATH=/bin:/usr/bin:$HOME/bin

cd $1
ls −l

for i in *
do        if test −f $i
          then      :
          else      dw $i
          fi
done
```

Figure 4.2 The dw command

The sequence

```
if command₁
then      command₂
fi
```

may also be written

command$_1$ && command$_2$

Conversely,

command$_1$ || command$_2$

executes command$_2$ only if command$_1$ fails. In each case the value returned is that of the last simple command executed.

4.1.8 Command grouping

Commands may be grouped in two ways,

{ command-list ; }

and

(command-list)

In the first, command-list is simply executed. The second form executes command-list by a separate shell process. For example,

(cd x; rm junk)

executes rm junk in the directory x without changing the current directory of the invoking shell.

The commands

cd x; rm junk

have the same effect but leave the invoking shell in the directory x.

For historical reasons the parentheses are special characters like | and ; and will be recognized anywhere unless quoted. The braces are reserved words and, like if and do, will only be recognized following a newline or ;.

4.1.9 Debugging shell procedures

The shell provides two mechanisms to help when debugging shell procedures. The first may be invoked within the procedure as

set −v

(v for verbose) and causes lines of the procedure to be printed as they are read. It is useful to help isolate syntax errors. It may be invoked without modifying the procedure by saying

sh −v proc ...

where proc is the name of the shell procedure. Unwanted side-effects may be avoided using the −n flag that prevents execution of commands. (set −n at a terminal will render the terminal useless until an end-of-file is typed.)

The command

set −x

will produce an execution trace. Following parameter substitution each command is printed as it is executed.

Checking for unset shell variables is provided by the −u flag. Using this flag, any attempt to substitute for a variable that has not been set will cause an error message to be printed and execution will stop. (Try these at the terminal to see what effect they have.) All flags may be turned off by saying

```
set −
```

and the current setting of the shell flags is available as $−.

4.1.10 The man command

Figure 4.3 is a version of the man command that prints sections of the *Programmer's Manual*. It is called, for example, as

```
man sh
man −t ed
man 2 fork
```

The first line prints the manual section for sh. Since no section is specified, section 1 is used. The second line will typeset (−t option) the manual section for ed. The last line prints the fork manual page from section 2.

```
cd /usr/man

N=n s=1 # default is nroff ($N), section 1 ($s)

for i
do      case $i in
        [1−9]*)    s=$i ;;
        −t)        N=t ;;·
        −n)        N=n ;;
        −*)        echo "$i: unknown flag" ;;
        *)         if test −f man$s/$i.$s
                   then     ${N}roff −man man$s/$i.$s
                   else     # look through all manual sections
                            found=no
                            for j in 1 2 3 4 5 6 7 8
                            do      if test −f man$j/$i.$j
                                    then     man $j $i
                                             found=yes
                                    fi
                            done
                            case $found in
                            no) echo "$i: manual page not found"
                            esac
                   fi
        esac
done
```

Figure 4.3 A version of the man command

4.2 Advanced use

4.2.1 Parameter transmission

Shell variables may be given values by assignment or when a shell procedure is invoked. An argument to a shell procedure of the form name=value that precedes the command name causes value to be assigned to name before execution of the procedure begins. The value of name in the invoking shell is not affected. For example,

    user=fred command

will execute command with user set to fred. The −k flag causes arguments of the form name=value to be interpreted in this way anywhere in the argument list. Such names are sometimes called keyword parameters. If any arguments remain they are available as positional parameters $1, $2, ...

The set command may also be used to set positional parameters from within a procedure. For example,

    set − *

will set $1 to the first file name in the current directory, $2 to the next, and so on. The first argument, −, ensures correct treatment when the first file name begins with a −.

The *environment* of a process is a list of name-value pairs that is passed to an executed program in the same way as a normal argument list. The shell interacts with the environment in several ways. On invocation, the shell scans the environment and creates a variable for each name found, giving it the corresponding value. Executed commands inherit the same environment. If the user modifies the values of these variables or creates new ones, none of these affects the environment unless the export command is used to bind the shell's parameter to the environment. The environment seen by any executed command is composed of any unmodified name-value pairs originally inherited by the shell, plus any modifications or additions made to exported variables.

When a shell procedure is invoked both positional and keyword parameters may be supplied with the call. Keyword parameters are also made available implicitly to a shell procedure by specifying in advance that such parameters are to be exported. For example,

    export user box

marks the variables user and box for export. When a shell procedure is invoked copies are made of all exported variables for use within the invoked procedure. Modification of such variables within the procedure does not affect the values in the invoking shell. It is generally true of a shell procedure that it may not modify the state of its caller without explicit request by the caller. (Shared file descriptors are an exception to this rule.)

A name whose value is intended to remain constant may be declared readonly. The form of this command is the same as that of the export command, readonly name ...

Subsequent attempts to set readonly variables are rejected.

4.2.2 Parameter substitution

If a shell parameter is not set then the null string is substituted for it. For example, if the variable d is not set

echo $d

or

echo ${d}

will echo nothing. A default string may be given as in

echo ${d−.}

that will echo the value of the variable d if it is set and . otherwise. The default string is evaluated using the usual quoting conventions so that

echo ${d−'*'}

will echo * if the variable d is not set. Similarly

echo ${d−$1}

will echo the value of d if it is set and the value (if any) of $1 otherwise. A variable may be assigned a default value using the notation

echo ${d=.}

that substitutes the same string as

echo ${d−.}

and if d were not previously set then it will be set to the string .. The notation ${...=...} is not available for positional parameters.

If a value must be provided and no default is available, the notation

echo ${d?message}

may be used to echo the value of the variable d if it has one. Otherwise message is printed by the shell and execution of the shell procedure is abandoned. If message is absent then a standard message is printed. A shell procedure that requires some parameters to be set might start as follows.

: ${user?} ${acct?} ${bin?}

...

: is a command that is built into the shell and does nothing once its arguments have been evaluated. If any of the variables user, acct or bin is not set then the shell will abandon execution of the procedure.

The above notation tests unset shell variables. An additional notation is provided that tests shell variables that are either unset or set to the null string. A : is written preceding −, =, or ?. For example,

${d:−.}

will substitute the value of d if it is set and non-null, and . otherwise.

4.2.3 Command substitution

The standard output from a command can be substituted in a similar way to parameters. The command pwd prints on its standard output the name of the current directory. For example, if the current directory is /usr/fred/bin then the command

    d=`pwd`

is equivalent to

    d=/usr/fred/bin

The entire string between grave accents (`...`) is taken as the command to be executed and is replaced with the output from the command. The command is written using the usual quoting conventions except that a ` must be escaped using \. For example,

    ls `echo "$1"`

is equivalent to

    ls $1

Command substitution occurs in all contexts where parameter substitution occurs (including here documents) and the treatment of the resulting text is the same in both cases. This mechanism allows string processing commands to be used within shell procedures. An example of such a command is basename that removes a specified suffix from a string. For example,

    basename main.c .c

will print the string main. Its use is illustrated by the following fragment from a cc command:

    case $A in
        . . .
        *.c)   B=`basename $A .c`
        . . .
    esac

that sets B to the part of $A with the suffix .c stripped.

Here are some composite examples:

    for i in `ls −t`; do . . .
            The variable i is set to the names of files in time order, most recent
            first.
    set `date`; echo $6 $2 $3, $4
            Print, e.g. 1970 Feb 3, 11:59:59. The output from date is Tue Feb 3
            11:59:59 GMT 1970 and the shell breaks up this output as arguments
            for the set command. The result is assigned to the positional param-
            eters.
    a=`expr $a + 1`
            Increment the shell variable a by 1.

4.2.4 Evaluation and quoting

The shell is a macro processor providing parameter substitution, command substitution and file name generation for the arguments to commands. This section discusses the order in which these evaluations occur and the effects of the various quoting mechanisms.

Before a command is executed the following substitutions occur.

- *Parameter substitution*
  $user is an example of parameter substitution. Only one evaluation occurs and the shell does not rescan the substitution string for further substitutions. To illustrate, if the value of the variable X is the string $y then

      echo $X

  will echo $y.

- *Command substitution*
  `pwd` is an example of command substitution. For example, within a profile, the HOME variable might be set as

      HOME=`pwd`

  making the profile independent of the login directory.

- *Blank interpretation*
  Following the above substitutions the resulting characters are broken into non-blank words *(blank interpretation)*. For this purpose blanks are the characters of the string $IFS. By default, this string consists of space, tab and newline. The null string is not regarded as a word unless it is quoted. For example,

      echo ""

  will pass on the null string as the first argument to echo, whereas

      echo $null

  will call echo with no arguments if the variable null is not set or set to the null string.

- *File name generation*
  Each word is finally scanned for the file pattern characters *, ?, and [...] and an alphabetical list of file names is generated to replace the word. Each generated file name is a separate argument.

The evaluations described above also occur in the list of words associated with a for loop. Only parameter and command substitution occurs in the word used for a case branch.

As well as the quoting mechanisms described in section 2.6.3 using \ and ´...´ a third quoting mechanism is provided using double quotes. Within double quotes, parameter and command substitution occurs but file name generation and the interpretation of blanks does not. The following characters have a special meaning within double quotes but may be quoted using \.

$	Parameter substitution.
`	Command substitution.
"	End the quoted string.
\	Quote the special characters $ ` " \.

For example,

```
echo "$x"
```

will pass the value of the variable x as a single argument to echo. Similarly,

```
echo "$*"
```

will pass the positional parameters as a single argument and is equivalent to

```
echo "$1 $2 ..."
```

The notation $@ is the same as $* except when it is quoted.

```
echo "$@"
```

will pass the positional parameters, unevaluated, to echo and is equivalent to

```
echo "$1" "$2" ...
```

When no parameters are present this notation provides a null argument that is useful in the following script.

```
for i in "$@"
do cat $i
done
```

The null argument guarantees that the loop is executed once. In this example, each file is processed, and if no files are provided as arguments the standard input is copied.

Figure 4.4 gives, for each quoting mechanism, the shell metacharacters that are evaluated.

Metacharacter					
	´	"	`	\	$	*
´	t	n	n	n	n	n
"	n	t	y	y	y	n
`	n	n	t	y	n	n

Key: t   terminator
        y   interpreted
        n   not interpreted

Figure 4.4 Shell quoting mechanisms

In cases where more than one evaluation of a string is required, the built-in command eval may be used. For example, if the variable X has the value $y, and if y has the value pqr then eval echo $X

will echo the string pqr.

    In general the eval command evaluates its arguments (as do all commands)
and treats the result as input to the shell. The input is read and the resulting
command(s) executed. For example, if the variable subscript has the value user,
then

    eval echo \$L_$subscript

is equivalent to

    echo $L_user

In this example, eval is required since there is no re-interpretation of the $ charac-
ter after substitution.

    An eval may also be used when syntactic characters, such as |, are to be
evaluated following substitution.

4.2.5 Error handling

The treatment of errors detected by the shell depends on the type of error and on
whether the shell is being used interactively. An interactive shell is one whose input and output are connected to a terminal (as determined by the gtty system call).
A shell invoked with the −i flag is also interactive.

    Execution of a command (see also section 4.2.7) may fail for any of the fol-
lowing reasons.

- Input-output redirection may fail, for example, if a file does not exist or
  cannot be created.
- The command itself does not exist or cannot be executed.
- The command terminates abnormally, for example, with a bus error or a
  memory fault. See figure 4.5 for a list of signals of most interest to shell
  programs. The quit signal produces a core dump if not caught. However, the only external signal that can cause a core dump is quit and this
  signal is ignored by the shell.
- The command terminates normally but returns a non-zero exit status.

Signal	Description
1	hangup
2	interrupt
3	quit
9	kill (cannot be caught or ignored)
15	software termination (from the kill command)

Figure 4.5 UNIX system signals for shell programs

    In all cases the shell will go on to execute the next command. Except for the
last case, an error message will be printed by the shell. All remaining errors cause
the shell to exit from a command procedure. An interactive shell will return to
read another command from the terminal. Such errors include the following.

- Syntax errors, e.g. if ... then ... done where done should be fi.
- A signal such as interrupt. The shell waits for the current command, if any, to finish execution and then either exits or returns to the terminal. The trap command is used to alter this default action on interrupt.
- Failure of any of the built-in commands such as cd.

The shell flag −e causes the shell to terminate if any error is detected.

4.2.6 Fault handling

Shell procedures normally terminate when an interrupt is received from the terminal. The trap command is used if some cleaning up is required, such as removing temporary files. The first argument to trap is the command to be executed. Subsequent arguments indicate signal numbers. For example,

    trap ´rm /tmp/ps$$; exit´ 2

sets a trap for signal 2 (terminal interrupt), and if this signal is received will execute the commands

    rm /tmp/ps$$; exit

exit is another built-in command that terminates execution of a shell procedure. The exit is required in this example; otherwise, after the trap has been taken, the shell will resume executing the procedure at the place where it was interrupted.

Signals can be handled in one of three ways. They can be ignored, in which case the signal is never sent to the process. They can be caught, in which case the process must decide what action to take when the signal is received. Lastly, signals can be left to cause termination of the process without the process having to take any further action. If a signal is being ignored on entry to the shell procedure, for example, by invoking the procedure in the background (see section 4.2.7) then trap commands (and the signal) are ignored.

The use of trap is illustrated by the fragment of a command in figure 4.6. The cleanup action is to remove the file junk$$ and exit.

---

    trap ´rm −f junk$$; exit´ 0 1 2 3 15

Figure 4.6 An example of the use of the trap command

The trap command should appear before the creation of the temporary file; otherwise it would be possible for the process to die without removing the file.

Signal number 0 is not used by the system and so it is assigned by the shell to indicate exit from a shell procedure.

A procedure may elect to ignore signals by specifying the null string as the argument to trap. The following fragment is taken from the nohup command.

    trap ´´ 1 2 3 15

and causes hangup, interrupt, quit and kill to be ignored both by the procedure and by invoked commands.

Traps may be reset by saying, for example,

trap 2 3

that resets the traps for signals 2 and 3 to their default values. A list of the current values of traps may be obtained by writing

trap

There is no need for a trap command to include an exit. The procedure scan (figure 4.7) is an example of the use of trap where execution resumes once the trap has been executed. scan takes each directory in the current directory, prompts with its name, and then executes commands typed at the terminal until an end-of-file or an interrupt is received. The : command does nothing once its arguments have been evaluated, so that

trap : 2

causes interrupts to be effectively ignored while executing eval $x. When waiting for input, executing the statement read x,

trap exit 2

is in effect.

```
d=`pwd`
for i in *
do        if test −d $d/$i
          then    cd $d/$i
                  while     echo "$i:"
                            trap exit 2
                            read x
                  do trap : 2; eval $x; done
          fi
done
```

Figure 4.7 The scan command

read x is a built-in command that reads one line from the standard input and places the result in the variable x. It returns a non-zero exit status if either an end-of-file is read or an interrupt is received.

4.2.7 Command execution

To run most commands the shell first creates a new process using the system call fork. Commands requiring a new process include simple commands, commands enclosed in parentheses, and shell constructs such as while and for, with input-output redirection present. A command is either built into the shell, a defined function, or is assumed to exist in the search path. No new process is created for built-in commands or functions.

The *execution environment* for a command includes open files, the umask value, the current directory, and the states of signals, and is established in the child process before the command is executed. The built-in command exec is used when a new process is not needed and simply replaces the shell with a new command. For example, a simple version of the nohup command is

```
trap '' 1 2 3 15
exec "${@?}"
```

The trap turns off the signals specified so that they are ignored by subsequently created commands and exec replaces the shell by the command specified as arguments.

4.2.8 Input-output redirection

Most forms of input-output redirection have already been described. In the following, word is only subject to parameter and command substitution. No file name generation or blank interpretation takes place so that, for example,

```
echo ... >*.c
```

will write its output into a file whose name is *.c. Input-output specifications are evaluated left to right as they appear in the command. If word is the null string then no redirection occurs. For example,

```
cat <$1
```

Is the same as cat with no redirection if $1 is unset or the null string.

> word   The standard output (file descriptor 1) is sent to the file word that is created if it does not already exist.

>> word   The standard output is sent to the file word. If the file exists then output is appended (by seeking to the end); otherwise the file is created.

< word   The standard input (file descriptor 0) is taken from the file word.

<< word   The standard input is taken from the lines of shell input that follow up to but not including a line consisting only of word. If word is quoted then no interpretation of the here document occurs. If word is not quoted then parameter and command substitution occur and \ quotes the characters \, $, ` and the first character of word. In the latter case \newline is ignored (cf. quoted strings). If word is the null string then an empty line terminates input. If word begins with − white space is removed from the start of each line of the here document.

>& digit   The file descriptor digit is duplicated using the system call dup and the result is used as the standard output.

<& digit   The standard input is duplicated from the file descriptor digit.

<&−   The standard input is closed.

>&−   The standard output is closed.

Any of the above may be preceded by a digit in which case the file descriptor created is that specified by the digit instead of the default 0 or 1. For example,

```
... 2>file
```

runs a command with error output (file descriptor 2) directed to file.

```
... 2>&1
```

runs a command with its standard output and error output merged. (Strictly speaking file descriptor 2 is created by duplicating file descriptor 1 but the effect is usually to merge the two streams.)

Within a shell procedure the standard input, output and error output may be redirected using the above forms and the exec command. For example,

```
exec >stdout 2>errout
```

redirects the standard output to the file stdout and the error output to errout. These are the default outputs for subsequently executed commands.

The environment for a command run in the background such as

```
list *.c | lpr &
```

is modified in two ways. Firstly, the default standard input for such a command is the empty file /dev/null. This prevents two processes (the shell and the command) that are running in parallel, from trying to read the same input. Chaos would ensue if this were not the case. For example,

```
ed file &
```

would allow both the editor and the shell to read from the same input at the same time.

The other modification to the environment of a background command is to turn off the quit and interrupt signals so that they are ignored by the command. This allows these signals to be used at the terminal without causing background commands to terminate. The hangup signal is not automatically ignored by background processes. The nohup command is provided for this purpose. Consequently, the convention for a signal is that if it is set to 1 (ignored) then it is never changed even for a short time. The shell command trap has no effect for an ignored signal.

4.2.9 Invoking the shell

The following flags are interpreted by the shell when it is invoked. If the first character of argument zero is − commands are read from the system profile /etc/profile followed by the user file .profile. Shell output is written to file descriptor 2.

−c s   If the −c flag is present then commands are read from the string s. This form is often used by C programs that pass commands to the shell for execution. This is how ed implements the ! request.

−s   If the −s flag is present or if no arguments remain then commands are read from the standard input.

−i   If the −i flag is present or if the shell input and output are attached to a terminal (as told by gtty) then this shell is *interactive*. The terminate signal is ignored (so that kill 0 does not kill an interactive shell) and the interrupt signal is caught and ignored (so that wait can be interrupted). The quit signal is always ignored by the shell.

Errors detected by the shell, such as syntax errors cause the shell to return a non-zero exit status. If the shell is being used non-interactively then execution of the shell file is abandoned. Otherwise, the shell returns the exit status of the last command executed (see also exit).

4.3 Built-in commands

Certain functions are built into the shell, either of necessity, or for efficiency reasons. These commands are executed in the shell process and except where specified no input-output redirection is permitted.

:   No effect; the command does nothing and returns zero exit status.

. file   Read and execute commands from file and return. The search path $PATH is used to find the directory containing file.

break [n] Exit from the enclosing for or while loop, if any. If n is specified then break n levels.

continue [n]
            Resume the next iteration of the enclosing for or while loop. If n is specified then resume at the n-th enclosing loop.

cd [arg] Change the current directory to arg. The shell parameter $HOME is the default arg. Also, the shell variable CDPATH is used to search for directories containing arg. This is fully described in section 4.1.4.

echo [arg ...]
            Echo arguments. See the echo command.

eval [arg ...]
            The arguments are read as input to the shell and the resulting command(s) executed.

exec [arg ...]
            The command specified by the arguments is executed in place of this shell without creating a new process. Input-output arguments may appear and, if no other arguments are given, cause the shell input-output to be modified.

exit [n] Causes the shell to exit with exit status n. If n is omitted then the exit status is that of the last command executed. (An end-of-file will also exit from the shell.)

export [name ...]
            The given names are marked for automatic export to the environment of subsequently executed commands. If no arguments are given then the exported variable names are listed.

hash [−r] [name ...]
            The shell maintains a hash table for each command executed that records where the command was found in the search path. The hash command provides information about this hash table. Names may be added to this table using the form hash name. All names in the table are removed by hash −r.

            If no arguments are given, information about remembered commands is presented. hits is the number of times a command has been invoked by this shell process. cost is a measure of the work required to locate a command in the search path. The hash table entries can become out of date, for example, when the entry is relative to the current directory and the current directory is changed. Such entries are indicated by an asterisk (*) adjacent to the hits information. cost is incremented when the recalculation is done.

newgrp [arg . . .]

Equivalent to exec newgrp arg . . . . See the newgrp command.

pwd   Print the current working directory. See the pwd command.

read name . . .

One line is read from the standard input; successive words of the input are assigned to the variables name in order; any remaining words are assigned to the last variable. The return code is 0 unless an end-of-file is encountered.

readonly [name . . .]

The value of the given names may not be changed by subsequent assignment. If no arguments are given then a list of all readonly names is printed.

return [n]Causes a function to exit with the return value specified by n. If n is omitted, the return status is that of the last command executed.

set [−aefhkntuvx [arg . . .]]

   −a   Mark variables which are modified or created for export.
   −e   If non-interactive then exit immediately if a command fails.
   −f   Disable file name generation.
   −h   Locate and remember function commands as functions are defined.
   −k   All keyword arguments are placed in the environment for a command, not only those that precede the command name.
   −n   Read commands but do not execute them.
   −t   Exit after reading and executing one command.
   −u   Treat unset variables as an error when substituting.
   −v   Print shell input lines as they are read.
   −x   Print commands and their arguments as they are executed.
   −   Turn off the −x and −v options.

Using + rather than − causes these flags to be turned off. These flags can also be used on invocation of the shell. The setting of flags may be found in $−. Remaining arguments to the set command are assigned, in order, to $1, $2, ... If no arguments are given then the values of all names are printed.

shift [n]   The positional parameters from $n+1 . . . are renamed $1 . . . . If n is not given, it is assumed to be 1.

test   Evaluate conditional expressions. See the test command.

times   Print the accumulated user and system times for processes run from the shell.

trap [arg] [n] . . .

arg is a command to be read and executed when the shell receives signal(s) n. arg is evaluated once when the trap is set and once when the trap is taken. Trap commands are executed in order of signal number. Any attempt to set a trap on a signal that was ignored on entry to the current shell is ineffective. An attempt to trap on signal 11 (memory fault) produces an error. If arg is absent then all trap(s) n are reset to their original values. If arg is the null string then this signal is ignored by the shell and by invoked commands. If n is 0 then the command arg is executed on exit from the shell. trap with no arguments prints a list of commands associated with each signal number.

type [name ...]

For each name, indicate how it would be interpreted if used as a command name.

ulimit [−fp] [n]

Imposes a size of limit n.

−f   Imposes a size limit of n blocks on files written by child processes (files of any size may be read). With no argument, the current limit is printed.

−p   Changes the pipe size to n.

If no option is given, −f is assumed.

umask [ddd]

The user file creation mask is set to the octal value ddd (see the umask system call). If ddd is omitted, the current value of the mask is printed.

unset [name ...]

For each name, remove the corresponding variable or function. The variables PATH, PS1, PS2, MAILCHECK, and IFS cannot be unset.

wait [n]   Wait for the specified process and report its termination status. If n is not given then all currently active child processes are waited for. The return code from this command is that of the process waited for.

Chapter 5 **The C Programming Language**

C is the programming language used to write the UNIX operating system and most of its commands. The language was developed at the same time as the system was being written and has evolved to its current state over a decade. Both machine dependent and machine portable programs may be written and compilers for the language exist for many different machines although the first compiler was written for a PDP 11/45.

Historically C was influenced by BCPL, a language developed at M.I.T. and later at Cambridge University. The link between these two languages was through the language B.

BCPL is a typeless language that supports only one object, the machine word. All language operations are defined on words and storage is also allocated on this basis. The language is appealing because of its simplicity. A portable compiler was available in the late 1960s and it was used for writing operating systems.

The historical origins of C help explain some aspects of the language design. It was intended for systems programming and similarity to the machine was considered important. For example, the ++ operator has a direct equivalent in the PDP 11 instruction set. Features allowing portable programs to be written, such as unions, were added to the language in the late 1970s. Traces of the typeless origin of C can still be seen in the ease with which integers and characters, or pointers and integers, can be mixed in some implementations. Type checking is also absent when parameters are passed to functions.

C provides different basic data objects such as int, char, float and double and also has types derived by aggregation using arrays and structures. Other derived types include enumerations, pointers, unions and structures. The type structure of C is similar to languages like ALGOL 68 and Pascal. C differs in the strictness with which type mismatches are treated. Some C compilers will, for example, permit the assignment of a pointer value to an integer variable. In Pascal no semantics are defined for this operation and it is, therefore, not implemented. The permissive approach to types adopted in C allows programs such as storage allocators to be written provided some information is available about the implementation.

C provides standard control flow primitives such as if and switch for selection and while and for for iteration. In addition, functions may be defined to return values and can be called recursively. A function that returns no value may be declared void in a similar way to ALGOL 68.

This chapter introduces C as a language and also describes ways that C programs can be organized, maintained and debugged. C is used to describe the UNIX system calls in the next chapter.

The next section of this chapter describes briefly, and with examples, the main elements of the C language. Since this language has evolved over many years there are different versions of the compiler in existence.

5.1 Sample C programs

5.1.1 A simple program

The following simple C program

```
main( )
{
        printf("It works.\n");
}
```

will print the text

    It works.

on the standard output.

The source text of the program must be placed in a file whose name ends with .c, such as simple.c. To compile this program the C compiler is invoked by the cc command

    cc simple.c

that produces an executable program called a.out. Alternatively, using the −o option of the cc command

    cc −o simple simple.c

produces the executable program in the file simple. The executable program can then be executed by typing the command

    simple

Let us return to the original C program. All C programs, by convention, have a function called main where execution of the program begins. In this program it is the only function defined. The parentheses ( ) indicate that no parameters are used by main. The text of main is enclosed between { and }. There is only a single statement terminated by a ; calling the function printf to format output. Character strings are enclosed within double quotes as in the example above. In strings, \n denotes the newline character and causes a new line to be started on the output.

5.1.2 An octal dump

The program in figure 5.1 is a simplified version of the od command that reads its standard input and prints each character as an octal integer (base 8) on the standard output. After every 10 characters a new line is started.

This program illustrates several new features of C. The functions getchar and putchar are the two basic input-output routines defined in the C system library. getchar returns the integer equivalent of the next input character from the standard input. Conversely, putchar takes an integer as its argument and prints the corresponding character on the standard output.

The first line of the program is the #include statement incorporating the definitions required when using the standard input-output library. The value returned by
getchar when an end-of-file is reached is denoted by the symbolic constant EOF
that is defined in the *header* file <stdio.h>.

```
#include <stdio.h>

int main()
{
        int c, n;

        n = 1;
        while ((c = getchar()) != EOF) {
                printf("%o ", c);
                if (n++ >= 10) {
                        n = 1;
                        printf("\n");
                }else{
                        printf(" ");
                }
        }
        if (n != 1) {
                /* end unfinished line */
                printf("\n");
        }
        return(0);
} /* main */
```

Figure 5.1 A simple octal dump command

The body of main consists of declarations and statements in that order. Let us
examine the various parts in some detail:

main()   Declare the function main required in all C programs as the starting
            point of execution.

int c, n;   Declare two integer variables called c and n.

n=1;   Assign 1 to n.

(c = getchar())!=EOF
            The expression c=getchar() is an assignment that can also be used as
            part of an expression. Its value within the expression is the quantity
            assigned to c. The operator != tests for inequality so that (...)!=EOF
            returns true if the next character read is not the end-of-file.

while (...) {...}
            The condition in parentheses is evaluated and, if true, the loop body
            enclosed in {...} is executed. This process is repeated until the con-
            dition is false. The loop body is the statement enclosed between
            braces.

```
printf("%o", c);
```
>   Print c according to the octal format %o.

n++
>   Add 1 to n. The value of this expression is the value of n before being incremented.

n++ >= 10;
>   Compare the value of n with 10 and return true or false; 1 is added to n after its value has been used in the comparison.

if (...) {...}
>   The condition in parentheses is evaluated and, if true, the statements enclosed between the braces are executed. Otherwise, the statement following else is executed.

5.1.3 Average distances

The game Star Trek is played on a 9×9 board divided into quadrants. In this game it is an advantage to know the average distance of a star base from every quadrant before starting to play. In deciding whether to play a particular game it is useful to know the average distance of any point from every other point on a grid. The program in figure 5.2 prints averages for a grid of size 9×9.

- The #include and #define statements are interpreted by the C preprocessor, cpp. #include has already been introduced in the previous example and is used here to obtain the declaration of sqrt() from the standard mathematical library. #define is a constant declaration. Whenever XMAX is used in the program it is replaced by 9.

- The declaration

```
double average();
```

  introduces the function and its result type double. This allows the function to be used before it is defined later in the program.

- The declaration

```
double sum = 0.0;
```

  introduces the real variable sum and initializes its value to zero. All variables must be declared and the declaration must precede the first use.

- The for statement

```
for (x=0; x<XMAX; x++) {
        statements;
}
```

  is equivalent to the while statement

```
x=0;
while (x<XMAX) {
        statements;
        x++;
}
```

  and repeatedly executes statement until x exceeds or equals XMAX.

```
#include <math.h>

#define XMAX 9
#define YMAX 9

double average();

int main()
{
        int x, y;
        double sum = 0.0;

        for (x=0; x<XMAX; x++) {
                printf("%d: ", x);
                for (y=0; y<YMAX; y++) {
                        double s=average(x, y);
                        sum+=s;
                        printf("%.2f ", s);
                }
                printf("\n");
        }
        printf("average=%f\n", sum/(YMAX*XMAX));
} /* main */

double average(x0, y0)
        int x0, y0;
{
        int x, y;
        double sum = 0.0;

        for (x=0; x<XMAX; x++) {
                for (y=0; y<YMAX; y++) {
                        double d = (x-x0)*(x-x0)+(y-y0)*(y-y0);
                        sum += sqrt(d);
                }
        }
        sum /= (XMAX*YMAX-1);
        return(sum);
} /* average */
```

Figure 5.2 The program average

● The output statement

    printf("%d: ", x);

.prints x as a decimal integer followed by : . The first argument to printf is
a string that is printed except for embedded *formats*.

The format determines how the remaining arguments are interpolated within the printed string. A *format* such as %d is replaced by the decimal representation of the next integer argument. Within this program the formats %f and %.2f are also used; the former prints a floating-point number using a default format, whereas in the latter case the floating-point number has two digits after the decimal point. The format %6.2f requests a field of width 6 with two places after the decimal point.

- The statement

```
double s = average(x, y);
```

declares the variable s and initializes it to the value returned by the function average, called with parameters x and y.

- The statement

```
sum += s;
```

introduces the assignment operator += and is equivalent to

```
sum = sum+s;
```

Similarly, in the function average

```
sum /= (XMAX*YMAX−1);
```

is equivalent to

```
sum = sum/(XMAX*YMAX−1);
```

- The definition of average declares its result type as double and the two parameters required, x0 and y0. The statement

```
return(sum);
```

exits from the function with the resulting value sum.

The program average is compiled as

```
cc −o average average.c −lm
```

The argument −lm instructs cc to load the mathematical subroutine library containing the definition of the sqrt function.

5.2 The language

This section presents the details of the C programming language starting with identifiers, constants, basic data types, expressions, and followed by flow of control, function declarations, arrays and pointers and finally, storage classes.

5.2.1 Lexical considerations

Comments and spaces

Comments start with the characters /* and end with the next occurrence of */. Within a comment /* is not treated specially so that nesting is not permitted. Spaces, tabs and newlines are also used to separate identifiers and reserved words.

Identifiers

Identifiers are used for variables, labels and function names. An identifier consists of a sequence of letters or digits starting with a letter; an _ is also considered to be a letter; upper and lower case letters are distinct.

External identifiers (used in more than one program file) are often limited to 6, 7 or 8 characters in length and there may be no distinction between upper and lower case letters. These details depend on the implementation.

Certain identifiers are reserved for use as language keywords and may not be used as variable names. The list of reserved keywords is shown in figure 5.3. In some implementations asm and fortran are also reserved.

auto	do	for	return	typedef
break	double	goto	short	union
case	else	if	sizeof	unsigned
char	enum	int	static	void
continue	extern	long	struct	while
default	float	register	switch	

Figure 5.3 Reserved words in C

Basic data types

The language supports several basic data types. Briefly, the type determines how the object in an identifier's storage is to be interpreted.

A character variable will store any object from the available character set and its value is that of the equivalent integer (ASCII or EBCDIC) character code.

Up to three sizes of integers are available: short int, int, and long int. Longer integers provide at least as much storage as shorter integers. Unsigned integers are written unsigned short int, unsigned int, or unsigned long int. The int may be omitted when unsigned is present. Unsigned integers obey the laws of arithmetic modulo 2^n where n depends on the implementation.

Single precision floating-point numbers have type float and double precision floating-point numbers have type double.

Figure 5.4 illustrates typical storage requirements for the basic data types for the PDP 11/45 and VAX 11/780. On both machines ASCII is the character code used.

Type	PDP 11/45	VAX 11/780
char	8	8
short int	16	16
int	16	32
long int	32	32
float	32	32
double	64	64

Figure 5.4 Sizes of objects in C

Constants

An integer constant is a sequence of digits. The constant is a decimal number unless the sequence of digits starts with a leading zero; then the constant is regarded as an octal number. If the string of digits is preceded by 0x or 0X (0 being the digit zero) the digits that follow are assumed to be hexadecimal where a–f or A–F are the digits corresponding to 10 through 15, respectively.

When an octal, decimal or hexadecimal constant exceeds the largest unsigned machine integer it is considered to be long. Long constants are written by placing an l or L immediately after the usual form. For example 0L is a long zero.

Character constants are enclosed within single quotes, thus ´c´. The value of a character constant is the numerical value in the character set of the machine. A \ is used as an escape character to introduce certain special characters as shown below:

Character	Escape
newline	\n
horizontal tab	\t
vertical tab	\v
backspace	\b
carriage return	\r
formfeed	\f
backslash	\\
single quote	\´
null	\0

Any character can be written as \ddd where d is an octal digit. If a \ is followed by any character other than those mentioned above then the \ is ignored.

String constants are written as a sequence of characters enclosed between double quotes, as in "...".´ Within a string the same escape character conventions described for character constants apply. A digit following the null character should be written \000d where d is the digit. Additionally, \" is used for the double quote character itself, and \newline is ignored allowing long strings to be continued over more than one line. The null character ´\0´ is automatically inserted at the end of string constants.

Floating-point constants contain either a decimal point or an exponent part and possibly both. The general form is

integer-part . fractional-part e $\pm$ *exponent*

All floating point constants are implemented as double-precision. The following are examples of floating point constants.

0.0
3.14159
3e10

5.2.2 Expressions and operators

Expressions in C are formed from constants, identifiers, subscripted variables, structure or union references, and function calls combined using both unary and binary operators.

Binary operators are left associative, unless otherwise stated, so that

```
a − b − c
```

is interpreted as

```
( a − b ) − c
```

The binary operators can be grouped under the following categories.

Arithmetic operators

The binary arithmetic operators are, +, −, *, and /, together with the modulus operator % for integers. Whenever / is used between integers, integer division takes place; the decimal point and all subsequent digits of the result are omitted. If positive integers are divided, the quotient is truncated toward zero; if either operand is negative the result is machine dependent.

Relational operators

The operators >, >=, <=, and < are the relational operators, greater-than, greater-than-or-equal-to, less-than-or-equal-to, and less-than respectively. These operators return 0 if the comparison is false and 1 if it is true.

Equality operators

The equality operator is == and the inequality operator is !=. The value returned is 0 if the result is false and 1 if it is true.

Shift operators

The two operators ≪ and ≫ allow a bit pattern (the left operand) to be shifted by n places left or right, respectively; n must be non-negative and less than the size of the objects in bits. If the quantity is signed, either zeros or ones fill vacated positions for a right shift depending on the implementation. If the quantity being shifted is unsigned then zeros are always used to fill vacated positions.

Bitwise operators

There are three bitwise operators &, |, and ^. The & operator performs the AND operation on corresponding bits. The | operator performs the inclusive OR operation on corresponding bits. The ^ operator performs the exclusive OR on corresponding bits.

Logical operators

There are two logical operators && and ||. The logical AND operator && returns 1 if both operands are non-zero, and 0 otherwise. The && operator differs from & in that the right operand is evaluated only if the left operand is non-zero.

The logical OR operator | | returns 1 if each of the operands is non-zero, and 0 otherwise. Again a left-to-right evaluation is used; the second operand is not evaluated if the first operand is non-zero.

Comma operator

exp_1 , exp_2

exp_1 is evaluated and its result discarded; the result delivered is exp_2. The comma operator is useful when the evaluation of exp_1 can influence the result of exp_2, as in

    while (reserv++, word( )!=´\n´) ...

but the language syntax requires a single expression. In this example, reserv is used by the function word.

Assignment operators

An assignment has the form

    lvalue = *rvalue*

where an *lvalue* is one of the following:

    identifier
    * *expression*
    expression . field
    expression -> field
    expression [*expression*]
    (*lvalue*)

and an *rvalue* is any C expression. The left hand and right hand sides of the assignment are evaluated and the rvalue is stored in the location specified by the lvalue.

When a value is assigned to a variable, truncation may occur. For example, in the context of the declaration

    int i;
    char c;

the assignment

    c = i;

may lose some information in the value stored in c. This is sometimes called truncation. The program checker lint will detect this potential problem.

The operator += is defined so that

    x += y

is equivalent to

    x = x + y

The result of the operation is the value stored in the left hand variable following the assignment.

The operator += is a special case of a set of assignment operators that include =, −=, *=, /=, %=, >>=, <<=, &=, ^=, and |=. Operators of this form are defined so that

    x op= y

and

    x = x op y

are equivalent except that x is evaluated only once.

Conditional operator

The conditional operator ? : takes the form

    exp ? exp₁ : exp₂

If exp is non-zero, the result is the value of exp₁, otherwise it is exp₂. If the types of exp₁ and exp₂ are different, conversion will occur to yield the result. Mixing arithmetic and non-arithmetic values for exp₁ and exp₂ should be avoided.

A conditional expression may not be used directly on the left hand side of an assignment since it does not deliver an lvalue.

Unary operators

The unary operators are listed below. e represents an expression; v denotes an lvalue.

Operator	Description
*e	Contents of e, for use with pointers.
&v	Address of v, for use with pointers.
−e	Unary minus.
!e	Logical (Boolean) negation.
~e	Bitwise complement of e.
++v	Equivalent to v=v+1.
−−v	Equivalent to v=v−1.
v++	Produces the value of v and then increases v by 1.
v−−	Produces the value of v and then decreases v by 1.
(type)e	Cast e to the specified type.
sizeof(e)	The number of bytes occupied by e.
sizeof(type)	The number of bytes occupied by items of this type.

Conversion of values

Conversion of values from one type to another is available explicitly using the cast operator. Conversion also occurs automatically when an expression appears as a function argument or as an operand. The rules for the conversion of arithmetic values are described below. Pointers are discussed in section 5.2.5.

●   A char or a short is converted to int. A character is considered signed, and sign extension occurs during the conversion to integer. Unsigned short integers should be used where appropriate. A float is similarly converted to double.

- Then, if either operand is double the other is converted to double.
- Otherwise, if either operand is long the other is converted to long.
- Otherwise, if either operand is unsigned the other is converted to unsigned.
- Otherwise both operands are int.

When passing arguments to functions no type checking occurs. However in this context, a short or char value is always converted to an int and a float to a double. It is advisable to be sure that the necessary type conversions have been performed. For example, sin(3) is incorrect since the sin function expects a double as its argument and not an int. Correct forms for this call are sin((double)3) or sin(3.0).

Operator precedence and associativity

Figure 5.5 summarizes the operators from higher to lower precedence. Operators on the same line have the same precedence level. When several operators of the same precedence level appear together, they usually associate left-to-right. However, exceptions to this rule are listed. When in doubt, or if the expression is complicated, use parentheses.

Operator	*Associativity*
( ) [ ] –> . ! ~ ++ –– – * & * / % + – ≪ ≫ < <= > >= == != & ^ | && || ? : = += ... ,	right to left right to left right to left

Figure 5.5 Operator precedence in C

The order of evaluation of expression operands and function arguments is not defined by C. As a result the order of side-effects when calling functions cannot be relied upon. Further, expressions involving the commutative operators

    *   +   & | ^

may be arbitrarily rearranged by the compiler, so that

    a + b + c

may be evaluated as (a + b) + c or as a + (b + c).

5.2.3 Control flow

C provides a range of control flow facilities. Normal sequencing of statements is provided by juxtaposition. Branching is provided by if and switch and iteration by for, while and do.

The conditional statement

The form of the conditional statement is

    if (expression) statement₁ **else** statement₂

The expression is evaluated and if it is non-zero statement₁ is executed; otherwise statement₂ is executed. Both statement₁ and statement₂ can be a block or compound statement of the form

    {
                optional-declarations
                statements
    }

The **else** statement can be omitted producing

    if (expression) statement₁

The statement

    if (expression₁)
                if (expression₂)
                            statement₁
                else
                            statement₂

is potentially ambiguous since the else part could be associated with either the first or second if. C chooses to associate the else with the inner if so that the indented layout shown is particularly misleading. This form should be avoided by using the compound statement, as in,

    if (expression) {
                . . .
    }

The switch statement

The switch statement provides a multi-way branch of the form

    switch (expression)
                statement

The expression is evaluated to produce an integer result. The statement normally takes the form of a compound statement several of whose statements may be labeled by

case constant-expression:

The constant-expression may be an integer or character constant such as 1 or ´A´ possibly combined with the operators

    ~ − * / % + −
    ≪ ≫ & ^ | ?:
    < <= > >= == !=

The statement labeled by a constant-expression is executed if the integer value of the switch expression is equal to the constant-expression. If no match is found control is transferred to the default statement, if any. At most one statement may be labeled

default:

Execution continues from one case to the next and the break statement

break;

is required to exit from within the switch to the statement following the switch.

Iteration

The while loop has the form

while (expression)
        statement

The expression is evaluated and if it is non-zero, statement is executed. This process is repeated until a zero value is returned by expression. The statement of a while loop can be compound.

The general form of the for statement is convenient for loops that have an initial condition, an increment and an exit condition. Its form is

for (expression$_1$; expression$_2$; expression$_3$)
        statement

Formally, this is equivalent to

expression$_1$;
while (expression$_2$) {
        statement;
        expression$_3$
}

The for and while loop statements evaluate the condition that terminates the loop at the start of the loop. The do...while form of loop tests an expression after the statement is executed. Thus,

do statement
while (expression);

executes the statement and then checks the value of expression before repetition.

To terminate a loop during execution the break statement is used. The effect of

break;

is to terminate the innermost enclosing for, while, or do loop, or switch statement. The break statement does not permit a jump outside several nested loops. To achieve this effect the goto statement is used. Thus

goto error;

where error is a label marking a statement, as in

error: statement

A label has the same form as an identifier and it must be defined in the same function body as its accompanying goto. Thus jumps from one function to another are not permitted. The subroutines setjmp and longjmp described in section 5.2.9 provide for 'non-local' jumps.

The continue statement avoids the use of goto and causes the current execution of the loop body to terminate and the next iteration to begin. It is equivalent to a jump to the end of the loop body, but not out of the loop itself.

5.2.4 Functions

Functions in C are similar to routines in ALGOL 68 or to procedures in PL/I. A body of program can be named and then invoked elsewhere as many times as needed. A function may be defined, even if it is only called once, simply to identify an activity.

All functions need a definition that introduces the result type, argument types, formal parameter names, and the body. If a function is to be used textually before it is defined a declaration may be made specifying the result type and function name, as in the example of the function average in section 5.1.3. Otherwise, only a definition is needed.

The general form of a definition is

result-type function-name (argument-names)
       argument-declarations
{
       function-body
}

If there is no result, the result-type void is used and no value should be returned. If the result-type is omitted then int is assumed. Functions that are called before they are defined or declared are also assumed to return an int value.

The statements in the function body begin with declarations of local variables. Subsequent program statements may contain the return statement. If no return statement is present then the function will end after the last statement in its body.

A return statement of the form

    return;

exits from the function to the place where the call occurred but no value is returned. If the caller expects a value to be returned then the statement

    return expression;

should be used.

Function calls

Functions may be called either as a statement or as part of an expression. When
used as a statement any value returned is discarded. If a function is used within an
expression a value should be returned.

Function arguments (or parameters) are passed by value. Each argument is
evaluated and a copy made available to the called function. This allows the formal
parameters of a function to be used as variables within the function body without
affecting the values of variables where the function is called. Some functions,
such as printf, accept a variable number of arguments of differing types. However,
printf assumes that the format string and the number and type of the arguments is in
agreement. If not, unexpected results can occur.

No type checking is performed to ensure that the type of the formal and actual
parameters match. However, lint does perform these checks.

A single result may be returned using the return statement. Results may also
be returned through parameters using pointers.

When a function does not deliver a result it should only be called as a statement. Functions may be recursive, even mutually recursive. However, function
definitions may not be nested.

5.2.5 Arrays and pointers

Arrays

Arrays provide a set of variables of the same kind. Thus

    int a[10];

makes available 10 integer variables a[0], a[1], ..., a[9]. The square brackets select
an element of the array. Subscripted variables such as a[i] or a[2*i+4] are lvalues
and can appear in expressions, be passed to functions and be assigned to, as in,

    a[i]=4;

In a similar way,

    char c[100];

makes available 100 character variables c[0], c[1], ..., c[99].

Multi-dimensional arrays are introduced, as in,

    int matrix[10][100];

thereby creating the elements matrix[i][j] for $0 \leq i \leq 9$, $0 \leq j \leq 99$.

The bounds of arrays are constant and fixed at compile time. The C preprocessor is normally used to define constants for use as array bounds.

Arrays can be passed as parameters to functions. However, unlike Pascal, bounds for one-dimensional arrays may be omitted from the parameter specifications, as in,

```
int length(buffer, size)
        char buffer[];
        int size;
{
        int i=0;

        while (i<size && (buffer[i]!=' ') ) {
                i++;
        }
        return(i);
} /* length */
```

No space is allocated for the array itself when it appears as a function parameter. When the function is called the value passed is a pointer to the first element of an array. In this example, it is assumed that the number of elements in buffer is passed as the separate argument size. One way to ensure this is to write, for example,

```
length(array, sizeof(array))
```

Only the first bound may be omitted from an array parameter, so that a two-dimensional array is declared, for example,

```
void invert(matrix)
        int matrix[][10];
...
```

Strings are arrays of characters. Conventionally, strings in C end with the null character '\0' (\ followed by zero). The existence of this null character makes string copying particularly simple. For example,

```
void copystr (str1, str2)
        char str1[], str2[];
{
        int i;
        for (i=0; (str2[i]=str1[i]) != '\0'; i++)
                ;
}
```

copies str1 into str2. The body of the for loop is the null statement and the copying is performed by the assignment str2[i]=str1[i] as a side-effect of evaluating the loop termination condition.

Pointers

String manipulation can be simplified using pointers. A pointer is a variable whose value is the address of another variable. If pn is a pointer to the variable n that holds the integer 5, this can be expressed pictorially as shown in figure 5.6. Each box is labeled by its lvalue; the contents being the value of the corresponding variable.

When pointers are declared the indirection operator * appears in the declaration. For example, pn is declared as

    int *pn;

The rationale for this form of declaration is that *pn is an integral value and the notation follows the use of * for indirection.

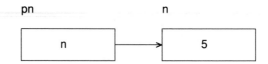

Figure 5.6 Pointers in C

The *address-of* operator & produces the address of a variable. For example,

    &n

yields the address of the variable n.

    pn = &n;

results in pn pointing to the address of the variable n.

    *pn = 5;

would then result in the variable n being assigned the value 5. However, the assignment

    pn = n;

is illegal since pn is·offered the integral value of n whereas the address of an integer variable is required.

Pointers and arrays are closely related. In the context of

    char *cp;
    char buffer[100];

the statements

    cp = &buffer[0];

and

    cp = buffer;

are equivalent. The pointer addresses the zero-th element of the buffer. In a similar way

    cp = &buffer[4];

and

```
cp = buffer+4;
```

assign to cp the address of the fourth element of the array.

A string constant may be assigned to a character pointer since the value of the constant is the address of its first element. For example,

```
char *cp = "...";
```

In general, a pointer p and integer i can be added to yield the address of the i-th element beyond the array element pointed at by p. Thus if cp points to buffer[0], then

```
buffer[i]
```

is equivalent to

```
*(cp+i)
```

The result is an lvalue.

Subtraction of an integer from a pointer is similarly defined. Further, two pointers to objects of the same type may be subtracted to yield an integer corresponding to the number of objects between them. Usually, the two pointers will be pointing to the same array.

The increment and decrement operators are defined for pointer variables. cp++ increments cp by the size of the object pointed to; the value of cp is used in the expression and then the value of cp is incremented. cp−− is similar, except that the variable is decremented.

++cp also increments cp by the size of the object pointed to and the incremented value may then be used in an expression. −−cp is similarly defined.

Examples

The next two examples illustrate the use of pointers. The function swap is defined as

```
void swap(x, y)
        int *x, *y;
{
        int temp;
        temp = *x;
        *x = *y;
        *y = temp;
}
```

and is called as

```
swap(&a, &b);
```

where a and b were originally defined by

```
int a, b;
```

The effect is to interchange the values of the two integer variables.

The following example illustrates another implementation of string copying:

```
void copy(str1, str2)
        char *str1, *str2;
{
        while (*str1++ = *str2++)
                ;
}
```

This function is more efficient than that produced by our earlier string copying function. The test for '\0' has been deliberately omitted since this is the default test in a condition.

5.2.6 Structures and unions

Structures group together pieces of related information. For example, the name, age, and weight may be used to characterize a person. Thus

```
struct{
        char name[30];
        int age;
        float weight;
} someone;
```

defines someone to be a structure having three members (or fields), namely name, age and weight. To access a structure member the field selection operator . is used, so that,

```
someone.age = 21;
```

or

```
copystr("Spike", someone.name);
```

assigns to the individual fields age and name respectively.

To avoid repeated writing of a structure declaration an abbreviation can be used. A declaration such as

```
struct person{
        char name[30];
        int age;
        float weight;
};
```

makes available the *structure tag* person, equivalent to the type struct{. . .} used previously. Using this structure tag the above declaration may be written

```
struct person someone;
```

An alternative abbreviation introduces a name for the type using the typedef statement. The form of this statement is the same as a declaration except that it is preceded by the keyword typedef; the identifier declared is not a variable but a name for the type.

For example,

```
typedef struct{...} person;
```

defines person to be equivalent to struct{...}. The declaration

```
struct{
            char name[30];
           .int age;
            float weight;
} someone;
```

can then be replaced by

```
person someone;
```

Besides application of the operators . and &, no other operator can be applied to structures. Some versions of C allow structures to be assigned or passed as arguments to functions; however, structures are usually manipulated by pointers. The size of the structure is automatically taken into account when structure pointers and integers are added or subtracted.

If ptr is a pointer to a structure, such as person already defined, then

```
ptr -> age
```

is defined as

```
( * ptr ) . age
```

and is an lvalue pointing to the age member of person.

Self-referential structures can be defined. For example,

```
struct node
{
            struct node *left;
            struct node *right;
            int val;
};
```

The definition of node makes use of node itself; it does not contain a member of type node but includes pointers left and right to objects of type node. Pointers to such structures are common and, for each structure defined, it is convenient to define nodeptr as

```
typedef struct node *nodeptr;
```

for use with the definition of node above.

To determine how much space is occupied by a particular structure, the sizeof function is used.

```
sizeof(object)
```

or

```
sizeof(type)
```

returns the number of bytes occupied by the object or an object of the specified type.

To create binary trees such as node defined above, storage allocation facilities are required. In C storage allocation and deallocation is the responsibility of the programmer. Two routines are provided.

```
malloc(n)
```

allocates n contiguous bytes of store and returns the address (of type char *) of the first of these; as, for example, in

```
struct node *ptr;
ptr = (nodeptr)malloc(sizeof(struct node));
```

The cast

```
(nodeptr) . . .
```

is used to convert the result delivered by malloc into a value suitable for the assignment. Since malloc guarantees that the pointer returned is non-zero the value zero is used to denote the nil pointer value, as in,

```
#define nilnode ((nodeptr)0)
```

Storage is returned to the free pool using the statement

```
free((char*)ptr);
```

The value ptr must have been obtained by an earlier call of malloc.

The example shown below illustrates the use of structures, pointers and the storage allocator malloc and uses the definitions introduced so far for node. In this example the function new is defined to take an integer value and return a pointer to a newly created tree node containing that value:

```
nodeptr new(v)
        int       v;
{
        nodeptr n = (nodeptr)malloc(sizeof(struct node));

        n–>left = n–>right = nilnode;
        newval = n–>val = v;
        return(n);
} /* new */
```

The variable newval is set to the last value created and will be used shortly.

Another function required is to print a tree and this is defined as

```
void print(n)
        nodeptr   n;
{
        if(n != nilnode) {
                print(n–>left);
                printf("%d\n", n–>val);
                print(n–>right);
        }
} /* print */
```

The remainder of the program is shown in figure 5.7 and consists of a function called split that sorts a new node into the tree, given the root, and the function main that provides the overall organization. split is unusual in that it keeps the most recently accessed nodes near the root of the tree.

```
int        newval;

void split(ladr, radr, tree)
        nodeptr   *ladr, *radr;
        nodeptr   tree;
{
        if( tree == nilnode ) {
                *ladr = *radr = nilnode;
        }
        else if(newval > tree->val) {
                *ladr = tree;
                split(&tree->right, radr, tree->right);
        }else{
                *radr = tree;
                split(ladr, &tree->left, tree->left);
        }
} /* split */

main(argc, argv)
        int argc;
        char *argv[];
{
        nodeptr root=new(0);

        while(argc-- > 1) {
                nodeptr r = new(atoi(argv[1]));
                split(&r->left, &r->right, root);
                root = r;
                argv++;
        }
        print(root);
} /* main */
```

Figure 5.7 Tree sorting program

Unions

Variables provide for the storage of a particular type of value. For example, a float cannot be assigned to (stored in) a variable i declared as an int. In a program that allocates a significant amount of storage it is often necessary to be able to use the same variable to store different types of values. The union type is provided for this purpose.

For example,

```
union number {
        int i;
        float f;
} x;
```

declares storage for the variable x that is large enough for either an int or float
value. Only one value at a time may be kept in x. If x contains an int value it can
be accessed as x.i and if it is a float value it is accessed as x.f.

The language itself does not keep track of the type of the value stored in x.
This is the responsibility of the user. Either an integer variable can be used for this
purpose or it may be possible to deduce the type of x from other information available when writing the program.

5.2.7 The C preprocessor

The C compiler automatically invokes the preprocessor cpp when a program is
compiled. Lines beginning with the # character are interpreted by the preprocessor. Several facilities are provided.

Constant definition and macro expansion

A line of the form

```
#define identifier token ...
```

causes identifier to be replaced throughout the remainder of the file by one or more
tokens, where each token is an identifier, keyword, constant, string, operator, or
punctuation such as ;. For example,

```
#define BUFSIZ 512
```

allows BUFSIZ to be used in the program and is replaced by 512 wherever it appears. Replacement of defined constants does not occur within string constants.

Macros may also be defined and may have parameters.

```
#define identifier(arg₁, arg₂, ..., argₙ) token-string
```

causes all subsequent occurrences of identifier(p_1, p_2, ..., p_n) to be replaced by the
token-string with arg_1 replaced by p_1, arg_2 by p_2, ..., and arg_n by p_n. The argument
list can be empty, however the macro preprocessor checks that the number sup-
plied and the number defined agree.

Macros are sometimes used to replace function definitions, usually for efficiency reasons. A macro argument, unlike a function argument, is evaluated once
each time it appears in the definition, so that using the definition

```
#define max(a, b) ((a)>(b) ? (a) : (b))
```

the call

```
max(i++, j++)
```

will increment either i or j twice.

Parentheses surround the arguments in the definition to avoid possible ambiguities. Since macros are evaluated by the C preprocessor, unexpected results could occur resulting from operator precedence. For example, without any parentheses in the above definition,

```
max(p?q:r,s)
```

would expand into

```
p ? q : r > s ? p ? q : r : s
```

that is understood by C to be the same as

```
( p ? q : ( (r>s) ? (p?q:r) : s ) )
```

File inclusion

The contents of a file (usually containing some definitions) can be included in a C program by the statement

```
#include "filename"
```

that causes the statement to be replaced by the entire contents of the file filename. The file is sought first in the directory holding the original C program; if it is not there then some standard system directories are searched.

```
#include <filename>
```

also causes the line to be replaced by the file contents; however, the file name is sought only in standard directories, *not* in the directory of the original C program.

Conditional compilation

Conditional statements allow part of a program to be compiled depending on some condition. Typically the decision depends on which machine is being used or on whether a program is at a debugging stage.

Conditional compilation is written in the form

```
#if ...
        section one
#else
        section two
#endif
```

or the form

```
#if ...
        section one
#endif
```

The test can take the following forms.

    #if constant-expression

tests the value of the constant expression (section 5.2.3) and, if zero, the text that
follows is included.

    #ifdef identifier

includes the following text if identifier has already been defined to the preprocessor
by a #define line.

    #ifndef identifier

includes text that follows if identifier is currently undefined to the preprocessor.
The statement

    #undef identifier

removes identifier from the list of defined identifiers if it is currently defined.

The identifiers listed below are defined in most implementations and should
be avoided except to determine the kind of machine you are compiling for. Also,
the lint command uses the identifier lint.

| gcos | ibm | interdata | os | pdp11 | RES |
| RT | tss | u370 | u3b | unix | vax |

5.2.8 Language structure

C is a block-structured language similar to ALGOL 60. However, it differs in one
important respect; functions cannot be declared inside the body of another function. In C, blocks are sequences of declarations and statements enclosed by { and
}; when declarations are absent this construction is called a compound statement.
Within blocks or compound statements, individual statements themselves can be
blocks or compound statements.

The normal scope rules associated with block-structured languages apply. If a
variable x is declared in an inner block that definition causes other outer declarations of x to be superseded until the end of its block. In these circumstances the
outer x can still be accessed indirectly, for example, by use of a pointer.

Storage class specifiers convey information about the storage requirements
and scope of variables. In C there are several such specifiers. These include auto,
static, extern, register, and typedef and they qualify declarations. Thus

    static int a[20];

or

    auto char c;

Of these, typedef is called a storage class specifier for convenience; no storage is
reserved. Further, a register declaration is similar to auto. It suggests to the compiler that associated variables should be placed in registers for efficiency purposes;

only limited numbers of register variables are available on a given machine and then only for variables of certain types, e.g. integers or pointers.

At most one storage class specifier may accompany each declaration. If the specifier is missing, auto is assumed inside a function and extern outside a function.

Let us first consider external variables. If a function accesses any global variable that variable must be an external variable. It must be defined outside the function, perhaps in another file; the definition allocates storage. The variable may also be declared within the function, as in,

```
char line[80];
main()
{
        extern char line[];

        . . .

}
```

Variables that are not external are said to be internal.

Each variable that is local to a routine is called an automatic variable, and has storage class auto. Such variables typically are allocated space from a stack. They are created on entry to the function and removed on exit. Care should be taken with pointers to such variables since they have only a limited lifetime.

Finally there is the storage class static. Static variables may be internal or external. Internal static variables, i.e. those declared inside functions, are like the own variables of ALGOL 60. The value of the variable persists from one call of the function to the next, unlike an automatic variable. External static variables are declared outside functions and are known throughout the remainder of the file in which they are declared, but are not available in any other file. Functions may be declared static and then are limited in scope to the file in which the definition occurs. This is useful for restricting the availability of the function.

Declarations can contain an initialization of the variables declared.

- Static and external variables are always initialized to 0.
- All expressions that initialize static or external variables must be constant expressions or expressions that reduce to the address of a previously declared variable possibly offset by some constant amount.
- Automatic and register variables may be initialized by arbitrary expressions containing constants and previously declared variables and functions.
- Automatic arrays, structures and unions may not be initialized.

The following examples illustrate initializations:

```
int prime[] = {2, 3, 5, 7};
```
                Since no bounds are present the size of the array is determined from the size of the aggregate thus creating prime[0], . . ., prime[3].
```
char message[] = "You have mail.\n";
```
                The string initializes the array message and provides the bounds; note that '\0' is added at the end of the array.

```
int table[4][3] = {{2, 3, 5},
                   {7, 9, 11},
                   {13, 17, 19},
                   {0, 0, 0}};
```

5.2.9 The standard C library

The standard input-output library

The functions provided in the standard input-output (stdio) library constitute an efficient user-level input-output library. The in-line macros getc and putc read and write characters quickly. The higher level routines gets, fgets, scanf, fscanf, fread, puts, fputs, printf, fprintf, fwrite can be freely intermixed with the lower level operations getc and putc.

A file with associated buffering is called a *stream,* and is declared to be a pointer to a defined type FILE. fopen creates descriptive data for a stream and returns a pointer to designate the stream in all further transactions. There are three normally open streams with constant pointers declared in the header file, stdio.h, and associated with the standard open files:

stdin	The standard input file.
stdout	The standard output file.
stderr	The standard error output file.

The constant NULL designates no stream at all.

The integer constant EOF is returned upon end-of-file or upon error by integer functions that deal with streams and is defined in the header file <stdio.h>. Any program that uses the standard input-output package should include this header file.

For efficiency, the standard library buffers a line of output to a terminal by default and attempts to do this transparently by flushing the output whenever a read from the standard input is necessary. This is almost always transparent, but may cause confusion or malfunctioning of programs which use standard input-output routines but use read themselves to read from the standard input.

An example using the stdio input and output can be found in section 8.4.

The function printf

The function printf formats output according to a control string and was introduced in section 5.1.2. Available formats are as follows:

%c	Character.
%d	Decimal integer.
%f	Floating-point number.
%o	Octal integer.
%s	String.
%x	Hexadecimal integer.
%%	The % character itself.

Any of the numeric formats may be preceded by the letter l to indicate long. A format may also include field width specifications. A − indicates a left adjusted field. A number following the % character denotes the minimum field width for the converted value. A second number may be specified separated by . from the first and indicates the maximum field width. For example:

%2d   Print decimal, padding with spaces on the right to ensure a minimum of two characters output.

%−3d   Print in decimal with spaces on the left to ensure a minimum width of 3 characters.

%.12s   Print a string with a maximum of 12 characters printed.

%ld   Print a long integer. The l modifier applies to all the numeric formats.

The function scanf

The function corresponding to printf for input is called scanf. The format specification is similar but the remaining arguments are the addresses of variables where the converted values are to be stored. Blanks are usually ignored and any literal character in the control argument is matched with the corresponding character in the input. For example,

```
double d;

scanf("%lf", &d);
```

will read into the variable d the value of the next floating-point constant in the input.

As another example,

```
int i, n; float x; char name[50];

n = scanf("%d%f%s", &i, &x, name);
```

with the input line

```
371     26.48E−2 morgan
```

will assign to i the value 371, x the value 0.2648, and name will contain morgan\0. Using the same declarations

```
scanf("%2d%f%*d%[1234567890]", &i, &x, name);
```

with input

```
56789 0123 56a72
```

will assign 56 to i, 789.0 to x, skip 0123, and place the string 56\0 in name. The next call to getchar will return the character a.

The scanf function returns the number of input items read; missing or illegal data items are not counted. If end-of-file is encountered EOF is returned.

String functions

A complete set of string copying and comparison functions is available and is described in appendix 3.

Error recovery routines

Two standard library routines setjmp and longjmp are provided for error recovery.
The routine setjmp is declared as

```
int setjmp(where)
        jmp_buf where;
```

and, when called, saves the program state for use by longjmp. The value returned is
0.

The routine used to recover the saved program state is

```
void longjmp(where, val)
        jmp_buf where;
        int val;
```

After a call to longjmp execution resumes at the original call of setjmp. The value
returned to setjmp is val. A system header file is used to declare the data type
jmp_buf.

These routines are useful for interactive programs that need to recover from
serious errors, return to a standard place in the program, and ask the user for
further instructions.

5.2.10 Postscript

The following dogma is observed by most C programs written in the standard distributed system. Sometimes the only important attribute of a particular rule is that
many people use it. Other rules represent techniques that make the programs
easier to read or write.

- Use typedef and avoid complicated declarations.
- Use #define for constants and use upper case names. In particular, avoid
  integer constants in a program for buffer sizes and other quantities that
  can reasonably be varied.
- Avoid using macros for functions except where efficiency is important.
- Always declare the result type of functions and use an explicit return
  statement. Always return a value from main since it is the exit status of
  the command.
- Check the returned value from system calls for an error condition.
- Use system header files such as <math.h> and <stdio.h> in section 5.1.
  Do not assume the values for constants such as EOF or for characters in
  the machine's character set.
- Avoid conditional expressions where the branches have non-numeric
  types.
- Adopt a consistent layout style and use braces for the control flow state-
  ments. A comment at the closing brace of a function definition helps if
  the function body extends over more than a page.
- Use casts to convert values returned by storage allocators to the ap-
  propriate type.
- Keep header files containing structure definitions separate from the main
  program. Do not use more than one copy of such declarations; refer to

header files using the #include statement. Keep related functions in the
same file and use the static definition for functions local to a file.

- Use ifdef as little as possible. Over-use makes programs unreadable.
- Run the lint command and understand its output.

5.3 Program organization and management

5.3.1 Compiling programs

C programs are compiled using the cc command. Simple programs, such as those
in the earlier examples, are easily maintained as a single file. For example,

```
cc average.c
```

compiles the program average.c leaving a corresponding executable a.out file.

```
cc −o average average.c
```

leaves the executable program in the file average. If this were part of a larger program split over two files average.c and main.c, the compilation for both files to produce an executable program is

```
cc −o average main.c average.c
```

To avoid recompiling both main.c and average.c each time a change is made,
an intermediate step can be introduced. This involves keeping the *object* files
main.o and average.o produced using the command

```
cc −c main.c average.c
```

The executable program average is then produced by

```
cc −o average main.o average.o
```

A program such as the shell consists of 35 files whose combined length is
4800 lines. Of these, 24 *source* files contain function definitions and the remaining
files are *header* files containing definitions used by one or more of the source files.
This organization is typical of UNIX programs. By splitting up the complete
source into functional subsections compilation time following a change can be reduced and the use of function names can be localized to a single subsection using
the static declaration. Reading and understanding the program may also be easier.

5.3.2 The make command

When developing a multi-file program with more than one source or header file,
keeping track of which files need to be recompiled following modifications can be
error prone and tedious. The make command is designed to relieve the user of this
book-keeping activity and serves to document the relationships between files.

make enables dependency information between files to be specified. When
invoked, make updates a *target file* if it depends on files that have been modified
since the target was last modified, or if the target does not exist. With each dependency an action can be specified, such as compiling a source file to produce the
corresponding object file or printing a file that has been changed since it was last
printed.

The description of the dependencies and actions is kept in the *makefile* called, by default, either makefile or Makefile. For example,

```
average:        main.o average.o
                cc −o average main.o average.o
```

is the makefile for the program average defined earlier in this chapter. The makefile should be read as

average *depends on* main.o *and* average.o

and if either .o file is more recent than the file average then execute the command

```
cc −o average main.o average.o
```

make already knows enough about .c and .o files to know that cc should be used if a .c source file is more recent than the corresponding .o object file.

A refinement of this makefile is needed if a header file such as defs.h were included in main.c and average.c. Additional dependency information might be

```
main.o average.o: defs.h
```

that would cause both files to be recompiled if defs.h were changed.

In general, a makefile contains a sequence of entries that specify dependencies. The first line of an entry is a list of targets separated by spaces, then a colon, then a list of files. Text following a semicolon, and all following lines that begin with a tab, are shell commands to be executed to update the target.

Using make, program development consists of the following steps:

- Think and edit.
- Make.
- Test and repeat.

Without arguments, make assumes that the first dependent file in the *makefile* is the *target* file. The target can be explicitly specified, so that

```
make main.o
```

would ensure that main.o is up to date.

make has some useful options. To discover those actions necessary but without executing any actions the command

```
make −n
```

is used. Normally, make prints each command before it is executed. This output can be suppressed using the −s option. Occasionally, a system of files can be up to date although the dates associated with the files are inconsistent. The command

```
make −t
```

will modify the dates of files to ensure consistency by *touching* the files concerned.

A makefile may also contain comment and string substitution requests. A comment begins with a # and ends with a newline.

Makefile entries of the form

```
string1 = string2
```

are macro definitions and subsequent appearances of $(string1) are replaced by string2. If string1 is a single character, the parentheses are optional.

make contains a list of suffixes that provide some default rules. The default list is

.SUFFIXES:; .out .o .c .e .r .f .y .l .s .p

The rule to create a file with suffix s2 that depends on a similarly named file with suffix s1 is specified as an entry for the *target* s1s2. In such an entry, the special macro $* stands for the target name with suffix deleted, $@ for the full target name, $< for the complete list of prerequisites, and $? for the list of files that are out of date. For example, a rule for making optimized .o files from .c files is

.c.o: ; cc −c −O −o $@ $*.c

5.3.3 The lint command

For programs longer than a few lines some additional tools are useful. The lint command has already been mentioned and is a program that is worth becoming familiar with. Although some of its messages may be irrelevant, others should be heeded as indicating questionable programming practice.

The consistency between function definitions and their calls is typically not checked by C compilers. Various other checks, often referred to as type checking, are also not performed. lint attempts to fill this gap. As well as checking for type consistency, unused variables and functions are listed, and some instances of variables used before they are set are detected.

Some constructions listed by lint as dubious are legal. For example,

if (1!=0)

reports 'constant in conditional context'. A more realistic example might be produced by insufficient parentheses, as in

if (x&1==0)

where

if ((x&1)==0)

was probably intended.

5.3.4 Program libraries

A program library in the C environment is stored as an *archive* file. Each member of the archive file is itself an object file, members being added, updated or removed using the ar command. By convention archive or library files have names ending with .a. For example, the library that is automatically invoked when compiling a C program using cc is kept in /lib/libc.a.

Within the distributed UNIX systems the standard libraries are documented in sections 2 and 3 of the manual. The default C library (libc) consists of the functions in section 2 (system calls), section 3C, and section 3S containing the standard input-output (stdio) package. If functions from 3S are used then the statement

#include <stdio.h>

should appear in the program.

Certain mathematical functions, such as exp(), are documented in section 3M of the manual and require

```
#include <math.h>
```

in source files. When producing an executable program that uses this mathematical library the cc command should include −lm, as in,

```
cc −o average main.o average.o −lm
```

Other libraries are used by naming the library (archive) file or using the −l... option of cc for standard libraries.

Library maintenance

A library allows a set of subroutines to be used by other programs. Libraries are created and maintained using the ar command and are conventionally kept in files with names ending in .a. The contents of a library are object files, sufficient information being present to enable the subroutine to be relocated and linked with the main program. The program ld is the link editor (or loader) used by the cc command to produce executable a.out files from object files and libraries.

A library file is only scanned once for undefined names. If the subroutines in the library itself refer to other names in the library, then these definitions must appear earlier than their corresponding definition. This imposes an ordering constraint on library file members.

Some versions of the UNIX system provide the program ranlib that creates a table of contents for a library archive enabling the link editor ld to access its members at random. In System V these functions have been incorporated into ar and ld. On older UNIX systems two tools lorder and tsort are provided for this purpose. Given a set of object files, lorder generates a list of dependent name pairs, and tsort takes such a list and produces a partial ordering of this list suitable for ld.

The archive program may also be used to consolidate a set of files into a single file.

5.3.5 Performance measurement

The time command

The overall time taken to execute a command may be determined using the time command. Using the average program from section 5.1.3 as an example,

```
time average
```

will first print the output of the average command, followed by

```
6.0 real          5.4 user          0.1 sys
```

The *real* time is the time elapsed on the clock for the entire execution. The *user* time is processor time spent executing the user's part of the program, and the *sys* time is the amount of time spent in the system executing system calls. Programs that perform a lot of input or output may use significant amounts of system time.

Profiling

A C program may be profiled to provide a count of function calls and how much time is spent in each function. No changes need be made to the program but it must be compiled with the −p option of the cc command. When the program is run the file mon.out is created containing the profile data and the prof command is used to print the data.

As an example, the command average from section 5.1.3 was recompiled with this option. The program was run and the output produced by

    prof average

is shown in figure 5.8.

Name	%Time	Seconds	Cumsecs	#Calls	msec/call
_sqrt	62.8	3.62	3.62		
_frexp	30.4	1.75	5.37		
_average	5.2	0.3	5.67	81	3.71
__doprnt	0.6	0.04	5.71		
__flsbuf	0.3	0.01	5.72		
_close	0.3	0.02	5.74		
_printf	0.3	0.02	5.76		
_write	0.3	0.01	5.77		
_main	0.0	0.00	5.77	1	0.00

Figure 5.8 The output from prof average

In this example, only the functions compiled with the −p option have been profiled.

5.3.6 Miscellaneous tools

Executable programs produced by cc contain a symbol table that can be used when debugging. Once a program is working this extra information can be removed (and file space saved) using the strip command, as in

    strip average

To discover the program and data sizes for an executable program

    size average

will print

    text−size + data−size + bss−size = total−size

The bss−size is the length of the uninitialized data segment.

To obtain a list of all the names used by a program

    nm average

is used. The output includes the name of every symbol and whether it is a data-symbol (variable) or text-symbol (program label or function name).

5.4 Debugging a C program

Most programs do not work the first time they are run. If you are fortunate you will have an idea from the program's behavior what is wrong with it. Otherwise, you are faced with a choice: think, add printf statements to print the values of key variables during execution, or use a debugger. If you choose to use a debugger, adb is available on PDP 11/45 or 11/70. On a VAX 11/780 sdb (see appendix 1) is available and provides more C oriented facilities. This section describes adb since it is more basic and more universally available, although the operation of sdb is similar.

A program can fail in the following ways:

- It can loop indefinitely.
- It can exit unexpectedly with a memory fault or other violation of the hardware.
- It runs although it has unexpected behavior and does not function properly.
- It can fail to get the resources (such as files) it needs.

A program that fails with one of the errors listed in section 6.6.1 may generate a core file containing the data and program from the aborted run. From a terminal generating the quit signal using a ∧\ terminates a process with a core dump unless that process has made arrangements to catch the signal.

adb provides requests to look at core image files resulting from aborted programs, print variables in a variety of formats, modify binary files, and run programs interactively with embedded breakpoints. It can be used to examine any file although it is intended for a.out and core files.

5.4.1 Debugging a core image

For debugging, adb is invoked as

    adb objfile corefile

where objfile is an executable file and corefile is a core image file. Frequently,

    adb

is sufficient, the defaults being a.out and core, respectively. An end-of-file or the request

    $q

will exit from adb.

The debugging request

    $c

gives a C backtrace of the subroutines called. The request

    $C

gives a C backtrace plus an interpretation of all the local variables in each function and their values (in octal). The request

    $e

prints out the values of all external variables. A specific external variable can also be printed (in decimal) using

    name/d

5.4.2 adb **requests**

adb has requests for examining locations in either the program file or the core file. The ? request examines the contents of objfile, the / request examines the corefile. The general form of these requests is

    address ? format

or

    address / format

    adb maintains a current address, called *dot*, similar to the current line in the editor ed. When an address is entered, *dot* is set to that location, so that

    0126?i

sets *dot* to octal 0126 and prints the instruction at that address. The request

    .,10/d

prints 10 decimal numbers starting at the current address. *dot* is the address of the last item printed. When used with the ? or / requests, the current address can be advanced and the next item printed by typing return; it can be decremented and an item printed by typing ^.

    An adb address is an expression made up from decimal, octal, and hexadecimal integers, and symbols from the program under test. Default input and output for integers is hexadecimal. These may be combined with the operators:

Operator	Description
+	Addition.
−	Subtraction.
*	Multiplication.
%	Integer division.
&	Bitwise conjunction.
|	Bitwise disjunction.
#	Round up to the next multiple.
~ a	Bitwise complement.
− a	Integer negation.
* a	Contents of a in corefile.
@ a	Contents of a in objfile.

Binary operators are left associative and are less binding than unary operations; there are no precedence rules and all arithmetic within adb is 32 bits.

5.4.3 adb **formats**

To print data, a format describes the printout. The following are the most commonly used format letters that follow the / and ? requests. Format letters are also available for long values, for example, D for long decimal, and F for double floating point. The last format is remembered so that a request without a format prints the requested location in the previous format.

Format	Description
b	One byte in octal.
c	One byte as a character.
o	One word in octal.
d	One word in decimal.
f	Two words in floating point.
i	A machine instruction.
s	A null terminated character string.
u	One word as unsigned integer.
w	Write a word to the file.

The most general form of a request is

address, count request modifier

that sets *dot* to address and executes the request count times.
The following table illustrates the adb requests.

Request	Description
?	Print contents from a.out file.
/	Print contents from core file.
=	Print value of the current address.
:	Breakpoint control.
$	Miscellaneous requests.
!	Escape to the shell.
>	Assign to adb variable.

adb catches signals, so that the quit signal cannot be used to exit from adb. An interrupt causes adb to abandon the current request and return to read another request. The request $q ($Q, or ^D) exits from adb.

5.4.4 **Setting breakpoints in** adb

A program may be executed under the control of adb.

adb a.out −

prepares a.out for testing. To start up the program under test, the request

:r ...

is used. Following the :r request, arguments can be supplied and some simple input-output redirection is permitted Control is now handed over to the program under test and adb waits either for the program to terminate or for it to receive a signal. When a signal is received, such as an interrupt from the terminal, or a memory fault, adb will regain control and the program is suspended. The program under test may also be stopped when a specific function is executed by planting a breakpoint. Breakpoints are set by

    address [, count] : b

where address is a C function name.

    To print the location of breakpoints type

    $b

The display will indicate a count field. A breakpoint is bypassed count-1 times before causing a stop.

    To delete a breakpoint

    address : d

is used.

    Whenever adb is in control, locations can be examined, breakpoints removed, variables modified, and the process resumed.

    The quit and interrupt signals act on adb itself rather than on the program being debugged. If such a signal occurs then the program being debugged is stopped and control is returned to adb. The signal is saved by adb and is passed on to the test program using

    :c

This can be used to test signal handling routines. The signal is not passed on to the test program if

    :c 0

is used instead.

    The program being debugged can be single stepped by

    :s

If necessary, this request will start up the program being debugged and stop executing after the first instruction. R S

5.4.5 Address mapping

The system provides several executable file formats. These are used to tell the system how to arrange the program in memory. adb interprets these file formats differently and provides access to the segments through a set of maps.

    A map is created for each file examined by adb and is used to translate addresses into locations within the file. The map for the a.out file is referenced by ? whereas the map for core file is referenced by /. Furthermore, a good rule of thumb is to use ? for instructions and / for data when looking at programs. To print out these maps type

$m

Each map contains two segments consisting of a base b1, b2, an extent e1, e2, and a file offset f1, f2. Given an address A, the location in the file is calculated as follows

$$b1 \leq A \leq e1 \qquad => \qquad \text{file address} = (A - b1) + f1$$
$$b2 \leq A \leq e2 \qquad => \qquad \text{file address} = (A - b2) + f2$$

Chapter 6 UNIX System Programming

This chapter describes the C interface to the UNIX programming environment. The problems of writing programs that interface directly with the UNIX system are discussed. The topics include creating and removing files, creating processes, handling interrupts, sending signals, and the use of pipes.

6.1 Argument conventions

Most commands are written either as shell procedures or as C programs. In both cases the arguments to the command are made available as strings of characters when the command is executed. A loosely defined set of argument conventions exists that should be followed when designing new commands. Initial arguments of the form

    −letter

frequently specify options. Other arguments are normally treated as file names. Consequently, it is unwise to use file names that begin with a minus-sign; they can cause considerable confusion. Commands vary in their treatment of arguments. Some check more carefully for consistency than others. Commands that do not expect arguments cannot be relied upon to check that none are supplied.

The general form of most command argument conventions is

    command-name [options] [files]

An option sometimes requires two arguments, as in the −o option of the cc command; for example,

    cc −o simple simple.c

There are some exceptions to the rule of treating arguments as options. The test command is described in chapter 4 and evaluates its arguments as an expression. Another example is the dd command, described in appendix 1, that converts and copies a file.

6.1.1 Argument handling in C programs

A C program begins execution with a call to the function main declared as

    int main(argc, argv, arge)
            int argc;
            char *argv[ ];
            char *arge[ ];

argv is a pointer to a vector of arguments expected by main and argc is the number of elements in argv. Suppose the corresponding command expects three arguments p1, p2, and p3, then

argc	is 4,
argv[0]	is the name of the command,
argv[1]	is a pointer to p1,
argv[2], argv[3]	
	are pointers to p2 and p3, respectively, and
argv[4]	is 0.

Each of the arguments accessed through argv[1], argv[2], and argv[3] is represented as a string of characters and is terminated by '\0'.

arge contains information about the environment. Many programs omit the declaration of arge and use the getenv subroutine to access environment values. This topic is discussed further in section 6.5.6.

Although C compilers permit arguments to be omitted if they are unused, it is good practice to declare them anyway. The C program checker lint checks for unused arguments.

As an example of argument handling a simple echo command is given in figure 6.1. echo prints its arguments separated by spaces on the standard output.

```
int main(argc, argv)
        int argc;
        char *argv[];
{
        while (−−argc>0) {
                printf("%s%c", *++argv, (argc>1) ? ´ ´ : '\n');
        }
        return(0);
} /* main */
```

Figure 6.1 The echo command

A more complete example of handling command arguments is illustrated in the outline of the cat command shown in figure 6.2. The −u option sets a flag that is used within the function copy. If no file name arguments are given, the standard input is copied. The function copy with a nil string is assumed to copy the standard input and is shown in figure 6.3.

The loop body examines each argument of the vector argv and discriminates on the first character. If a − is present, the argument is treated as an option; otherwise it represents a file name and is copied to the standard output. Adding options is easy, since the framework for argument handling is in place.

6.2 Basic input-output

The buffered input-output package (stdio) is summarized in chapter 5 and is usually adequate for simple input-output requirements. This section describes the lowest level of input-output available in the UNIX system.

```
int unbuff;

int main(argc, argv)
        int argc;
        char *argv[];
{
        char c;
        char *cp;
        int copied = 0;

        while (argc > 1) {
                switch (*argv[1]) {
                case '−': /* argv[1] is the option string */
                        cp = argv[1];
                        while(c = *++cp){
                                /* process each letter */
                                switch(c){
                                case 'u': unbuff++;
                                        break;
                                default:    /* unexpected letter */
                                        ;
                                }
                        }
                        break;

                default:    /* other arguments */
                        copy(argv[1]);
                        copied++;
                }
                argc−−; argv++;
        }
        if(copied==0){
                copy((char*)0);
        }
        return(0);
} /* main */
```

Figure 6.2 A skeleton of the cat command

Input-output operates with open files that are represented by file descriptors, each file descriptor being represented as an integer. Some file descriptors can be assumed to exist when any user program is run. These are:

0   Standard input (read only).
1   Standard output (write only).
2   Standard error output (read and write).

These are opened by login and may have been redirected by the shell. When a file has been opened or created by a program, the file descriptor will have to be remembered for use in input and output operations. File descriptors are used for both pipes and files.

A file may be opened for reading, writing or updating, i.e. both reading and writing simultaneously. Random access is available for files, but not for pipes. This topic is discussed in section 6.4.2.

Normally, input-output is sequential. If a particular byte was last written or read, the next input-output call implicitly refers to the next byte. For each open file the current position is maintained and this value is the address of the next byte to be read or written. If n bytes are read or written the current position is advanced by n bytes.

Objects other than characters may be stored in a file. For example,

```
int i;

while(...) {
        write(1, &i, sizeof(i));
}
```

will write a sequence of int values to the standard output. The same form should be used when reading the information from the file. Also, the same kind of computer should normally be used. The sequence of characters stored in the file is implementation dependent. These same constraints should be observed for any data type other than char.

To summarize: if bytes are written then bytes should be read; if integers are written, integers should be read.

6.2.1 The open system call

The open system call creates files or makes existing files available for reading or writing. It is declared as

```
int open(name, oflag [, mode ])
        char *name;
        int oflag, mode;
```

name is the address of a string of characters (terminated by '\0') representing the complete pathname of the file. The second argument oflag indicates

O_RDONLY   for reading,
O_WRONLY   for writing, and
O_RDWR   for reading and writing. These constants are defined in the
            include file <fcntl.h>.

An optional third argument, mode, specifies the mode of files created by open. See section 6.4.1 for a discussion of creation modes. The value returned by open is the file descriptor that is used for all input-output to the file. The current reading or writing position is initially set to the beginning of the file.

If the file cannot be opened, −1 is returned. Failure can result for any of the following reasons.

- The file does not exist.
- A directory in the pathname does not exist.
- Too many files are already open.
- The file is not readable or writable, as necessary.

To discover whether a file descriptor corresponds to an open file, the dup system call may be used. The call

    dup(filedescriptor)

returns a new (duplicate) file descriptor if its argument is an open file. If filedescriptor is invalid or there are too many files already open, then −1 is returned. Another way to test the status of an open file is to use the fstat system call (section 6.4.3).

6.2.2 Reading and writing files

Once a file has been opened, reading and writing can take place using the functions read and write.

The function read takes the form

```
int read(filedescriptor, buffer, nbytes)
        int filedescriptor;
        char *buffer;
        int nbytes;
```

A call of read places nbytes characters in the location pointed to by buffer. The value returned by read is either

- the number of characters read if an end-of-file is not reached, or
- zero if the end-of-file is reached.

read may return fewer characters than requested.

The character ⌃D at a terminal causes any partially constructed line to be transmitted to the program waiting for a read system call. (See also section 6.4.4.) If no characters are available to be read then the call of read returns a zero. By convention, this is the end-of-file indication. Further reading may return more characters although this practice should be avoided.

The function write takes the form

```
int write(filedescriptor, buffer, nbytes)
        int filedescriptor;
        char *buffer;
        int nbytes;
```

and outputs nbytes characters from the array buffer to the file described by filedescriptor. For efficiency, buffers of size 64 bytes or more are recommended although any length can be used within the limits of available memory and the size of the array. If an error occurs, such as a bad file descriptor or a bad buffer address, write returns −1. When writing robust programs it is advisable to include checks for error conditions to take account of events such as running out of file space.

To illustrate the use of read and write the following program copies its standard input to its standard output a character at a time.

```
char c[1];

while (read(0, c, 1)==1) {
        write(1, c, 1);
}
```

The identifier c is declared to be a character array since this does not require the appearance of & in the uses of c. The address of the char c[0] is automatically used as the argument.

The value returned by read is 1 if a character is read. If some other value is returned an error has occurred or the end-of-file reached.

The program given above is inefficient since it invokes a system call for each character read and written. The program in figure 6.3 is considerably more efficient since it avoids this overhead. The function copy defined below is used by the cat command described in figure 6.2.

```
#define BUFSIZ 512

copy(s)
        char *s;
{
        char buffer[BUFSIZ];
        int length;
        int fd = 0;             /* assume standard input */

        if (s) {
                fd = open(s, 0);
        }
        do{     length = read(fd, buffer, BUFSIZ);
                write(1, buffer, length);
        } while (length > 0);

        return(0);
} /* copy */
```

Figure 6.3 The copy subroutine

When read reaches the end-of-file and there is nothing more to read it returns 0 as previously described. However, read may fail for other reasons such as an interrupt being received or the file descriptor being invalid. A complete list of errors resulting from failure of system calls is given in the errno section of appendix 2. The symbolic names of these errors are obtained by including the file errno.h.

The system call close completes the introduction to system calls dealing with file descriptors.

    close(filedescriptor)

ends the association between the filedescriptor and its associated file (or pipe). Normally all files are closed automatically when their associated process dies, but since the number of open files per process is limited it is sometimes necessary to do this by program. close returns 0 if successful and −1 if the file descriptor is unknown.

6.3 The file system revisited

6.3.1 File permissions

Each file has an associated set of permissions that determines who can access the file and whether the access is restricted to read (r), write (w) or execute (x) or some combination. There are three classes of users that are used to decide access rights.

u	The owner or creator of the file (user).
g	The members of a group.
o	The general user population (other people).

In each class, permissions are established by the owner of the file. A complete set of current information about an individual file (or directory) may be obtained using the −l option of the ls command. For example,

    ls −l /etc/motd

produces

    rw−rw−r−−   1 adm   adm   0   Jul 28 20:03   /etc/motd

The string rw−rw−r−− represents the *protection mode* of the file /etc/motd. The first three characters, rw−, are the access rights for the owner of the file, the next three are the group access (see below for groups) and the last three, r−−, are the access rights for all other users. In this example, the owner and group members can read and write the file and other users can only read the file. The next field is the number of links and is 1 for newly created files. adm is the login-name of the file owner. The next field is the number of bytes in (or the size of) the file. In this example, the file has zero length. The date is the last time the file was written or modified and the last field is the file name.

Files that are intended for execution (binary programs or shell procedures) need the execute flag to be set in the file mode. The executable program /bin/sh is listed by ls −l as

```
rwx--x--x    1 bin          bin          24272    Jan 10 18:03    /bin/sh
```

indicating that it is executable for all three classes of users but is readable and writable only by the owner.

Executable programs may also have the *set-user-id* or *set-group-id* mode and this is discussed in section 6.5.4.

The access rights for the owner of a file are determined only by the owner part of the mode, even though the user may also be a group member. A file whose mode is

```
---r--rwx
```

cannot be written by the owner or group members but is fully accessible to other users. Modes of this kind are not very useful.

6.3.2 Changing file modes

The mode of a file can be changed by its owner using the chmod command. Early versions of this command only allowed explicit absolute numeric modes to be specified as octal numbers (like those used in umask below). For example,

```
chmod 751 run
```

would result in run having mode

```
rwxr-x--x
```

allowing the owner full access but restricting group members to read and execute and other users to execute only.

chmod allows both relative and absolute specifications. For example,

```
u-r        Remove user (owner) read permission.
g+w        Add write permission for groups.
o=x        Set execute permission for others.
```

To make run executable by everyone

```
chmod +x run
```

is sufficient. In this example, run could be replaced by a list of files, in which case, all would be made executable.

The mode of a file is determined when it is created and may be modified by its owner thereafter. A maximum set of permissions given, by default, to any files created by a user can be specified using the umask command.

```
umask 0
```

is equivalent to no restriction and created files would have mode rwxrwxrwx.

```
umask 22
```

is the default on some systems and specifies maximum access permission of rwxr–xr–x. The chmod command ignores the current umask setting.

The following script will list the mode of a file created with the current umask setting.

```
>/tmp/$$
ls −l /tmp/$$
rm /tmp/$$
```

Many systems are run with a friendly and cooperative user community and in these circumstances it may be normal to allow everyone to read all files. In an environment where privacy is important, umask 77 would restrict files created to the mode rwx−−−−−− thus providing only the owner with accessibility.

Ordinary users can change the ownership of files or directories that they own. However, for files this can sometimes be circumvented by copying the file, removing the original and renaming the copy. One side-effect of this operation is to change the created time of the file.

6.3.3 Directory access

The interpretation of read, write and execute for directories is somewhat different than for files.

r   Allow the directory to be read as if it were a file. This is used, for example, by file name expansion in the shell.

x   Allow access to the names (files and directories) in this directory.

w   Allow directory entries to be created and removed. (These two operations are not distinguished in the UNIX system.)

To print the permissions associated with a directory the −d option of ls must be used, otherwise ls lists the entries in the directory rather than the directory itself. For example, the current directory is listed by

```
ls −ld .
```

The output has the form

```
drwxrwxr−x    5 srb        srb        496      May 5 18:06
```

where the initial d indicates that the entry is to be interpreted as a directory. On some systems the group name of the file or directory is also listed by the ls command.

The access restrictions for files and directories apply to all normal users. One user, called the *super-user,* is exempt from security checks. Certain system calls such as directory creation are limited to the super-user. mkdir is implemented as a set-uid command rather than as part of the operating system. Also, changing the owner or group of a file, is restricted to the super-user or the owner of the file. The login-name root is normally reserved for the super-user.

6.3.4 Groups

As with ownership, the group identity of a file is determined at creation time.
When you log in you will have been assigned to a group. On some systems all
users are, by default, assigned to a single group. The group identity of a file can be
printed using the −g option of ls, so that,

    ls −lg /etc/motd

might print

    rw−rw−r−−   1 adm   0   Mar 30 20:03   /etc/motd

where adm is the group name. During a terminal session you can change your
group using the command

    newgrp group-name

if you are a member of the group group-name. A new shell is invoked, replacing
the current shell. Exported variables retain their value after invoking newgrp.
Other variables are either set to default values or unset. If the first argument to
newgrp is − the login environment is instantiated.

New groups are created by system administrators and can be used for users
involved in a particular project where access to files needs to be restricted to the
group. The mechanism is cumbersome and does not lend itself to flexible usage.

Files have both a user (owner) and group identity called the *user-id* and
group-id respectively. These are represented as integers within the file system and
are mapped into names such as srb and root by programs such as ls. These map-
pings together with some additional information are kept in the two files,
/etc/passwd and /etc/group.

The password file /etc/passwd contains entries such as

    srb:yKohajlbawhyg:142:3:mh5967,m044:/usr/srb:

each field being separated by a :. The first field is the login-name, the second field
the encrypted password. The third and fourth fields are the (numeric) user-id and
group-id. The next field contains information that, historically, was used to contain
remote job submission information including the login-name and account number
for the local computer center system. The sixth field contains the initial working
directory following logging in. This is the home directory referred to earlier. The
last field is often empty but is used when a user requests a different command interpreter than /bin/sh.

The group file called /etc/group has a similar format and consists of entries
such as

    a68::3:srb,a68

each field being separated by a : as with the password file.

The first field is the group-name, the next field is the password used by
newgrp, and the third field is the group-id. The last field is a comma separated list

of login-names of users who are group members. The newgrp command is similar to login and changes the group-id of the process.

6.4 Advanced input-output

6.4.1 Creating and removing files

Programs are able to create files when necessary. The creat system call is declared as

```
int creat(name, mode)
        char *name;
        int mode;
```

A call of creat causes either a new file to be brought into existence or a previously existing file is prepared for overwriting (it is truncated to zero length). In either case the file is opened for writing.

Recall that in the file system there are nine protection bits controlling the read, write and execute permission for the owner, the owner's group and for all other users; the access mode is normally represented as a three digit octal integer. The access mode described by the mode argument of creat is modified by the mode mask, umask of the process that attempts the creation. In effect,

```
( ~umask ) & mode
```

is used. creat will return a file descriptor if successful and −1 otherwise.

A file may be removed by the unlink system call, declared as,

```
int unlink(name)
        char *name;
```

This usually returns 0, but −1 indicates that the associated file does not exist or could not be removed.

The creat system call will not create directories. Instead a call of the mkdir command is used. Similarly, directories can be removed only by executing the rmdir command.

A physical file may have more than one associated file name. The first name is associated when the file is created. Subsequent names are attached using the link system call,

```
int link(name1, name2)
        char *name1, *name2;
```

where $name_2$ is an alternate for $name_1$. link will fail if $name_2$ already exists.

The ln command is a direct reflection of the system call.

```
ln file newname
```

will make a link called newname to the existing file.

Creating a lock file

To end this section we look at two more examples. A lock file is the exclusive possession of its owner and may be used to ensure exclusive access to a resource. For example, the program that controls the line printer creates a lock file when it is started. If, by accident, another instance of the same program is started it will discover the existence of the lock file and exit.

Such a file can be created as shown in figure 6.4. The method used is to create and open a file, as in

```
creat("lock", 0);
```

The second argument 0 is the mode of the created file, —————. Creating the file so that it cannot be read ensures that another attempt to open it for reading will fail. If creat is successful then the lock has been claimed. Otherwise, another process has the file open.

This version can fail if used by the super-user, since read permission will not be denied. Another technique that can be used is to link to a file that already exists with the name of the lock.

```
/*
 *   mklock file . . .
 */
int main(argc, argv)
        int argc;
        char *argv[];
{
        int      rc = 0;
        char     *n;
        int      f;

        while (argc-- > 1) {
                if ((f = creat(*++argv, 0)) < 0) {
                        rc++;
                }else{
                        close(f);
                }
        }
        return(rc);
} /* main */
```

Figure 6.4 The mklock command

The cp command

The implementation of a simplified version of the cp command is shown in figure 6.5. The program first checks that the correct number of arguments is supplied. If not, it returns from main, and consequently exits from the program. Otherwise, the input and output files are opened. If successful, the copying is implemented within the while loop. A check has also been inserted to detect failure of the write call. This is the subject of further discussion in section 6.6.3. The function strlen is part of the standard C system library and returns the length of its argument string.

```
#define BUFSIZ 512
#define MODE 0644 /* rw- for user, r-- for group and others */
int errflg;

void error(s)
        char s[ ];
{
        write(2, s, strlen(s));
        errflg++;
} /* error */

int main(argc, argv)
        int argc;
        char *argv[ ];
{
        int rd, wt, n;
        char b[BUFSIZ];

        if (argc!=3) {          /* wrong number of arguments */
                error("usage: cp fromfile tofile\n");
                return(1);
        }

        if ((rd=open(argv[1], 0)) == -1)
                error("cp: cannot open input\n");

        if ((wt=creat(argv[2], MODE)) == -1)
                error("cp: cannot create output\n");

        if (errflg==0) {
                while ((n=read(rd, b, BUFSIZ)) > 0) {
                        if (write(wt, b, n)!=n) {
                                error("cp: write error\n");
                                break;
                        }
                }
        }
        return(errflg);
} /* main */
```

Figure 6.5 A simplified version of the cp command

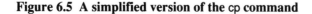

Creating a temporary file

Temporary files are often created within shell scripts for use within the script. Two directories, /tmp and /usr/tmp, are available in which temporary files may be created by anyone. Files created in these directories should be removed by the program that creates them. When the system is rebooted these directories are usually emptied.

```
#include <stdio.h>
/*
 *        mktemp -- create temp file
 */

char *mktemp();

int main(argc, argv)
        int argc;
        char *argv[];
{
        int rc = 0;
        char *n;
        int f;

        while(argc-- > 1) {
                n = mktemp(*++argv);
                if((f = creat(n, 0644)) < 0) {
                        fprintf(stderr,
                            "mktemp: cannot create ´%s´\n", n);
                        rc++;
                } else {
                        fprintf(stdout, "%s\n", n);
                        close(f);
                }
        }
        return(rc);
} /* main */
```

Figure 6.6 Creating a temporary file

One convention often used in shell scripts is to create files called

/tmp/$$

This is safe provided everyone follows the convention.

The command mktemp described in figure 6.6 uses the standard C library function mktemp to generate files that do not (already) exist. A typical call of mktemp is mktemp /tmp/XXXXXX

The name of the file created is printed, as for example,

/tmp/a22780

This output is then available for use by shell procedures. For example,

tmp=`mktemp /tmp/XXXXXX`
...

will set the shell variable tmp to the name of the temporary file created by mktemp.

6.4.2 Random access input-output

A file consists of a sequence of characters and access to a file is often sequential. However, a file can be read or written non-sequentially by positioning within a file using the system call lseek.

lseek is defined as

```
long lseek(filedescriptor, offset, whence)
            int filedes;
            long offset;
            int whence;
```

and the current position in the file associated with filedescriptor is moved to the position offset, taken relative to the location specified by whence. Subsequent reading or writing will begin at this position. The argument offset is a long integer, the filedescriptor and whence are both integers and whence may be 0, 1 or 2. These three possibilities are as follows:

0   The offset from the start of the file.
1   The current position + offset.
2   The end-of-file + offset.

For example,

lseek(filedescriptor, 0L, 2)
        The current position is moved to the end of the file.
lseek(filedescriptor, 0L, 0)
        The file is rewound to the beginning without loss of information. (In early UNIX systems seek was used instead of lseek; the difference being that seek did not use the long integer argument.)

In error situations, such as,

- an undefined file descriptor,
- an attempt to seek on a pipe, or
- an attempt to seek to a position before the start of the file,

the call of lseek returns −1.

Using lseek it is possible to create files with 'holes'. By writing to a certain point and then seeking beyond the end-of-file a section of file space is created containing no data. In certain applications, such as a large hash sort, this may be useful. No file space is actually used by these holes.

6.4.3 Status of files

```
struct     stat
{
           dev_t      st_dev;
           ino_t      st_ino;
           ushort     st_mode;
           short      st_nlink;
           ushort     st_uid;
           ushort     st_gid;
           dev_t      st_rdev;
           off_t      st_size;
           time_t     st_atime;
           time_t     st_mtime;
           time_t     st_ctime;
};
#define    S_IFMT     0170000 /* mask for the file type */
#define    S_IFDIR      0040000 /* directory */
#define    S_IFCHR      0020000 /* character special */
#define    S_IFBLK      0060000 /* block special */
#define    S_IFREG      0100000 /* regular */
#define    S_IFMPC      0030000 /* multiplexed char special */
#define    S_IFMPB      0070000 /* multiplexed block special */
#define    S_ISUID    0004000 /* set user id on execution */
#define    S_ISGID    0002000 /* set group id on execution */
#define    S_ISVTX    0001000 /* save swapped text */
#define    S_IREAD    0000400 /* read permission, owner */
#define    S_IWRITE   0000200 /* write permission, owner */
#define    S_IEXEC    0000100 /* execute/search permission, owner */
```

Figure 6.7 The system include file <sys/stat.h>

The status of files can be determined using the stat and fstat system calls. A call of
stat provides information about any named file. A call of fstat accepts a file
descriptor and returns information about open files or pipes. Only stat is described
since fstat is otherwise identical. The declarations of the two calls are

```
int stat(name, buf)
          char *name;
          struct stat *buf;
```

and

```
int fstat(filedescriptor, buf);
          int filedescriptor;
          struct stat *buf;
```

The structure stat is declared in the system include file <sys/stat.h>. Also defined in this file are the constants to be used when interpreting the fields. Figure 6.7 shows the contents of this system include file. The fields have the following interpretations:

st_mode   The type of the file, i.e. whether it is an ordinary file like any user file, a directory, a block special file (unbuffered) or a character special file (buffered).

st_uid   The user's identification.

st_gid   The user's group identification.

st_size   The last (relative) address written to.

st_atime   The time when the file was last read (or accessed). This is not set when a directory is searched.

st_mtime   The time when the file was last written or created; this is unaffected by changes of owner, group or mode.

st_ctime   Set by writing the file or by changing the mode, owner or group.

The ls command provides this information given suitable options. The use of this status information is illustrated by the program chksum in figure 6.8. For each argument chksum produces a line of the form

    chksum.c 170242   Thu Dec 16 03:32:55 1982

```
/*
 * chksum a list of files
 */
#include <sys/types.h>
#include <sys/stat.h>

char *ctime( );

struct stat STATBUF[1];
int fd;
char buf[512];

int main(argc, argv)
        int argc;
        char *argv[ ];
{
        int i;

        for(i = 1; i < argc; i++) {
                close(fd);
                if ((fd = open(argv[i], 0)) < 0)
                        printf("%s: cannot open\n", argv[i]);
                else{
                        fstat(fd, STATBUF);
                        chksum(argv[i]);
                }
        }
        return(0);
```

```
} /* main */

chksum(nam)
        char *nam;
{
        register int p, e;
        register unsigned short sum = 0;
        char *c;

        while(e = readb()) {
                for(p = 0; p < e; p++) {
                        if(sum&01) {
                                sum = (sum≫1) | 0x8000;
                        }
                        else{
                                sum ≫= 1;
                        }
                        sum ^= buf[p];
                }
        }
        c = ctime(&STATBUF->st_mtime);
        if((STATBUF->st_mode&S_IFMT) == S_IFREG) {
                printf("%–14s %o\t%s", nam, sum, c);
        }
} /* chksum */

int readb()
{
        register int r;

        r = read(fd, buf, sizeof(buf));
        return((r <=.0) ? 0 : r);
} /* readb */
```

Figure 6.8 The chksum **command**

The constant S_IFREG is defined in the system header file and denotes the value of (st_mode&S_IFMT) for a regular file. The field st_mode first has to be masked with S_IFMT since the field also contains the permission bits.

6.4.4 Terminal input-output

The file /dev/tty is, in each process, the control terminal associated with the process. It can be used by programs that wish to be sure of sending a message to the terminal, even though the standard and error output have been redirected. It can also be used when input or output is needed from or to the terminal and a command requires a file name.

The first terminal file opened by a process becomes the *control terminal* for that process. Normally, the open occurs during login and processes that are forked inherit the same control terminal. The control terminal can generate quit and interrupt signals as discussed below. The set of processes that share a control terminal is called a *process group*. The control terminal is inherited by a child process during the fork system call. The association can be changed using the setpgrp system call.

Any terminal associated with one of these files operates in full-duplex. Characters typed at the terminal are transmitted to the host computer where they are passed on to the program and also reflected back to the terminal by the system. Characters may be input at any time, even while output is taking place. There is a limit (usually 256) determined by system buffer sizes on the maximum number of characters that can be typed before they are read by a process. Beyond this limit characters are simply lost.

Input from a terminal is collected a line at a time, so that a read will halt the program until an entire line has been entered. Even if more characters are requested by the read only a single line will be returned. If fewer characters are requested they will be returned without losing any information. A program can also request input to be read before a full line has been typed using an option of the ioctl system call.

During input, erase and kill processing is normally performed. The character # erases previous characters typed up to the beginning of a line and @ kills the entire line typed so far. These two characters may be changed via an ioctl system call.

Other characters, listed below, also have a special meaning and are not passed on to the reading program except in *raw mode* where they lose their special character.

^D	Generate an end-of-file from a terminal. All characters waiting to be read are passed to the program without waiting for a return and the ^D is discarded. If no characters are waiting, zero characters will be returned by read and this is the standard end-of-file indication.
del	Send an interrupt signal to all processes associated with the control terminal. Unless other arrangements have been made, the processes will terminate.
^\	Generate the quit signal. This signal is identical to an interrupt except that a core image is generated unless the signal is caught. The core file is only written provided that it exists and has write permission or can be created in the current directory.
^S	Delay printing on the terminal until a character is typed.
^Q	This character is ignored except after ^S when printing is resumed.

When a terminal hangs up, the hangup signal is sent to all processes in its group. This signal is generated, for example, if the carrier signal from a dataset drops. If the hangup signal is ignored then any further read will return an end-of-file indication.

The treatment of the terminal by the system includes the following:

- Input and output baud rate.

- The parity allowed on input.
- Timing delays for various characters such as tab, newline.
- Expand tabs into spaces on input and output.
- The characters used for erase, kill, and interrupt.

These options can be read and rewritten using the ioctl system call. This system call is used by stty command. In the Sixth Edition UNIX system there were two system calls stty and gtty. In subsequent systems they were replaced by the single ioctl call and stty and gtty were implemented as library subroutines using ioctl.

6.4.5 Pipes

Data may be sent between two processes via an inter-process channel called a *pipe*. A pipe is uni-directional and has two ends. These two ends are represented by the file descriptors p[0] and p[1] returned by the call

```
pipe (p);
```

where p is declared as

```
int p[2];
```

The file descriptor p[0] is the reading end and p[1] the writing end of the pipe. The value returned by pipe itself is zero if successful and −1 otherwise. A process that reads on a pipe is halted if the pipe is empty and will wait for some characters to be written into the pipe. Similarly, if a process writes to a pipe that is full, it will block until some characters are read by the process at the other end.

Pipes are usually created by a common ancestor of two processes. The shell, for example, when executing the pipeline

```
a | b
```

first creates the pipe and then forks to create the processes for the commands a and b. In the process created to execute the command a, the standard output is closed and the pipe duplicated to take the place of the standard output as shown in the following code

```
close(1);
dup(p[1]);
close(p[1]);
```

The dup system call uses the lowest number file descriptor available; it being assumed that file descriptor 0 is already assigned as the standard input. A similar sequence is executed for the command b. Once the standard input and output are suitably redirected the exec system call is used to invoke the commands a and b.

The notation provided by the shell is adequate for most needs; however, the shell only allows a simple chain of commands to be connected with pipes and more complex connections are not provided.

6.5 Processes

Using the terminology of Ritchie and Thompson (Ritchie, 1978) an *image* is a computer execution environment. This includes the program, associated data, the states of open files, and the current directory. Some attributes of images such as the user-id and group-id are directly accessible to the user via the system calls getuid and getgid. Other properties, such as the list of child processes are only available (indirectly) via a system call such as wait.

A *process* is the execution of an image. Within the system there is a list of processes maintained by the system. Most of these processes are waiting, either for input from a terminal or file, or for some system function to complete. This list may be printed using the ps command. There is a per user and a system wide limit to the number of processes that may be in existence at one time. For a typical VAX 11/780 these two limits are 50 and 250 respectively.

6.5.1 Process execution

During execution a process has three parts to its address space.

- The program text itself is often shared and therefore write protected. This avoids accidental self destruction. (C programs are not self modifying.)
- A data segment that is writable by the user and not shared with, or accessible by, other users. This area begins where the program ends and may be expanded or contracted by the user using the brk system call.
- A non-shared stack segment that grows down from the top of memory. This region is automatically extended when it is exhausted.

The address space of each process is distinct from that of other processes within the system. Communication between processes is possible using pipes and signals.

Four system calls are provided to manage processes: fork, exec, wait and exit.

6.5.2 The fork system call

The system call fork creates two nearly identical copies of a process. One copy is called the parent and the other the child. In the *parent* process, fork returns the process number of the child. The value returned in the child is zero. If fork cannot create a new process then a −1 is returned. This can happen, for example, when the system process table is full, or if the fork call is interrupted.

All parts of the image of the parent process are inherited by the child, including open files. The forked process has its own data and stack segments. The only resources shared by a parent and child are the files that were open when the parent forked. If the parent waits for the child to finish then this presents no problem. However, if the child executes in parallel with its parent then some agreement must be reached to decide to whom these open files belong.

For example, when the shell executes the command

    a &

a process is created using fork and the standard input is then redirected from /dev/null. The shell thus keeps the terminal for its own use.

6.5.3 The wait system call

Once a process has been created by fork, the parent may elect for the child process to execute independently or it may wait for the child to terminate.

The wait system call will halt the caller until one of its children finishes execution. When more than one child is executing, the order of finish is not defined and to wait for a particular child the following loop is required.

```
int        status;
int        childpid;

while (wait(&status)!=childpid)
           ;
```

A command may not assume that the only children that will be reported by wait have been created by itself. A command may inherit children from a previous user of the process. A command could create children using fork and then invoke another command using exec.

Only a parent may wait for its children and, if the parent dies, the processes are inherited by process 1.

6.5.4 The exec system call

The exec system call overlays the process that is running with a new program and begins execution of the program at its *entry point*. The process-id is unchanged by exec. If successful, this call does not return and the calling program image is lost. There are various forms of exec, the simplest of which is

```
int execv(name, argv)
        char *name;
        char *argv[];
```

The name argument is the file name of the program (a.out file) to be executed and argv is a zero-terminated list of pointers to the argument strings that will be available to the called program. By convention, argv[0] is the name of the command being executed.

The second form of exec that is available is declared as

```
int execl(name, arg₀, arg₁, ..., argₙ, 0);
        char *name;
```

and provides the arguments explicitly.

Unless the appropriate option of ioctl is used, files remain open across an exec call. This allows the parent (e.g. the shell) to open files for the child. Also the states of signals are left unchanged unless they are being caught, then they are reset to zero. The real user-id and group-id are also left unchanged by exec. However, if the file to be executed has either the *set-user-id* or *set-group-id* mode then the *effective* user-id or group-id is set to that specified by the file.

As an example, the shell provides input-output redirection by closing and opening files before exec is called. If the command is run in the background the standard input is also opened from /dev/null to avoid confusion over input and terminal generated signals are turned off.

The most frequent reason for exec to fail is likely to be that name does not exist or is non-executable. Another common reason, especially when using * for file name generation in the shell, is that the space occupied by the argument list exceeds 5,120 bytes. Other reasons include insufficient address space to start execution (more likely on a PDP 11/45 or 11/70 than on the VAX 11/780).

Most programs need not concern themselves with process management; this can be left to the shell using shell scripts. For programs that need to execute a sub-command the system subroutine provided in the standard C library may well suffice.

6.5.5 The exit system call

A process can finish execution (terminate) either voluntarily using the system call exit or, involuntarily, by receiving a signal. The argument to exit is interpreted as the status of the terminating process. By convention a zero means that the command succeeded and a non-zero value indicates failure.

From a C program the exit call may be used directly, or the program can return a value from the main function.

```
int status, signal;

while (wait(&status) != childpid)
        ;

if (status&0200) {
        /* Core file was produced */
}
if (status == 0177) {
        /* Child process has been stopped and can be restarted.
         * This is mostly for debuggers that use the ptrace
         * system call to control and monitor another process.
         */
}
signal = status&0177;
if (signal == 0) {
        rc = (status>>8)&0377;
        /* Process terminated normally with exit status in rc. */
}else{
        /* Process terminated abnormally as a result of signal. */
}
```

Figure 6.9 Status returns by a process

When a process terminates the status returned to the parent by wait distinguishes various cases. Figure 6.9 shows a program that distinguishes the status values returned by processes. childpid is assumed to contain the process-id of the child process. This program fragment is executed by the parent.

6.5.6 The environment of a process

argv and argc represent explicit (positional) arguments supplied by the exec call. An additional array of strings called the *environment* of a process is also made available by exec when a process begins. The most frequently used names from the environment are discussed in chapter 4.

Conventionally these strings have the form

```
name = value
```

execv passes this environment unchanged. A modified or new environment can be passed using the call

```
int execve(name, argv, envp)
        char *name;
        char *argv[];
        char *envp[];
```

The argument envp is a zero terminated array of pointers to strings containing the *environment* and is made available to the called program in the external variable environ, declared as

```
extern char **environ;
```

From C programs values may be retrieved from the environment using the getenv subroutine declared as

```
char *getenv(name)
        char *name;
```

getenv searches for a string of the form name = value in the environment list and returns a pointer to value if the name is found and zero otherwise.

6.6 Signals and interrupts

Various events, such as terminal break, are reported to a program via an asynchronous *signal*. Other events include a program error (e.g. memory fault), and the request of another program (kill). The normal action caused by a signal is to terminate the process. Except for SIGKILL all signals can be either ignored or will cause a jump to a specified C function within the process. Some signals (see list below) will leave a core file so that an investigation of the fault can be pursued using adb or sdb. This can be prevented, for example, by creating a core file that cannot be written.

6.6.1 Signals

A complete list of signals follows. The names used are defined in the system header file <signal.h>. Signal numbers marked by an asterisk will generate a core file unless the signal is caught or ignored.

1   SIGHUP
    A hangup from the terminal. Usually results from loss of carrier on a phone line and can also be generated using

        stty 0 >/dev/tty

2   SIGINT
    Terminal interrupt. Either del or break from a terminal keyboard.

3* SIGQUIT
    Quit. This is the usual way to abort a program when a core dump is required. Generated using fs (^\) from a terminal.

4* SIGILL
    Illegal instruction.

5* SIGTRAP
    Trace trap. (Used by adb.)

6* SIGIOT
    IOT instruction. (Used by adb.) This signal is sometimes referred to as *abort*.

7* SIGEMT
    EMT instruction. Used on some machines without floating point.

8* SIGFPE
    Floating point exception. Overflow has occurred or a zero divisor is used in floating point arithmetic.

9   SIGKILL
    Kill. This signal can be safely used to get rid of any of your processes. It cannot be caught or ignored by any process.

10* SIGBUS
    Bus error. This usually results from an illegal pointer indirection in C.

11* SIGSEGV
    Segmentation violation. This signal can also result from an illegal pointer reference or an array bound error.

12* SIGSYS
    Bad argument to a system call. This should not occur for C programs.

13 SIGPIPE
    Write on a pipe with no process to read it. This occurs when a process on the receiving end of a pipe terminates, leaving the writer with a *broken pipe*.

14 SIGALRM
    Alarm clock. This is generated following the pause system call (see appendix 2).

15 SIGTERM
    Software termination signal. This signal is the default for the kill com-

mand and allows processes receiving it to clean up temporary files and exit gracefully. If this fails, try kill –9 to send a SIGKILL.

16   SIGUSR1
     User-defined signal 1.
17   SIGUSR2
     User-defined signal 2.
18   SIGCLD
     This is generated at the death of a child process, and is reset when caught.
19   SIGPWR
     Power failure.

6.6.2 Sending signals

The kill command uses the kill system call to send a signal to a process with the same effective user-id.

```
int kill(pid, sig)
          int pid;
          int sig;
```

will send the process whose number is pid the signal sig. If pid is zero then all processes with the same effective user-id will be sent the signal. If sig is out of range or the process does not exist then kill returns a –1. Only processes with the same effective user-id can send signals using kill.

6.6.3 Catching signals

```
#include <signal.h>

int sigcnt;

handler(a)
          /* The value of `a´ is SIGINT. */
{
          /* Reset the signal so that it can be caught again. */
          signal (a, handler);

          /* Record the interrupt and resume. */
          sigcnt ++;
} /* handler */

main()
{
          signal(SIGINT, handler);
          . . .
} /* main */
```

Figure 6.10 Signal handler

A process can elect to catch a signal, ignore it completely, or allow the system default action. Normally all signals cause termination of the receiving process. The
signal system call allows a signal to be caught, ignored or the system default action
to be restored. If the signal is caught then control will be transferred to a user
specified location (function in C). For example, the program shown in figure 6.10
catches SIGINT using the function handler. When the program receives the signal,
the function handler is called with its argument set to the signal number. This example counts how many times the signal occurs.

Most signals are reset to the default action when they occur. If it is required
to catch every signal, the handler must issue another signal call. To reset a signal
to the system default action the call is, for example,

```
signal(SIGINT, SIG_DFL);
```

A signal may be ignored completely using

```
signal(SIGINT, SIG_IGN);
```

The value returned by a call of signal is the previous state of the signal.

Otherwise, the program is only disturbed by possibly failed system calls.
These system calls can be retried if they fail with errno set to EINTR. For example,
if the program cp in figure 6.5 were interrupted it would still print a message.

```
if(errno != EINTR)
        error("...");
```

restricts the message to other errors.

6.6.4 Background processes

The states of the signals of a process are inherited by a child process via fork. By
convention if a signal is being ignored when a process starts (following exec) then
it is never changed. This allows processes to be started up at a terminal and then
executed in the background without interference from terminal generated signals,
such as interrupt and quit. To ensure that this convention is not violated even for a
short time the safe way to set signals is illustrated in the following code:

```
if (signal(SIGINT, SIG_IGN)!=SIG_IGN)
        signal(SIGINT, handler);
```

thus leaving it set to SIG_IGN if it is already set that way.

The subroutine in figure 6.11 may be used from within any C program to execute a sub-command. While it is waiting for the child process to finish, interrupts
(and quits) are ignored; for the child they are inherited from the parent. When the
child terminates, the parent signals are reset to their original values and the subroutine returns.

```
#include <signal.h>

int system(name, argv)
        char *name;
        char *argv[];
{
        int     pid;
        int     status;
        int     *del;
        int     *quit;

        /* ignore signals in parent */
        del = signal(SIGINT, SIG_IGN);
        quit = signal(SIGQUIT, SIG_IGN);
        switch (pid = fork()) {

        case 0:  /* This is the child branch */
                 /* signals are reset for child */
                 signal(SIGINT, del);
                 signal(SIGQUIT, quit);
                 exec(name, argv);

                 /* exec failed after the fork */
                 /* the reason is in errno */
                 exit(1);

        case -1: /* fork has failed */
                 status = 0;
                 break;

        default:  /* Wait for the child to terminate. */
                  /* This is the parent branch. */
                  while (wait(&status)!=pid);
        }
        signal(SIGINT, del);
        signal(SIGQUIT, quit);
        return(status);
} /* system */
```

Figure 6.11 The system **subroutine**

Chapter 7 **Document Preparation**

The preparation of text for letters, reports or books is a time consuming activity requiring considerable attention to detail. The UNIX system provides a set of tools to aid document preparation. These tools include text formatting programs that enable page size, line length, margins, spacing between lines and type fonts to be specified. Other tools combine with these formatters allowing tables and mathematical equations to be produced.

These tools together with a text editor allow documents to be drafted and corrected with considerable ease. Programs are also available to check for correct spelling, make indices or look for wordy or misused phrases. Generally, a high quality result can be achieved with a reasonable expenditure of effort. If a particular tool is not available, it can often be constructed with relatively little effort using the techniques shown in this chapter.

7.1 nroff **and** troff

The basic tools are the text formatters called troff (pronounced *tee-roff*) and nroff. For typewriter quality output nroff is used and for print quality output troff is used. Both programs are descendants of an early text formatter called roff, that was available with the CTSS system (Crisman, 1965). The input contains both text and instructions describing the expected format of the output. The output is suitable for devices ranging from simple ASCII terminals to high-resolution phototypesetters. Much of this chapter is concerned with nroff that is used mainly for typewriter-like terminals, such as the DASI-450 or the Diablo Hiterm, or for a line printer. With a little care, nroff and troff are compatible and the same input can be used for both. Documents can be printed using a variety of devices including a matrix printer such as the Versatec V80, an Imagen laser printer, or a phototypesetter such as the APS-5.

Throughout this chapter references to nroff should be understood to include troff as well. troff is only referred to when the facility, such as a font change, is not available in nroff. When a facility is available only in troff, nroff will usually continue processing. A summary of troff requests is given in appendix 7.

nroff provides control over the formatting process including the page size, line length, vertical line spacing, and provides facilities for arbitrary horizontal or vertical movement, indentation, and tabulation. Line filling modes (ragged or smooth) and the level of hyphenation can also be specified. In troff control over different fonts and character size is also provided and finer resolution is available.

nroff provides direct access to these formatting capabilities. In addition there are features that enable nroff to be programmed. String variables and conditional requests are provided as well as numerical registers and the normal arithmetic operations. Macros can be defined and invoked allowing libraries of requests to be encapsulated. Traps can be set to execute a predefined sequence of requests when a given place in a page is reached. Text can be diverted into a named buffer, enabling footnotes to be accumulated and output when the end of the page is reached.

7.1.1 Guidelines for preparing documents

Material submitted to troff contains both text and instructions (or requests) indicating how the text is to be printed. troff requests begin with a special character, either a . or a ´. Even when there are no requests, troff will format the output using some primitive defaults. Requests could then be added to produce the required output. This approach is rarely used. Documents are produced with packaged requests that provide for a consistent treatment of paragraphs, titles, displays and headings.

Before entering a document into the machine, you should consider how it is to be formatted and the macro package you intend to use. Macro packages for general use have been written and are suitable for a wide variety of applications. The −mm package is distributed with UNIX System V. Your own installation may support its own package conforming to local conventions.

Macros should be used to introduce headings, paragraphs, and displays. For example, in this book

    .SH 2.1 "..."

is used for major section headings;

    .LP

appears on the line preceding text for a left blocked paragraph and, similarly,

    .PP

is used before a paragraph with an indented first line. An indented paragraph with a hanging label (a) such as,

    (a)   ...

             ...

would be written as

    .IP (a)

        ...

The use of macros allows final formatting decisions to be delayed, and subsequently varied, to suit individual requirements. When using a macro package care should be taken when using nroff requests directly. Where possible, their use should be avoided since it may interfere with the working of the macro package itself. In any case check with the definitions first to see if the function you need is available.

This chapter introduces some of the capabilities of nroff and troff including a description of the macro library used to format this book. It also provides enough information to allow nroff and troff to be used for simple formatting applications, such as letter writing or viewgraph production. However, writing nroff macros for complex formatting tasks, such as double column output, requires considerable expertise and should be undertaken only by a competent (nroff or troff) programmer.

When preparing documents for nroff, individual lines should be kept reasonably short. Each sentence should begin on a new line and ending a line on each punctuation mark allows modifications to be made more easily. A large document should be split into more than one file. Each chapter of this book, for example, is kept in a separate file enabling text to be easily identified with its chapter when using tools like grep.

The incorporation of the formatting macros into the text is straightforward. Documents can be composed directly at a terminal or entered from the author's handwritten copy, introducing macro requests as needed.

Invoking nroff

nroff is invoked as

    nroff [options ...] document

and the whole document will be printed beginning, by default, at page 1. Some of the options available include the following:

−m *p*	Use the macro package specified by *p*.
−n *q*	Set the first page number to *q*.
−o *list*	Print only the pages listed by number.
−s *n*	Stop after every *n* pages.

For example,

    troff −o3−5,8,12− chapter1

or

    nroff −s1 chapter4

The −o option prints only the pages listed. In the first example, pages 3 through 5, page 8, and pages 12 through to the end of the document will be printed. In the second example, the −s1 option causes nroff to stop printing after every page and wait for a return to be typed. This may be used, for example, when special paper is to be loaded into the typewriter.

7.1.2 Simple requests

In its simplest form nroff absorbs input lines until enough words have been assembled to fill one output line. If an input line begins with white space, any output waiting will be flushed and a new output line is begun preceded by the same number of spaces. A new output line is also started if a blank line appears in the input.

Formatting requests to nroff appear alone on a line and start with a . at the beginning of a line. For example,

    .sp

is equivalent to a blank input line.

Functions are similar to requests and appear within the text introduced by the character \. For example, a comment to nroff is written using a \" as in,

```
.sp        \" output a blank line
```

All requests and functions are embedded within the text of the document and consist of one or two character names. Macro names follow the same rule. Requests may take one or more arguments separated by spaces.

```
.sp 5
```

will move 5 lines down the page and resume output at the start of a new line.

Normally output lines are single spaced. When producing a draft of a document a double spaced format allows room for marking corrections. The request

```
.ls 2
```

sets double spaced output and single spacing can be restored using

```
.ls 1
```

Input lines may be centered using the .ce request. For example,

```
.ce
4. The Shell
```

produces the heading

4. The Shell

Several lines can be centered using the .ce request followed by an integer. In nroff the heading can be underlined using the .ul request, as in,

```
.ce
.ul
4. The Shell
```

In troff this request produces the heading in italic, as in

4. The Shell

Margin control

Both the left and right margins can be controlled. The position of the left margin is altered by the indent request.

```
.in 4
```

indents to the fourth character position on the line.

```
.in +4
```

increases the indentation level by four character positions and

```
.in −4
```

will decrease the indentation level by four positions. At the start of a paragraph the first line is often indented relative to the body. The temporary indent request applies the specified indentation to the next output line only. For example,

.ti +3

moves the left margin three character positions to the right.

The right hand margin is controlled by specifying the line length.

.ll 4i

sets the output line to 4 inches wide. The initial line width is 6.5 inches. The line length can be increased or decreased using a + or −, as in

.ll −8

that decreases the line length by 8 characters.

Filling and adjusting lines

Once enough words have been read by nroff to fill a line, spaces are inserted between words so that the right hand margin is straight and the line is output. In troff the space between words can be as little as one third the width of the letter m. A ragged (non-adjusted) right margin is requested using the

.na

request. In this mode no extra spaces are added between words. To restore the right margin alignment, the request

.ad

is used. For a block of text the

.nf

request prevents filling of lines during output. Output lines are neither filled nor adjusted following this request; input lines are copied directly to the output without regard for the current line length or word spacing. To resume fill mode, the re-quest

.fi

is used. To break up output text between two lines the .br request is used and causes a *break* to occur; the current line is output and a new output line started.

To adjust the position of the output relative to the physical page the whole page can be offset using the request

.po

Initially, the page offset is set to zero in nroff and to 26/27 inches in troff.

The relationship between line length, indentation, centering and the page offset is illustrated in figure 7.1. The line length is measured from the left margin to the right margin. The current indentation is also measured from the left margin.

Figure 7.1 nroff **margins**

Without an argument the requests ll, in, and po restore the previous setting. There is only one value remembered so that nesting is most effectively dealt with using an increment and decrement.

nroff normally hyphenates its output. This can be prevented using

.nh

or, for an individual word

.hw word

prevents hyphenation. Preferred hyphenations may also be provided, as in

.hw in—di—vid—ual

Vertical positioning

Vertical movement may be specified relative to the current position or from the start of the current page. For example,

.sp 1.5i

moves 1.5 inches down the page starting at the present position, whereas

.sp |1.5i

moves to 1.5 inches from the top of the current page. To move back one line a negative distance is used, as in,

.sp —1

The page length is normally set to 11 inches, by default and may be changed by the

.pl

request. Only movement within the current page is allowed.

Since some devices do not have reverse or half-line feed a special filter, col, is provided to buffer a page and print the lines in order.

Distances

Movements are performed using whatever resolution is available on the output device. A line printer may only be able to resolve to a single line, whereas a Diablo Hiterm has a vertical resolution of 1/48 inches. The CAT typesetter originally used to develop troff is accurate to 1/144 inches vertically and 1/432 inches horizontally. The internal unit size for troff depends on the output device; for the Linotronic 300, used in this document, 1/723 inches is used. For nroff the unit is 1/240 inches.

Requests that specify distances may use the units defined in figure 7.2. When no units are specified the default depends on the request. For horizontally oriented requests the width of the letter m (an *em*) is used. In troff the size of an em is relative to the current character size. For vertically oriented requests a line space is used as the default unit. The line spacing may also be changed using the .vs request (q.v.). Decimal fractions may be used and arithmetic performed. The results are always rounded to the resolution of the output device. Parentheses and the arithmetic operators +, −, /, *, and % (mod) are available within expressions. There is no operator precedence in nroff expressions; parentheses should be used.

Unit	Meaning	Size
i	inch	
c	centimeter	2.54 inches
p	point	1/72 inch
P	pica	1/6 inch
u	basic unit	device dependent
m	em	the width of an 'm'
n	en	the width of an 'n' (1/2 an em)
v	vertical line space	variable

Figure 7.2 nroff **unit values**

Since nroff rounds distances to the horizontal or vertical resolution of the output device inaccuracies can occur, particularly when using absolute specifications, such as

.sp | 6.751i

Tabs and columns

Tables and columns of figures are sometimes simple enough to be formatted using nroff directly. However, it is usually better to use a preprocessor such as tbl that was designed specifically for tables.

A tab character in an input line is converted on output into enough unpaddable spaces to move to the next column. The default tab settings in nroff occur every 8 characters, in troff every 0.5 inches. Tabs may be reset. For example,

.ta 8 40 60

sets the tab positions at 8, 40 and 60 ems. On a typewriter with mechanical tabs, if text is already past a tab position the carriage automatically moves to the next tab. The behavior of nroff is similar. Also, by default, tabs are left justified. For numbers right justified columns are provided and centered columns are also available. For example,

```
.nf
.ta .5i 1.5i 3.5iR
.ul
Ⓣ Name Ⓣ Supplier Ⓣ Cost
Ⓣ Kubik Ⓣ Computer  Technology Ⓣ $183
Ⓣ Anderson Ⓣ System  Memories Ⓣ $79
.fi
```

(where Ⓣ represents a tab character) causes the third field to be right justified at character position 3.5 inches, as in

Name	Supplier	Cost
Kubik	Computer Technology	$183
Anderson	System Memories	$79

To center a field the C postfix is used.

The fill character used by tabs is usually a space, but may be changed using the tc request. For example,

```
.nf
.ta 20
.ul
Name ⓣ Phone
.tc .
Hal Alles ⓣ xxxx
. . .
.fi
```

produces

Name	Phone
Hal Alles...xxxx	

. . .

To reset the tab character to space use .tc with no argument. .nf appears at the start of the table to prevent output lines from being filled.

Page control

The length of a page is normally 11 inches and may be changed using the page length request, as in,

```
.pl 6i
```

When an explicit page break is required, the request .bp may be used. Page breaks are normally used from within a page end trap (see section 7.1.3). For tabular output it may be required that no page break occurs in the middle of the table. To prevent such a split the .ne request is used. For example,

```
.ne 6
```

continues output if 6 lines are left on the current page, otherwise a break to the next page occurs.

Page titles

The .tl request prints a three part title. The first part of the title is left justified, the second is centered and the last is right justified. For example, the request

```
.tl ´February 3, 1982´DRAFT´Chapter 7´
```

will print

```
February 3, 1982                    ´DRAFT                    Chapter 7
```

The delimiter used, in this case a ´, is arbitrary and is the first non-blank character after the request.

The line length and title length are independent. The current indentation does not affect the title but a page offset does. To set the length of the title the .lt request is used.

7.1.3 Advanced requests

Macros

A macro allows a group of requests or plain text to be given a name and invoked using that name. A macro should be defined before it is used, since undefined macros names are ignored. When defining a macro, use can be made of existing definitions. For example, the first version of the control requests for a paragraph in this book was

```
.sp
.ti 4
.ne 2
```

requesting a blank line and a temporary indent of 4 ems. These requests are defined in the macro PP as

```
.de PP
.sp
.ti 4
.ne 2
..
```

The first line, .de PP, is the start of the definition and gives the name of the macro, PP. The end of the definition is marked by .. on a line by itself; the line may not contain a comment. Each paragraph of the subsequent text then starts with a call of PP, as in

```
.PP
Upper case names ...
```

Upper case names are used in many macro libraries to avoid conflict with nroff reserved names. Care should be taken to avoid names that are used by troff or by your macro library. To obtain a list of the names defined in a library the .pm request may be used.

Macros may be supplied with parameters on the same line as the call. For example, the section heading macro used in this book is called as

```
.SH 7.2 "Production tools"
```

White space separates arguments and an argument may be enclosed in double quotes if it contains a space or tab. In the example, the first argument is 7.2 and the second argument is Production tools. In the definition up to 9 arguments are available as \$1 \$2, ... Arguments that are not provided are assumed to be the null string.

In this example, SH is defined as

```
.de SH    \" section heading: .SH section-number heading
.sp
\&\\$1 \\$2
. .
```

The definition also contains a comment introduced by \" describing the macro and its arguments.

A macro definition is read twice, once when it is defined and once when it is called. In both cases nroff requests are executed as they appear in the macro text. In the above definition of SH the \ is needed before \$1 to prevent the interpretation of \$1 during the definition scan. Further, if the first argument was an nroff request, such as .bp, a page break would occur. The escape character \& is provided to hide the . at the start of a line.

A pair of double quotes in a quoted argument will be passed to the definition as single double quote. For example,

```
.SH ... "The treatment of the "" character in troff"
```

Page traps

Using the requests introduced so far, ordinary text can be formatted readily although the lack of page control is soon apparent. No direct provision is made within nroff for titles at the top and bottom of the page. Instead, a *trap* may be set at specified vertical positions within the page and when the vertical position is reached the specified request is executed. Often two traps are set, one at the top of the page as

```
.wh 0 ...
```

and the other near the bottom of the page. For example,

```
.wh −5 PE
```

sets a trap 5 lines from the bottom of each page. After the line is output 5 lines before the end of the page, the macro PE is invoked. The definition of the page end macro PE is separate from the trap specification. For example,

```
.de PE
´sp 2
.tl :Unix Programmer´s Manual:First Edition 1971:Page %:
´bp
. .
```

defines PE to skip two lines and print a title. A : is used as the delimiter since a appears in the title string.

Requests introduced by a ´ rather than a . prevent any partially processed line from being output. The request ´sp 2 is otherwise identical to .sp 2 and skips two lines. When a . is used, nroff generates a break just as if a .br had been issued and using a ´ causes any partially constructed line to be held over to the next page.

A *break* occurs when a line begins with white space, a blank line occurs, or when one of the following requests is encountered:

```
.bp .br .ce .fi .nf .sp .in .ti
```

.tl may be used, as opposed to ´tl, since the .tl request does not cause a break, although using a ´ is equivalent.

The special character %, when used in a title, prints the current page number in decimal. Other print formats may be assigned to the page number character using the .af request. For example,

```
.af % i
```

causes the page number to be printed in lower case Roman numerals i, ii, iii, ...

Writing trap macros requires care, particularly when the title has font or character size changes. This is discussed further in the section on environments.

Horizontal and local vertical motion

Vertical motion within a line is available using \d, \u, or \v. Half a line downwards is provided by \d and upwards by \u. An arbitrary distance downwards is provided by the \v function, as in

```
\v´1i´
```

or upwards as

```
\v´−1i´
```

The half-line motion is useful when dealing with superscripts and subscripts. For example,

```
X\d1\u
```

produces

$$X_1$$

Up and down movements within a line should be balanced otherwise unexpected behavior may result.

Horizontal movement may be specified similarly using the function

```
\h´. . .´
```

For example, the shell here document symbol

```
≪
```

is written as

```
<\h´−.2m´<
```

bringing the two characters closer together to improve their appearance.

Computing the distance to be moved can be dependent on a string and the width function is provided for this purpose. For example,

```
\w´do´
```

yields the width of the string do in basic units. As an example, do\h´−\w´do´u´do

overstrikes the word do to embolden it on a printer. The word is printed once and
the \h function returns to the same place horizontally and prints it again. Point size
and font changes may occur within a \w function and have no effect on the sur-
rounding text. The u after the width function is strictly unnecessary since the result
of \w is in units already.

The same overstriking effect can be achieved using the \k function that marks
the current horizontal position on the line and stores the result in a register. For example,

\kxdo\h´| \nxu´do

will also overprint the word do. The function \kx marks the horizontal position in
the register x and the function \h´|...´ moves to the absolute horizontal position
specified.

The vertical place on the page may be marked using the .mk request. Output
can proceed and the .rt request used to return to the same vertical position within a
page. This is useful for producing multi-column output.

For example,

```
.mk
o
e
t
n
.rt
.in +4
The page number is odd.
The page number is even.
Using troff.
Using nroff.
.in −4
```

will print two columns, the first at the current indentation and the second indented
by 4 more ems as shown below.

o   The page number is odd.
e   The page number is even.
t   Using troff.
n   Using nroff.

If the vertical height of the two columns differs, arrangements must be made to return to the correct place after the second column is output.

Horizontal and vertical lines may be drawn. The function

\l´1i´

draws a horizontal line one inch long (like this: _____). The character
used to draw the line can also be specified, so that,

\l´1i.´

will produce

The function \L is similar but draws lines vertically.
    For example,

\kx\l´1i´\L´2´\l´−1i´\h´|\nx´\L´−2´

will produce a box 1 inch wide and 2 lines deep, as in

Conditionals

Requests and text can be processed conditionally, depending on the outcome of a
test. Both string and arithmetic comparisons may be specified. The simplest form
of a conditional is

    .if c anything

where, if the condition c is true, anything is used as input; anything could be text or
further nroff requests. The conditions provided by nroff are listed in figure 7.3.

Name	Condition
o	The current page number is odd.
e	The current page number is even.
t	The formatter is troff.
n	The formatter is nroff.

Figure 7.3 nroff **test conditions**

    For example

    .if e .tl ´%´´´
    .if o .tl ´´´%´

places the page number on the left for even pages and on the right for odd pages.
Other tests, such as the first page of a document, require the use of register variables provided by nroff.
    Several other forms of conditional are available.

    .if N anything

accepts anything if the numerical expression N is non-zero and positive.

    .if ´string$_1$´string$_2$´ anything

accepts anything if the two strings are the same. The ! operator may be used in a
conditional to negate the sense of the test, so that

    .if !N anything

accepts anything if $N \leq 0$.

An if-then-else form of conditional is also available of the form

.ie c anything$_1$
.el anything$_2$

If c is true then anything$_1$ is accepted; otherwise, anything$_2$ is accepted.

When several actions are required, the requests may be enclosed between the delimiters \{ and \} as shown in figure 7.4.

```
. ie \\n(sw \{
. nr sw 0
. in 0
. bp
. ns \}
. el \{
. nr sw 1
. rt
. in |3i \}
```

Figure 7.4 An example of a nroff conditional

String registers

Whenever a sequence of characters is used frequently it can be defined as a string. Like macros, strings have one or two character names. Strings and macros share the same set of names, so that if a string called xx is defined it will replace any macro of the same name. The define string request is written

.ds *xx string*

where string begins with the first non-blank character and ends at the end of the line. To permit initial blanks, an initial double quote is stripped off from *string*.

For example, a subscript 1 could be defined as

.ds s1 \d1\u

where \d and \u are half-line motions down and up, respectively. The string s1 is used in later text as

x*(s1

and would appear as x_1.

One character names can also be defined. For example, a bullet can be simulated in nroff as an o overstruck with + using the \o function, as in

.ds b \o´+o´

The string b is referred to within text as

*b

Horizontal movement may be embedded within a string. For example, the here document symbol, used in chapter 4, is defined as

.ds HE <\h´−.2m´<

and is used within text as *(HE.

Number registers

nroff provides a set of number registers for storing numerical values. These registers may be set, incremented and decremented, and used within text. Register names consist of one or two characters and are accessed either as

\n*x*

or

\n(*xx*

These names do not conflict with those used for macros and strings. Registers can be used within arithmetic expressions, or directly within text. For example, the day, month and year (since 1900) are maintained by nroff in the registers

dy, mo, yr

so that

19\n(yr \n(mo \n(dy

would print

1986 7 18

when the date is July 18, 1986.

The default conversion style for number registers is Roman numerals, as in the example. The af request is used to set the format and has the form

.af *R f*

where *R* is a register name and *f* is one of the formats listed below. If the format contains n digits then the field width is at least n digits.

Format	Numbering sequence
1	0, 1, 2, 3, 4, 5, ...
001	000, 001, 002, 003, 004, 005, ...
i	0, i, ii, iii, iv, v, ...
I	0, I, II, III, IV, V, ...
a	0, a, b, c, ..., z, aa, ab, ..., zz, aaa, ...
A	0, A, B, C, ..., Z, AA, AB, ..., ZZ, AAA, ...

nroff does not define a string for the name of the month but it can be provided as follows.

.if \n(mo−0 .ds MO January
.if \n(mo−1 .ds MO February

. . .

These requests define the string called MO as the current month name.

Number registers are set using the .nr request. For example,

    .nr IN 2m

sets IN to 2m units and

    .nr IN +2m

increases the value of IN by 2 ems.

Registers may be automatically incremented or decremented using the notation

\n+x	Add *m* to *x*.
\n+(xx	Add *m* to *xx*.
\n−x	Subtract *m* from *x*.
\n−(xx	Subtract *m* from *xx*.

The amount, *m,* added or subtracted is set using the .nr request. For example,

    .nr sn 0 1

sets the register sn to 0 and sets *m* to 1. This form is useful when providing automatic incrementing of section numbers.

Some requests like .mk also set registers. For example,

    .mk p1

sets the current vertical position, in units, into the register p1. The value of p1 set by this .mk request is 2688. The .sp request

    .sp |\n(p1u

may be used to return to this place where | requests absolute positioning within the page. The value stored in the register by .mk is in basic units and the letter u ensures that nroff treats the value accordingly. The default units for the .sp request are vertical line spaces and if the u were missing this would be the same as

    .sp |2688

requesting 2688 lines. (The numerical values printed in this section depend on the device to which output is being sent.)

To be safe, the u should always be used in arithmetic expressions. For example,

    .sp 1i/2

is the same as

    .sp 3u

since the 2 has been given vertical line spacing as the default units. The above request should be written

    .sp 1i/2u

to divide 1 inch by 2 and this is equivalent to

    .sp 288u

The following registers are set by nroff and are read only. The second column lists the values as they are set for this page using the Linotronic 300.

Name	Value	Description
.H	1	The available horizontal resolution in basic units.
.V	1	The available vertical resolution in basic units.
.c	2713	The number of input lines read.
.i	278	The current indentation.
.l	2678	The current line length.
.n	2281	The length of text on previous output line.
.o	555	The current page offset.
.p	6336	The current page length.
.s	10	The current point size.
.t	2944	The distance to the next trap.
.v	96	The current vertical spacing.

Further registers are set by troff and may be changed by the user. As in the previous table the second column lists the values as they are set for this page.

Name	Value	Descriptio ....
%	*159*	*The current page number.*
dw	*6*	*The day of the week (1-7).*
dy	*18*	*The day of the month (1-31).*
hp	*347*	*The current horizontal input position.*
ln	*0*	*The output line number.*
nl	*3536*	*The current vertical position.*
mo	*7*	*The month (1-12).*
yr	*86*	*The last two digits of the year (00-99).*

Fonts

So far, except for device resolution, all requests have applied equally well to both nroff and troff. Printed output of the quality in this book uses a number of different fonts, such as Times Roman, bold, and italic. The examples use Helvetica, a sans serif font, to distinguish them from the main text. Modern phototypesetters have anything from 4 to 32 fonts immediately accessible and others available by request and a professional printer may well have 1000 different styles of characters available.

troff assumes that Times Roman, italic and bold are the standard fonts. The current font may be changed using the .ft request. For example,

.ft I

causes text to appear in *Times italic,* whereas

```
.ft B
```

changes to the **Times bold** font. This font change may also be effected within a line as

```
\fB...
```

To return to the previous font

```
.ft
```

or

```
.ft P
```

may be used. Similarly, within a line

```
\f(HIxx\fP
```

would cause *xx* to appear in Helvetica italic and then revert to the previous font. To return to the Roman font

```
.ft R
```

or ...\fR is used.

Character size

The size of characters (like these) is usually 10 points, where a point is 1/72 inches. This may be increased or decreased, depending on the output device capabilities. The .ps request or, within text, the \s function is used. For example, to make the heading in the title smaller

```
.tl ´\s−2UNIX Manual\s0´...
```

decreases the point size by 2 and then reverts to the original size. To make the size of headings 12 points in the SH macro, it would be defined as

```
.de SH
.ps 12
\&\\$1
.ps
..
```

The .ps request without an argument or \s0 restores the previous font size.

As written this macro can produce unexpected results if there is a point size change as part of the argument \$1. Making the changes relative, as in

```
.de SH
.ps +2
\&\\$1
.ps −2
..
```

avoids this problem. Also, if the point size throughout the document were changed to 9, for example, the headings would still be 2 points larger.

This text has a vertical spacing of 96u (about 12 points) and was set using the request

.vs 12p

The default point size is 10 and the default vertical spacing is 12p. The vertical spacing is the distance between successive lines of text and is the default distance moved vertically by the .sp request.

When the point size is changed the vertical spacing between lines is not automatically changed. As a general rule, the vertical spacing should be about 20% larger than the current point size.

The current point size is available in the register .s and the current vertical spacing is in the register .v.

Special characters

Special characters, such as the Greek letters and certain mathematical symbols are input to troff in the form

\(*xx*

where *xx* is a two character name. The Greek letters all have the form

\(**x*

where *x* is the Roman letter equivalent. For example,

∫ ∇ u dτ

is written

\(is \(gr u d\(*t

and

$$\alpha^2 = k/\rho$$

is written

\(*a\u\s−22\s+2\d \(eq k \(sl \(*r

For applications such as this the eqn preprocessor should be used. The example here illustrates the troff requests to obtain special characters. A complete list of the troff special characters is given in appendix 7.

Escape sequences

With three exceptions, listed below, the ASCII characters are input as themselves.

ASCII input	troff *output*
′	'
`	'
−	-

Some special characters and functions have already been presented and are reviewed here; a complete list is given in appendix 7.

Character sequence	Effect
\e	Print the escape character.
\´	Print an acute accent.
\`	Print a grave accent.
\−	Print a minus sign.
\kx	Mark horizontal position in register x.
\o´...´	Overstrike the characters enclosed.
..	End of macro definition.
\&	Hide a dot at the start of a line.
\"	Introduce comment.
""	A double quote in macro arguments.

Environments

When crossing a page boundary the point size and font may need to be changed in the page title. Normally this processing is performed in a page-end trap where some text is being held over from the filling process for the next page. To avoid affecting the held over text nroff provides the *environment* mechanism. There are three environments; each containing independent versions of the page layout parameters, font, point size, title length, filling modes, and partially processed text. The request .ev *n* switches to environment *n* where *n* must be 0, 1, or 2. With no argument, .ev reverts to the previous environment; initially processing starts in environment 0.

For example, to change the title length and font for the page end macro PE, defined earlier, it could be rewritten,

```
.de PE
.ev 1
.lt 4i
.ps 12
.ft B
´sp 2
.tl :Unix Programmer´s Manual:First Edition 1971:Page %:
´bp
.ev
..
```

Diversions and traps

Once input text has been filled and adjusted, it is normally output. However, the text for footnotes needs to be stored until the end of a page. Also, the placement of footnotes, and the length of the running page text depends on the size of the accumulated footnote text. Diversions provide a mechanism suitable for footnotes and similar problems.

Output text may be diverted into a named macro enabling the text to be assembled for footnote processing and its size determined. The diverted text may be re-read as input at a later time by invoking the macro.

The request

.di *xx*

starts diverting output text into the macro named *xx* replacing the original contents of the macro. The diversion ends when the request .di with no arguments is read and the text collected may be input again by writing

.*xx*

The vertical and horizontal size of the most recently ended diversion is available in the registers dn and dl respectively.

nroff provides three types of trap: page traps, the diversion trap, and an input-line-count trap. The page trap has already been described. The diversion trap is set with the .dt request and allows processing to be interrupted when a given vertical position is reached in the current diversion. Its use is similar to the .wh request. For example,

.dt 1 DT

sets the diversion trap to execute the request .DT when one line of output has been collected in the current diversion. Only one diversion trap exists at any one time and a second .dt request replaces the trap.

The input-line-count trap is set by the .it request and specifies a macro to be invoked after some number of input lines has been read. A given trap is only executed once. For example,

.it 1 IT

invokes the macro IT after one (more) line of input is read. Using this mechanism, the italicize request .it can be defined as,

```
.de it
.it 1 IT
.ft I
..
.de IT
.ft P
..
```

7.1.4 A macro library

The use of a macro library is essential when preparing documents and standard packages are available that deal with many formatting needs. A general purpose package will allow output to be generated in a variety of formats. If one of these packages does not provide the required capabilities it is sometimes easier to modify the package than to rewrite it from scratch. This section demonstrates the programming techniques used when writing a macro package. The macros described here were used to format this book and are similar to those found in a macro library such as −mm. Throughout the discussion that follows reference will be made to appendix 9 that contains a complete listing of the macro library used to produce this book.

The requests provided by the macro library described here are described briefly in the following table. A more complete description is given in the text.

Request	Description
.AH 1 "Commands"	Appendix heading.
.CH 1 "Introduction"	Chapter heading.
.SH 1.1 "History"	Section heading.
.SS 6.3.1 "File permissions"	Subsection heading.
.MS "Use of backslash"	Minor section.
.BU	Bulleted paragraph.
.IP (a)	Indented paragraph with hanging text.
.LP	Blocked paragraph start.
.MP x++	Indented para with hanging program text.
.PP	Normal paragraph start.
.DS 13	Display start.
.DE	End display.
.EX 24	Start of example.
.XE	End example.
.FX 34	Start figure in the text.
.XF	End of figure in text.
.FC 6.3 "Create a lock file"	Caption of a figure.
.FG lock.c 13	Inclusion of figure file.
.RS	Relative section start.
.RE	Relative section end.
.VX	Contract vertical space.
.XV	Expand vertical space.
.CN "ls"	Command name in text.
.DN "mode"	Definition in text.
.SN "newline"	Symbol (character) name in text.
.HI "heading"	Subsection heading font.
.HL	Half line spacing.
.RU	Horizontal rule.
.CX arg1 arg2	Index arg1,arg2 and arg2,arg1.
.IX arg1 arg2 arg3	Index generation.

nroff is permissive when errors are made and usually allows processing to continue without an error message. This makes debugging difficult. To avoid these difficulties the library described here was constructed incrementally. A small part would be written and tested to provide a working base. Changes to the 'program', in this case nroff macros, were made one at a time. This technique is applicable to all program writing since many bugs will be introduced as a result of the last modification made to the program. If a large program were to be written without trying out any part of it, it would be difficult to know where to start looking for malfunctions. Starting with something small that works and iterating allows the machine to be used effectively as part of the program construction process.

The first macros written were the section heading and paragraph macros. New macros were added as required and macros already written were revised as deficiencies were found. In the examples that follow the 'final' version of a definition is not necessarily presented. Successive samples, starting with the first approximation, are shown. Appendix 9 lists the version used to format this book.

In common with other macro libraries, the macro definitions have upper case names to avoid potential conflict with nroff requests.

Section headings

The first version of the section heading definition is shown in figure 7.5. A call of this macro would take the form

.SH number heading

If the heading contains any spaces it should be enclosed between double quotes. The section number and heading were provided as separate arguments so that the horizontal distance between them could be adjusted. This allows changes to be made to the spacing between the section number and title without changing each macro call. In later versions this number was incorporated into the title at the top of each page.

No check is made within the definition to ensure that the correct number of arguments is provided.

```
. de SH             \" Section heading:   . SH number title
. sp 2              \" leave blank lines
. ft B              \" bold font (ignored in nroff)
. in 0              \" reset indent
\&\\$1 \\$2         \" first macro argument
. ft R              \" resume normal font
. sp
. .
```

Figure 7.5 The first version of section heading macro SH

Lines that begin with a . or a ´ or that contain a \ are processed by nroff each time they are read. For a macro definition this occurs once at the time the definition is assembled and once when it is called. Hence the use of

\&\\$1

to access the argument. The \& at the start of the line prevents an initial . or ´ in the argument from being processed again when the definition is invoked. The \ preceding the \$1 delays the interpretation of the argument until the macro is called.

The return to the Roman font using

.ft R

instead of .ft P guards against the possibility of a font change within the heading, as in,

.SH 7.1 "\fHnroff\fP and \fHtroff\fP"

It also assures that the Roman font is selected even if some other font was selected prior to the new section.

Subsequent additions to SH included a change in the point size and a request to ensure that at least 4 lines remain on the page when a new section is started. This prevents a section heading appearing on one page with its associated text on the next page. These are written

```
.ne 4
.ps +2
...
.ps −2
```

A final refinement to SH introduces the number register rs for the left margin.

The left margin is changed for an indented section by changing the value of the rs register. An indented section of text is introduced by the RS macro (Relative Start) and to enable uses of .RS to be nested the associated register is incremented and decremented. The macro definition consists of the request

```
.nr rs +2m
```

that increases the value of the register rs by 2 ems. The initial value is assigned to rs at the start of the macro library by the request

```
.nr rs 0
```

The end of an indented section is marked by the .RE request. No check is made to ensure that uses of .RS and .RE are matched. This is left to a separate program although it could be incorporated in the definitions as follows.

```
. de RS
. nr rs +2m
. nr rc +1
. .
. de RE
. ie \\n(rc \{
. nr rc −1
. nr rs −2m \}
. el \{
. tm "Unmatched RE"
. nr rc 0 \}
. .
```

The register rc is incremented by 1 each time RS is invoked and decremented when RE is invoked. If the value of this count becomes negative, the .tm request prints a message on the error output stream and the register is reset.

Chapter headings

Each chapter of this book is kept in a separate file and begins

```
.so maclib
.CH 7 "Document Preparation"
```

```
.de CH    \" chapter heading: .CH number text
\\.ds cf \\$1
\\.ds ct \\$2
.ce 2
\\$1
\\$2
.sp 8
..
```

Figure 7.6 The first version of the chapter heading macro CH

The .so request reads the file maclib and then resumes reading the file containing the .so request. The chapter heading and number are recorded by the CH macro for use later. The initial definition of CH is shown in figure 7.6. The chapter title is stored in the variable ct and the chapter number is stored in cf. The chapter name is

```
.de CH              \" chapter heading  .CH 1 "Introduction"
.}H "Chapter \\$1" "\\$2"
\\.ds sh \\$1

..
.de AH              \" appendix heading.AH 1 "Commands"
.}H "Appendix \\$1" "\\$2"

..
.de }H              \" macro for chapter and appendix headings
.tm ======== .}H "\\$1" "\\$2" \\n%
.sp 7
\\.ds cf \\$1
\\.ds ct \\$2
\\.ds pn \\n%
.ft H
.ps 24
.sp 24p
.ce 2
\\$1
.sp 2
\\$2
.sp 4
.ft
.ps
.mk

..
```

Figure 7.7 Chapter and appendix heading macros

required in the page top macro and the chapter number was used in the page bottom text on drafts; both are output at the center of the first page.

Later versions of this definition have been changed to allow headings for appendices to be provided. A third macro called }H is introduced as shown in figure 7.7.

Paragraphs

The first paragraph macros written were LP for left blocked paragraphs like this one, and PP for paragraphs with an indented first line.

The indented paragraph macro IP is for a completely indented paragraph with some text projecting into the left margin on the first line. The two additional macros MP and BU follow the same pattern.

```
. de IP    \" Indented paragraph:  . IP (a)
. sp \\n(pd
. in 6
. ta 4
. ti −4
\&\\$1\t\c
\. if \\w\`\\$1\´u−4m  . br
. .
```

Figure 7.8 The definition of the paragraph macro IP

The MP macro is for hanging text in the program text font, whereas the BU macro provides for a bullet, ●, as the hanging text. All three definitions were more difficult to write than the section or chapter heading macros. The definition of IP is typical and an initial approximation is shown in figure 7.8. The indentation for all but the first line of the paragraphs is provided by .in 6 . The argument to IP is processed by the line

    \&\\$1\t\c

The tab (\t) is used to reach the text margin and the label is indented toward the left margin using a negative temporary indent, .ti −4. The text of the label is provided as an argument and is preceded in the macro definition by \& to prevent interpretation of arguments that start with a .. The \c prevents a break from occurring so that text can continue on the same line even though there is a newline in the input. The break is provided, if required, by the request

    .if \w`\$1´u−4m .br

where one layer of \ has been removed to allow for the defining scan of the macro by nroff. The form shown here is the request that will be executed when the macro is called. The condition succeeds if the width of the argument $1 is larger than 4 ems. The u following \w`...´ ensures that the appropriate units are used although is not strictly needed since \w returns a size in basic units.

The version of MP in the macro library allows an additional, optional, argument to specify the indentation. The lines

```
.ie \\$2 .nr xi \\$2-\\n(ip
.el .nr xi 4
.in \\n(rs+\\n(xi+\\n(ip
.ta \\n(xi
.ti -\\n(xi
.if \\w'\\$1'u-\\n(xim .br
```

set the register xi to the indentation required. The subsequent instructions refer to the value in this register as \\n(xi .

Page layout

The top and bottom of each page contain text that is output by two macros. The request

```
.wh 0 aa
```

instructs troff to execute the macro aa when the position on the page is 0 units from the top of the page. The definition of aa is shown in figure 7.9.

```
.de aa
.ev 1
.lt 7i
.tl '--''--'
.ll 4.65i
.lt 4.65i
'sp 5
.ps 8
.ft R
if e .tl '%\h'2m'UNIX System V'\\*(sh'
if o .tl '\\*(sh'\\T(ct\h'2m'%'
.ev
'sp
.mk
..
```

Figure 7.9 A top of page macro definition

The first line switches to a new environment to avoid disturbing the existing text. The next two lines generate marks on the page that are useful for cutting up continuous paper output. Since the title length is different from the physical paper width the title length is reset to 7 inches and then restored to the normal value for headings.

Initially, page numbers were output both on the left and right of the page

using the special character %. A refinement added later was to print the left-hand
and right-hand titles depending on whether the page number was even or odd. The
even and odd conditions provided by nroff are used as illustrated.

```
.if e .tl ´%\h´2m´UNIX System V´´´
.if o .tl ´´´\\*(ct\h´2m´%´
```

The end of page activity follows a similar pattern. Another trap, zz, is set by
the requests

```
.if n .wh −5 zz
.if t .wh 9i zz
```

In nroff the trap is 5 lines from the bottom of the page, and in troff it is 9 inches from
the top.

Within macros executed by traps care is taken to use a ´ rather than a . for
those requests that cause a break. This prevents any partially accumulated line
from being flushed.

Displays

A display is a block of text that is to be kept on the same page and where line filling is not required. The figures in this text are a special kind of display that start
and end with a ruled line. The display macros described here require the user to
provide the length of the text and a gap is left if there is insufficient room left on
the current page.

Two basic macros are provided for displays called DS and DE for display start
and display end respectively. The definition of DS is approximately

```
.de DS   \" display start      .DS
´in +2m
´ta 4m 8m 12m 16m 20m 24m 28m 32m
.HL
´nf
´ne \\$1
..
```

The block of text is indented, and some default tabs are established. No fill mode
is set and a .ne request ensures that vertical space is reserved.

The DE request ends a display and is defined as

```
.de DE
.HL
.fi
.in −2m
.ft R
..
```

Fill mode is resumed and the indent is reduced by 2 ems. The request .HL generates a half-line space.

For displayed examples of programs, the requests .EX and .XE are defined as

```
.de EX
.ft H
.fl
.ss 20
´DS \\$1
..
.de XE
.DE
.ss 12
.ft R
..
```

Two new requests have been introduced in this example. The request .ss 20 sets the minimum spacing between words to be 20/36 ems. The default minimum spacing of 12/36 ems is too small for programs in the Helvetica font. The interpretation of character sizes is the last action taken by troff as output is being copied from its internal buffers into the output stream. The .fl request flushes any output in the buffer and is needed to prevent the change in the space character size from affecting any pending output.

The definitions of .FX and .XF are for figures, where a ruled line is required above and below the figure. Each of these macros is defined in terms of the basic display macros DS and DE.

The last item to note in appendix 9 is a set of string registers designed to provide characters that are more visually appealing than the defaults. For example, the character tilde normally appears as ˜ whereas for programs it is required to be at the same height as an equals =. Character sizes have also been adjusted for cosmetic reasons.

Index generation

An index can be generated by including with the text a macro containing the index item. The macro prints the index item on the error output stream using the .tm request. When nroff is run by the command

```
troff chapter 2>ix/chapter
```

the index items are saved in the file ix/chapter. A sub-directory is used to avoid cluttering the working directory with files that can be regenerated.

The index macro IX is defined as

```
.de IX    \" index macro
.tm \\$1 \\$2 \\$3 \\$4 \\$5 \\$6 \\$7 \\n%
..
```

and for convenience another macro, CX is defined as

```
.de CX
.IX "\\$1," "\\$2"
.IX "\\$2," "\\$1"
..
```

so that two items can be generated for the index with only a single request. For example,

```
.CX "index macro" \fHnroff\fP
```

will generate the two index items:

```
index macro, nroff  \n%
nroff, index macro  \n%
```

The index macro output automatically refers to the page number containing the index request. The output is postprocessed using the shell procedure index shown in section 7.2.

Page layout

Throughout this book care has been taken to ensure page breaks occur in suitable places. For example, figures are placed to avoid wasted space at the end of pages and single lines at the end or beginning of a page are avoided. Although text itself has a fixed vertical space between lines there are places where the amount of white space can be adjusted without being noticeable. For example, in tables or between sections.

The two macros, .XV and .VX increase or decrease a number register that is used when vertical spacing is needed.

7.2 Production tools

As a project progresses commands are developed and conventions established for naming files. For example, the file containing the index for a given chapter is kept in a sub-directory called ix. The page numbers, similarly are kept in another directory called page. The commands described in this section were generated and refined during the writing of this book. These include the following:

- Print a chapter using nroff, or troff for various output devices.
- Generate page numbers.
- Generate the index.

Print a chapter

The command to print a chapter has different names depending on the output device required. It is convenient to keep these variants in one command file since they all have a similar form and adding a new variant is then easy with the editor. The command is called by the names listed in the case branches in figure 7.10. Each name t, n, p, and ix is a link to the file. These links are created using the ln command.

```
args=`chapters`
for i in ${*−$args}
do          echo "$0 $$          $i          `date`" ≫log
            n=`cat page/$i`

            # use tbl and eqn for chapter 7
            case $i in
              t7)       tbl $i | eqn ;;
              *)        cat $i
            esac |

            case $0 in
            t)          # typeset
                        troff −n$n 2>ix/$i | linotronic
                        ;;
            n)          # use nroff
                        nroff −n$n 2>ix/$i
                        ;;
            p)          # proof output
                        troff −n$n 2>/dev/null | proof
                        ;;
            ix)         # generate index only
                        troff −n$n 2>ix/$i >/dev/null
                        ;;
            esac
            makepage $i
done
```

Figure 7.10 Printing chapters

t   Produce troff output in final, camera ready, form on the Linotronic 300
     phototypesetter.

n   Use nroff and print on the standard output. This is used for viewing the
     text on simple output devices.

p   Generate output using a troff simulator on a high resolution bit-map ter-
     minal. No index is generated with this version since it is used interac-
     tively and is often interrupted before all output has been generated.

ix   Only generate the index into the file ix/....

A log of activities is kept in the file log. The command name, $0, the process
number, $$, and the chapter name and date are all recorded.

The command chapters in figure 7.11 is a simple echo script and is useful
since it contains the chapters in the order they appear in the final production.
Some chapters are generated automatically by processing other files. These names
are capitalized to distinguish them from chapters that cannot be regenerated.

```
echo tp TC t1 t2 t3 t4 t5 t6 t7 t8
echo A1 A2 A3 a4 a5 a6 a7 a8 a9 a10 a11 tb TX
```

Figure 7.11 The names of the chapter files

The number of the starting page for each chapter is kept in the file page/*chapter* and is set in the shell variable n by the command

```
n=`cat page/$i`
```

Initially this file is created by hand and when troff is called the page number is passed via the −n option. Page numbers are automatically updated by the makepage command described in figure 7.12.

Page numbering

```
args=`chapters`
for i in ${*−$args}
do        set − `"grep LAST <ix/$i`
          start=`expr ${2−0} + 1`
          if test −f page/next$i
          then      next=`cat page/next$i`
                    echo $next did start at page `cat page/$next`
                    echo now starts at page $start
                    echo $start >page/$next
          fi
done
```

Figure 7.12 The makepage script

Each chapter is printed separately and the page numbers are sequential from one chapter to the next. The starting page number for each chapter is kept in the file page/*chapter* and is kept up-to-date by the command makepage listed in figure 7.12.

```
. .                       \" set end of file macro
.em ee
. .                       \" end of file macro
.de ee
.af % 1   \" ensure Roman font
.tm LAST \\n%
. .
```

Figure 7.13 The end macro request

The index item LAST is generated using the end macro request, .em, provided by nroff as shown in figure 7.13. The makepage script uses this index item to find the number of the last page for a given chapter. One is added to the page number using the expr command and the result stored in a file associated with the appropriate chapter.

The set command in the script stores the page number associated with LAST in the shell variable $2 and the variable start is set to the page number for the beginning of the next chapter.

The page directory contains two files for each chapter. One contains the starting page number and the other, called page/nextchapter is the file name of the next chapter.

Index postprocessing

The index is generated into files and needs to be sorted alphabetically by the index items, and formatted. The index command postprocesses the output from troff and generates troff input containing the final index. If there were no font or point size changes within the index the script would be simple. The sed script described below makes a complete copy of each line, and in the first removes the font and point size changes. This is sorted and then removed by a later sed script.

The cat command on the first line of figure 7.14, generates some fixed troff requests to include the macro library, set the tabs, no fill mode, and the point size. The for loop iterates over the argument file names provided, or uses the standard list.

An initial approximation would sort the index output directly, as in

```
sort ix/*
```

Unfortunately the font changes and point size changes embedded within the index items cause errors in the sorting.

The next approximation to the index uses the sed command and generates a file with two fields separated by some distinctive string, in this example, ~~~~. The first field is the index item with the point size and font change requests removed, the second field is the original item unchanged. The for loop in figure 7.14 generates such a list and the output is piped into sort; the first item being the key. The −uf option to sort removes duplicate entries and ignores (folds) the distinction between upper and lower case letters.

The final stage is to use the cross reference program, xrefb, described in chapter 8 to take lines of the form

index-item   page-number
. . .

and generate a list of the form

index-item   page-number$_1$ page-number$_2$ . . .

when an index-item has more than one reference.

```
cat ≪!
. so maclib
.}H "−" Index
. ta 12m 14m 16m 18m 20m 22m 24m 26m
. ps 8
. nf
!

args="`chapters` see"
for i in ${*−$args}
do        sed −e "s/   *//
                s/ . */&~~~~&/
                s/\\\s−* . \( . *\)~~~~/\1~~~~/g
                s/\\\s−* . \( . *\)~~~~/\1~~~~/g
                s/\\\s . \( . *\)~~~~/\1~~~~/g
                s/\\\s . \( . *\)~~~~/\1~~~~/g
                s/\\\f . \( . *\)~~~~/\1~~~~/g
                s/\\\f . \( . *\)~~~~/\1~~~~/g
                s/\\\f . \( . *\)~~~~/\1~~~~/g
                s/           /                          /g" <ix/$i
done |
  sort −uft`           ` +0 −1 +1n |
   sed −e ´s/ . *~~~~//´ |
    xrefb
```

Figure 7.14 The index **postprocessor**

7.3 Document processing tools

The tools described so far enable text to be created and formatted. Tools are also provided to check spelling, analyze writing style, and to preprocess text enabling tables and mathematical equations to be produced.

col   Postprocess nroff output to filter reverse line feeds.
eqn   Lay out equations and mathematical notation.
spell   Print dubious or incorrect spelling of words.
style   Compare the readability and sentence structure of each chapter.
tbl   Prepare tabular information.

The programs eqn and tbl accept data from the standard input and output modified text on the standard output. The input processed occurs between certain pairs of requests; the remaining text is copied, unaltered.

7.3.1 The col command

The col command accepts output generated by nroff containing reverse line feeds, such as those generated by the .rt request. This request is generated by the tbl preprocessor and by the multi-column options of some macro libraries. Other non-printing characters are also filtered out by the col command making its output suitable for simple printing devices.

The default output produced by nroff is suitable for a model 37 teletype (a mechanical wonder in its time but no longer in general use). An alternative to using col is to instruct nroff to produce output for a simple terminal such as the DASI-450. This option is invoked as

    nroff −T450 ...

7.3.2 The eqn command

The eqn preprocessor is used for typesetting mathematics on a phototypesetter. A related command, neqn, provides the same function for typewriter-like devices. Using eqn it is possible to produce symbols such as integral signs, summation signs, square roots, as well as complicated expressions. The ideas are simple enough for a non-mathematician to understand.

Text for eqn is enclosed by a pair of lines beginning with .EQ and .EN To take a simple example

    .EQ
    x=a+b
    .EN

produces the italicized version of the equation

$$x = a + b$$

eqn text may also be included between delimiter characters, defined, for example, as

    .EQ
    delim $$
    .EN

Thus,

    Let $ 2 pi omega $ be the ...

produces

    Let $2\pi\omega$ be the ...

eqn preprocesses the source text outputting instructions for nroff or troff. Other document preparing activities such as centering and left justification are performed using the nroff/troff requests, possibly using a package such as −mm.

Within eqn requests, spaces separate items; extra space in the output being produced using a ~. The input is free format and may straddle several lines if necessary. Items may be grouped together using { and }.

eqn also provides for subscripts, limits, partial derivative signs, big brackets for vectors and matrices, sigma signs for summation, and symbols for continued fractions. Some examples of eqn are given in figure 7.15 and a brief description follows.

Subscripts and superscripts are generated with the keywords sub and sup. Fractions are made with over. sqrt makes square roots. The keywords from and to introduce lower and upper limits on arbitrary things. Left and right brackets and braces of the right height are made with left and right. The right clause is optional. Legal characters after left and right are braces, brackets, bars, c and f for ceiling and floor, and "" for nothing at all (useful for a right-side-only bracket).

Vertical piles of things are made with pile, lpile, cpile, and rpile. There can be an arbitrary number of elements in a pile. lpile left justifies, pile and cpile center, with different vertical spacing, and rpile right justifies. Matrices are made with matrix. In addition, there is rcol for a right justified column.

Diacritical marks are made with dot, dotdot, hat, tilde, bar, vec, dyad, and under.

eqn *text*	*Output from* troff
x sub i	x_i
a sub i sup 2	a_i^2
e sup {x sup 2 + y sup 2}	$e^{x^2+y^2}$
a over b	$\dfrac{a}{b}$
x sup 2 over a sup 2	$\dfrac{x^2}{a^2}$
sqrt {ax sup 2 +bx+c}	$\sqrt{ax^2+bx+c}$
lim from {n—> inf } sum from 0 to n x sub i	$\lim\limits_{n\to\infty}\sum\limits_{0}^{n}x_i$
left [x sup 2 + y sup 2 over alpha right] ~=~1	$\left[x^2+\dfrac{y^2}{\alpha}\right]=1$
pile {a above b above c}	$\begin{matrix}a\\b\\c\end{matrix}$
matrix { lcol { x above y } ccol { 1 above 2 } }	$\begin{matrix}x & 1\\y & 2\end{matrix}$
x dot = f(t) bar	$\dot{x}=\overline{f(t)}$
y dotdot bar ~=~ n under	$\overline{\ddot{y}} = \underline{n}$
x vec ~=~ y dyad	$\vec{x} = \overset{\leftrightarrow}{y}$

Figure 7.15 Examples of the use of eqn

Sizes and fonts can be changed with size n or size ±n, roman, italic, bold, and font n. Size and fonts can be changed globally in a document by gsize n and gfont n, or by the command-line arguments −sn and −fn.

Normally subscripts and superscripts are reduced by 3 point sizes from the previous size; this may be changed by the command-line argument −pn.

Successive display arguments can be lined up. Place mark before the desired lineup point in the first equation; place lineup at the place that is to line up vertically in subsequent equations.

Keywords like sum ($\sum$), int ($\int$), inf (∞), and shorthands like >= ($\geq$), -> ($\rightarrow$), and != ($\neq$) are recognized.

```
.EQ
t ~=~ 2 pi int sub 0 sup 1
sin ( sqrt { x sup 2 + a sup 2 } ) dx
.EN
```

produces

$$t = 2\pi \int_0^1 \sin(\sqrt{x^2 + a^2})\,dx$$

Greek letters are spelled out in the desired case, as in alpha or GAMMA. Mathematical words like sin, cos, log are made Roman automatically. troff four-character escapes like \(dg (†) can be used anywhere. Strings enclosed in double quotes "..." are passed through untouched; this permits keywords to be entered as text, and can be used to communicate with troff when all else fails.

If both tables and equations are required tbl should be used first, as in

```
tbl chapter | eqn | troff −mm
```

7.3.3 ptx – permuted index generation

The permuted index at the front of the Seventh Edition of the *UNIX Programmer's Manual* was produced using the ptx command.

```
ptx <input >output
```

creates a permuted index of the records in input and produces the result on the file output. The option

```
−o keywords
```

is used to specify a file of keywords.

Each line of the input is shifted circularly so that a keyword appears at the start of the line. The file resulting from a complete set of operations of this kind is sorted. Finally the sorted lines are rotated so that the keyword comes to the middle of the page.

7.3.4 The spell command

The spell command checks the words in its input against an on-line dictionary of words. It is run as

```
spell document
```

or

```
spell −b document
```

The latter checks for British, as opposed to American, spelling.

The output is a list of those words not contained in the dictionary. This list may contain words that are correctly spelled but are not in the standard dictionary. By keeping your own file of strange words the comm command may be used to print only new spelling errors, as in the example below. In this example it is assumed that genuine spelling errors are corrected each time the command is run.

```
for i do
          mv spell/$i spell/$i.prev
          <$i spell >spell/$i
          comm −23 spell/$i spell/$i.prev
done
```

Such words could also be added to the standard dictionary by your system administrator or someone who has access to the dictionary file.

spell strips nroff/troff requests using the deroff filter before checking words against the dictionary.

7.3.5 The style command

The readability of a document may be analyzed using the command

```
style document
```

The percentage use of different grammatical forms is printed. It reports on readability, sentence length, sentence structure, word length, usage, verb type and methods of opening sentences. Although this information is structural and superficial to meaning it is particularly useful for comparing two documents and may also indicate over-use of a given grammatical form.

7.3.6 The tbl command

tbl accepts a simple description of a table and generates nroff requests to print the table. The input to tbl is text with information on the design of tables. Requests to tbl occur between the .TS (table start) and .TE (table end) requests, as in,

```
.TS
table description
.TE
```

tbl leaves all other text unaltered. The .TS and .TE lines are also left unaltered by tbl and may be used by other macro requests.

Tables are described as follows:

```
.TS
options governing table design;
format of columns and rows.
data for table
.TE
```

The ; and . are literal and should appear as shown to terminate the appropriate section. The format of the columns and rows generally follows a pattern similar to that of the table itself. In the following example, ⓉT denotes the tab character that separates the columns of the table.

```
.TS
center;
c s s s
c c c c
l l n n.
Bell Labs Locations
Name ⓉT Address ⓉT Area Code ⓉT Exchange
Holmdel ⓉT Holmdel, NJ 07733 ⓉT 201 ⓉT 949
Murray Hill ⓉT Murray Hill, NJ 07974 ⓉT 201 ⓉT 582
Whippany ⓉT Whippany, NJ 07981 ⓉT 201 ⓉT 386
Indian Hill ⓉT Naperville, IL 60540 ⓉT 312 ⓉT 690
.TE
```

This example produces a table of the form

	Bell Labs Locations		
Name	Address	Area Code	Exchange
Holmdel	Holmdel, NJ 07733	201	949
Murray Hill	Murray Hill, NJ 07974	201	582
Whippany	Whippany, NJ 07981	201	386
Indian Hill	Naperville, IL 60540	312	690

In the format section of the instructions to tbl the following options are available.

c   A centered column entry.

l   A left justified column entry.

n   A numerical quantity.

r   A right justified column entry.

s   A spanned heading, i.e. the entry from the previous column continues across into this column.

The center option causes the entire table to be centered on the page. The default is left justification. Other options include the following:

allbox   Draw a box around every table entry.

box   Draw a box around the entire table.

center   Center the table, default left justifies.

doublebox   Draw a double box around the table.

expand   Expand the table to use the current line length.

tab(x)   Use x instead of a tab to separate columns.

For example, the allbox request for the above table produces

Bell Labs Locations			
Name	Address	Area Code	Exchange
Holmdel	Holmdel, NJ 07733	201	949
Murray Hill	Murray Hill, NJ 07974	201	582
Whippany	Whippany, NJ 07981	201	386
Indian Hill	Naperville, IL 60540	312	690

The line

    c s s s

defines the fields of the first line of the table. The c indicates that the field is to be centered and an s says that the previous field is to continue in this column. The request

    c c c c

formats the second line with four centered headings.

The format of the remaining entries is described by

    l l n n

and a . ends the format section. The letter l indicates a left justified column and an n a numerical entry that is to be aligned on the units digits.

Chapter 8　**Data Manipulation Tools**

The UNIX system is well known for its data manipulation tools. These include:

awk	A pattern matching language and report generator.
cmp	Compare two files.
comm	Select lines common to two sorted files.
diff	Find the differences between two files.
grep	Match patterns in a set of files.
join	Combine two files by joining records with identical keys.
sed	A stream editor like ed but not interactive.
sort	Sort or merge files line by line.
tail	Print the last n lines of input.
tr	One-to-one character translation.
uniq	Remove successive duplicate lines from a file.

In this chapter the tools listed above will be described briefly and examples of their use given. The emphasis is on building new tools from those that already exist.

Combining these tools is achieved via the shell that acts as the glue. Shell scripts are easy to maintain and understand. Shell programming using commands as building blocks can be inefficient unless care is taken. However, it is often possible to produce a working system in a shorter time than if all the programs were written in C. If the design is successful and efficiency is required, parts of the system can be rewritten once it is working.

The following examples are described later in this chapter and illustrate applications well suited to these tools.

Telephone directory

The first example manages a list of phone numbers, names and addresses. A program to update the file with new information is shown. A number may be retrieved by giving a name, or part of a name. Similarly, given a number the associated name can be found. This example treats the file like a notebook.

C language cross-reference

This section illustrates how a C program and a lex program can combine to produce a line and file number cross-reference for C identifiers. Also, a typical makefile is used to keep the compiled versions up-to-date. The cross-reference program itself is a shell script that uses the two tools constructed. One of these tools is also used in chapter 7 to produce the index for this book.

Tennis ladder maintenance

This example describes a set of shell programs written to maintain a small data base.

Tennis ladder management typically involves keeping up-to-date player rankings. Each week results are reported and the ladder is updated according to some set of rules. Using the UNIX system most of this can be done automatically; updates will happen at a particular time each week without anyone having to issue a command directly.

8.1 Brief description of tools

In this section a brief discussion of the major tools is presented. The details, including the wide variety of available options, can be found in appendix 1, or from the man command.

In the discussion of some of the commands, such as join and sort, the term *fields* within records is used. A record is a line of text. Within a record, fields are separated by a field separator character. Frequently a tab is used as the field separator; this is convenient since it allows easy report generation using nroff. Some commands allow this character to be specified, others do not.

The tools described in some cases perform similar functions. For example, awk, ed, grep, lex, or sed will select lines according to a regular expression. The examples that follow illustrate uses for which these tools are well suited. As a general rule the more specialized the tool the more efficient it is for its stated purpose. For example, wc should be used for counting lines and grep, or egrep, used for selecting lines according to a pattern. sed is used when transformations of the input are required, such as the index generation example in section 7.2. awk is the most general but is slow to get started; lex requires that the C language environment be understood.

Regular expressions

The term *pattern* is used in this book to denote a set of strings. The set is specified using different forms depending on the application. For example, the shell uses a * to match zero or more characters, and ? to match a single character. The shell provides the weakest pattern matching capability. The commands awk, ed, grep, lex, and sed, provide patterns that match input strings. Sometimes the phrase *regular expression* is used to describe these patterns. A short description of regular expressions is given here; a more detailed discussion can be found in Aho, 1977.

A regular expression e is defined as follows, but see also section 3.1.5 for a description of ed patterns. In this description *character* excludes newline.

\c	A \ followed by a single character other than newline matches that character.
^ $	The character ^ ($) matches the beginning (end) of a line.
.	A . matches any character.
c	A single character not otherwise endowed with special meaning matches that character.
[...]	A string enclosed in brackets [] matches any single character from

the string. Ranges of ASCII character codes may be abbreviated as in a–z0–9. A] may occur only as the first character of the string. A literal – must be placed where it cannot be mistaken as a range indicator.

e*   A regular expression followed by * (+, ?) matches a sequence of 0 or more (1 or more, 0 or 1) occurrences of the regular expression.

e1 e2   Two regular expressions concatenated match the first followed by the second.

The expressions described so far are available in all the programs providing patterns, namely awk, ed, grep, lex, and sed. Further facilities are provided in awk, lex, and egrep as described below.

e1 | e2   Two regular expressions separated by | or newline matches either the first or the second expression.

(...)   A regular expression enclosed in parentheses matches the regular expression enclosed.

The order of precedence of operators at the same parenthesis level is [], *+?, concatenation, and | .

8.1.1 awk – report generator

awk is a filter that provides facilities for processing text. It is fully programmable, providing conditionals, loops, and variables with a notation similar to the C language. The command

awk program file$_1$ file$_2$ ...

executes the awk instructions in the string program with input from the files listed. If no files are given the standard input is used. Output from awk is normally sent to the standard output.

awk scans each input line for *selector* and when a match occurs an associated *action* is executed. The general form of a program is

```
BEGIN{   initial statements
}
selector { action }
...
END{     final statements
}
```

Several selector-action pairs may appear. An input line is read and each selector evaluated, in order. If the selector is true, the associated action is performed. The selector or action may be absent. If there is no selector the action is performed for every line of input and if the action is omitted the input line is copied onto the output.

An action may consist of several statements separated by ;. BEGIN and END introduce actions that are performed once at the beginning of the file and the end of file respectively.

awk reads each line or record of input and breaks it up into fields normally

separated by white space. In an expression $0 represents the entire current record
and $1, $2, ... represent the first field, second field, and so on. The number of
fields in the current record is available in the variable NF and the number of input
records read is available in NR.

The current input field separator and record separator are stored in the variables FS and RS. The default value for FS is white space (space or tab) and for RS
is a newline. To process a file with fields separated by a :, like /etc/passwd, the
statement

    FS=":"

should appear in the BEGIN section. To revert to the default, the null string should
be assigned to FS. The output field separator is, by default, a space and is kept in
the variable OFS. The name of the file being processed is kept in the variable
FILENAME. (Assigning to this variable will not change the input source.)

Examples

    awk '/srb/'
                        Print all records of the standard input containing srb.
    awk 'END{print NR}'
                        Print the number of input lines.
    awk 'print $3'
                        Print the third field from each record.

Expressions

Expressions take on string or numeric values as appropriate and, where necessary,
awk will convert strings to numbers. The operators +, −, *, /, %, and concatenation
(indicated by a space) and the C operators ++, −−, +=, −=, *=, /=, and %= are available in expressions. Variables may be scalars, array elements (denoted x[i]), or
field names $1, $2, ... Variables are initialized to the null string. The relational
operators consist of <, <=, ==, !=, >=, and > with the same meaning as in C. Both
strings and numbers are accepted as arguments to these operators. For example,

    NF > 5

is true for records with more than 5 fields.

    $1>"s"

is true when the first field in the line exceeds "s" lexicographically, e.g. for "st" and
"tom".

    $2>=0

is true whenever the second field is numerically positive.

The explicit pattern matching operators ~ and !~ are also provided. For example,

    $1 ~ /srb | SRB/

is true for records whose first field is srb or SRB, and

```
$1~/[Ss]treet/
```

is true whenever $1 matches the pattern [Ss]treet. The patterns provided by awk are
described in section 8.1.

The range of an action can be restricted using the , operator. For example,

```
/begin/ , /end/{. . .}
```

applies the statements enclosed between { and } over sections starting with the line
containing begin and ending with the line after that containing end.

Actions

An action in awk consists of one or more statements separated by a ; or newline. A
statement can be an assignment, conditional, loop or a built-in function such as
print. Generally, the syntax of awk and the set of operators is the same as in C.

A statement is one of the following:

```
if ( conditional ) statement [ else statement ]
while ( conditional ) statement
for ( expression ; conditional ; expression ) statement
for ( identifier in array ) statement
break
continue
{ [ statement ] ... }
variable = expression
print [ expression-list ] [ >expression ]
printf format [ , expression-list ] [ >expression ]
next        # skip remaining selectors on this input line
exit        # skip the rest of the input
```

Statements are terminated by semicolons, newlines or right-braces. An empty
expression-list stands for the whole line.

For example,

```
if ($2 > $1) {
        x = $1
        $1 = $2
        $2 = x
}
```

copies the standard input to the standard output and swaps $1 and $2 if $2 exceeds
$1. The comparison is numerical if possible and lexicographic otherwise.

Formatted printing

Formatted printing is available in awk using the two statements print, and printf.
Without arguments, print will output the entire current record. printf is more general than print and allows a C style format to be specified (see chapter 5).

For example,

```
i = 1
while (i <= NF) {
        printf "%s, ", $i
        i++
}
```

prints each field followed by a , . The print statement without arguments prints the entire current record and, with arguments, selected fields may be printed, as in

```
print $2, $1
```

that prints the second field and then the first field followed by a newline.

No output separators are produced automatically by printf; they must be provided as part of the format. For example,

```
printf "%s, %s\n", $1, $2
```

prints the first two fields separated by a , .

Arrays in awk can be indexed by strings thus providing an associative memory. For example, the first field of the password file contains a login-name. The following program checks that each login-name occurs only once.

```
awk ´
BEGIN{   FS=":"
}
{           if (user[$1]) {
                    print $1, "duplicated"
            }
            user[$1] = NR
}´ </etc/passwd
```

All elements of an associative array are accessible via a for statement. For example,

```
for (i in user)
        statement
```

loops over all subscripts of the array user.

Standard functions

The only functions available to an awk programmer are those that are already built-in to the language and are described below.

sqrt, log, exp, int
: The square root, logarithm to base e, exponential, and integer-part of the argument in parentheses.

length
: The length of its string argument. Without an argument the length of the entire current record is given.

substr(s, m, n)
: Produce a substring of s that starts at the m-th character (counting from 1), and that contains at most n characters.

index(s, t) The position of the first occurrence of t within s starting at 1. If t is not a substring of s, zero is returned.

8.1.2 cmp – **compare two files**

The command

cmp file₁ file₂

compares file₁ and file₂. If the files are identical then no output is produced; if they are not identical cmp responds by giving the byte and line number where the first difference occurs. cmp can be substantially faster than diff but will stop after the first difference is detected. The exit status returned is as follows:

0   The files are identical.
1   The files are different.
2   The files are inaccessible or arguments are missing.

8.1.3 comm – **select common lines**

This command selects or rejects lines common to two sorted files.

comm file₁ file₂

takes file₁ and file₂ that must both be sorted lexicographically. The output is in three columns consisting of lines only in file₁, lines only in file₂, and lines common to file₁ and file₂. Columns may be suppressed using the −[123] option. For example,

comm −23 f₁ f₂

suppresses columns 2 and 3, printing lines that are in the first file but not in the second, whereas

comm −12 f₁ f₂

prints only lines common to both files.
    For example,

```
for i do
          mv spell/$i spell/$i.prev
          <$i spell >spell/$i
          comm −23 spell/$i spell/$i.prev
done
```

is a script that keeps a file of the words rejected by spell. Each time the script is run the previous file is preserved and the file updated. comm prints the new spelling errors.

8.1.4 diff – **file differences**

diff is a differential file comparator. It lists the lines from two files that differ and attempts to minimize the length of the differences. It is called as

```
diff file₁ file₂
```

The output resembles that expected by the a, c and d requests to ed. Lines in the first file are preceded by a < and lines from the second by a >. The −e option generates ed requests that will change file₁ into file₂.

For example,

```
diff −e file1 file2 >diffs
```

will keep in the file diffs an ed script to convert file1 into file2.

The exit status from diff is:

    0   The files are the same.
    1   The files differ.
    2   An argument is inaccessible or missing.

8.1.5 grep – pattern selection

grep is the pattern matching filter that was introduced in chapter 2.

```
grep expression file ...
```

selects lines matching the given regular expression (or pattern) in one or more files. The expression specifies patterns as described in section 8.1.

A typical use of grep is to find a variable or function name in a set of C program source files. For example,

```
grep main *.c
```

will search all files with names ending in .c in the current directory, and print lines containing the string main. If more than one file is searched each output line is prefixed by the appropriate file name.

If the expression contains characters that have a special meaning to the shell, such as * or ∧, the expression should be quoted. For example,

```
grep ´∧[0−9][0−9]*´
```

The exit status of grep is:

    0   A match was found.
    1   No match was found.
    2   Files are inaccessible or there are syntax errors in expression.

The exit status of grep may be used to test for the presence of a string within a file. For example,

```
if grep expression file
then ...
fi
```

will look for *expression* in *file*. If the expression is found the then clause is executed.

grep does not provide alternatives within expression. egrep accepts full regular expressions that include | for alternation, + for one or more occurrences, ? for zero or one occurrence, and parentheses for grouping.

8.1.6 join – combine files

This command combines two files by joining records with identical keys, the key being a field of the file. A typical call is

    join file₁ file₂

where both file₁ and file₂ must be sorted lexicographically on the fields to be joined. The default key is the first field in each line.

There will be one line in the output corresponding to each pair of lines in file₁ and file₂ with identical key. By default, each output line will take the form

    common-field rest-of-line-from-file₁ rest-of-line-from-file₂

For example, suppose that the file dept contains lines of the form

    name ⓣ department

and the file cost contains lines of the form

    name ⓣ amount ⓣ date-of-purchase

ⓣ is used to represent the tab character and it is assumed that both files are sorted on the first field. The command

    join dept cost

will print a line of the form

    name department amount date-of-purchase

for each pair of lines in the two files that have the same name. To illustrate, suppose that the file dept contains

    Leo   13
    Shaw   12

and the file cost contains

    Leo $35   3/82
    Shaw $20   2/82
    Shaw $45   4/82

then the output from join dept cost will be

    Leo 13 $35 3/82
    Shaw 12 $20 2/82
    Shaw 12 $45 4/82

Various options are available. The output just produced is separated by spaces. If the field separator is changed with the –t´ⓣ´ option, both input and out-

put fields are separated by a tab. The −o option accepts a list of fields to be printed. For example,

    join −o 1.2 2.1 2.2 file₁ file₂

will print, in order, field 2 from the first file, and fields 1 and 2 from the second.
Using the above example, the output would be

    13 Leo $35
    12 Shaw $20
    12 Shaw $45

The fields to be joined can be specified by the −j option. The argument

    −jn m

causes joining on the m-th field of the n-th file. For example,

    join −j1 2 −j2 2 file₁ file₂

joins on the second field of both files.

When using join the most frequent problem is insufficient output. This can be
caused by an incorrect use of the options where white space is significant, or by
files not being sorted on the appropriate fields.

Using the two files dept and cost from the previous example, the script below
may be used to print those keys in the cost file not contained in the department file.
Again, the first field of each file contains the key.

    # list names in cost file that are not in dept file

    field 1 <cost | sort −u >/tmp/cost$$
    field 1 <dept | sort −u >/tmp/dept$$
    comm −23 /tmp/cost$$ /tmp/dept$$
    rm /tmp/cost$$ /tmp/dept$$

The first two lines produce a sorted list of the keys from each file with no duplicates.

The first version of this program was written as shown here but without the −u
option for sort. Unexpected results were produced and it took a little time to discover the problem. If this script had been constructed in two stages this might
have been avoided. The first stage would construct the temporary files. These
files could then be printed to check for unforeseen problems such as duplicated
lines.

8.1.7 sed – stream editor

sed is an editor that is used as a filter, not interactively. The operation of sed
resembles in many ways that of the awk pattern matcher discussed earlier. Each
line of its input is read and the requests that apply are executed. Requests to sed
are like those for ed. Repeated global substitutions are more efficient with sed
than ed.

    sed is invoked as

sed −e script

or

sed −f scriptfile

The requests from the script or scriptfile are applied to the standard input. The script may be quoted to prevent characters from being interpreted by the shell.

A general request takes the form

address$_1$,,address$_2$ request argument

If addresses are omitted the request is applied to every line. If two addresses are identical only one need be specified. Otherwise, the address delimits the part of the file that the edit request is applied to. Addresses can be specified numerically as decimal numbers or by context using regular expressions similar to those employed by ed and enclosed between / and /. The + and − operators are not available when addressing lines. Unlike ed, a request is applied to each line that matches address.

The requests available include:

s/.../.../	Substitute a string.
d	Delete a line.
a\	Append text after the current line.
i\	Insert text before the current line.
c\	Change the current line.

Each line of text following a, i or c is terminated by \ except for the last line. Requests for reading files, r, writing files, w, and printing, p, are also available.

```
# print full path name of command found in $PATH

for j do
            for i in `echo $PATH | sed −e ´s/:/ /g`
            do          if test −f $i/$j
                        then        echo $i/$j
                        fi
            done
done
```

Figure 8.1 The path command

The path command in figure 8.1 illustrates a typical use of the sed command. The outer loop sets j to each argument supplied to path. The inner loop sets i to each non-blank word in the output of the command

```
echo $PATH | sed −e ´s/:/ /g´
```

The output consists of a blank separated list of directory names from the shell variable PATH.

8.1.8 sort – **sort or merge files**

When applied in the form

```
sort file₁ file₂ ...
```

all lines of $file_1$, $file_2$, ... are sorted onto the standard output. If no files are specified the standard input is read so that sort can be used as a filter. By default, sorting is done on entire lines using lexical ordering by bytes in the host machine's collating sequence (usually ASCII). This ordering is termed *lexicographic* and is close to the dictionary order for words. An option provides numerical sorting.

The notation

```
+pos₁ −pos₂
```

restricts the sort key to a field beginning at position pos_1, and ending just before position pos_2. For example,

```
sort +0 −1 +3 −4
```

sorts on the first field followed by the fourth field. (Incorrectly specifying field numbers is a frequent error when using sort.) A starting position may be followed by n to specify numeric comparison for this field. For example,

```
sort +0n ...
```

specifies that sorting on the first field is numerical.

The default field separator is white space and may be changed using the −t option. Thus

```
sort −t: ...
```

sorts on fields separated by a :.

Other useful sort options include:

−n   Sort using the numerical value of the field.
−r   Reverse the sense of comparisons.
−u   Suppress all but one instance in each set of identical lines.

sort and join use a different notation for numbering the fields within a record and this can be confusing. In sort, +0 −1 means the first field. For join the first field is specified as 1.

8.1.9 tail – **last lines of a file**

The tail command is a filter that prints the last few lines of a file. The −n option, where n is a number, specifies that the last n lines are required.

8.1.10 tr – translate characters

The command

    tr string₁ string₂

copies and translates characters from the standard input to the standard output. All the characters in string₁ are mapped onto the corresponding characters in string₂. If string₂ is shorter than string₁, it is padded to the length of string₁ by repeating the last character as often as necessary.

The command lower in figure 8.2 converts all upper case letters into lower case. Note that the arguments to the shell are quoted to avoid being interpreted as file name patterns.

---

    tr ´[A–Z]´ ´[a–z]´

Figure 8.2 The lower command

8.1.11 uniq – remove duplicate lines

This command accepts sorted input and compares adjacent lines. When invoked as

    uniq file

the second and later copies of repeated adjacent lines are removed from file and printed on the standard output. The standard input is read if no file is specified. Identical lines must be adjacent to be found; therefore the sort command may be needed before uniq is invoked. The −u option of sort has a similar specification although sort does not provide some of the options of uniq.

The following options are available:

−c   Print the number of occurrences of each line followed by the line.

−d   Only a single copy of duplicated lines is printed.

The following program generates a list of words from a set of files and produces a frequency count for each word. If no arguments are supplied, the for loop executes once with i set to the null string, causing the standard input to be read by tr.

```
for i in "$@"
do        <$i tr −cs A–Za–z ´\012´
done |
  sort −f |
  uniq −c
```

8.1.12 field – select columns

The field command is a basic tool, although it is not provided with standard versions of the UNIX system. The implementation of this command is given in section 8.4 and is used as an example to show how new tools are engineered. The arguments to field are the column numbers to be copied from each record. For example, when invoked as field 2 4 3

the standard input is read and produces on the standard output fields 2, 4 and 3 separated by a TAB. The awk script

awk ´{print $2, $4, $3}´

has a similar effect but separates the output by a space.

8.1.13 lex **and** yacc

This section mentions two compiler writing tools lex and yacc. lex accepts a set of regular expressions and associated C program fragments corresponding to actions. A program is produced that partitions its input according to these expressions and executes the associated actions. It is used for the lexical analysis of programming languages such as C, and is particularly well suited as an interface to yacc.

yacc accepts an LALR(1) grammar as input together with fragments of C program and generates a program to partition its input according to the grammar. When a rule is recognized the user program fragment supplied with the rule is executed. yacc expects its input to have been broken up into tokens by a lexical analyzer such as lex.

An example of the use of lex is given in section 8.2.2.

8.2 Simple examples

8.2.1 Maintaining a simple data base

In this example a program is designed to update a file containing names, addresses, and phone numbers. The command is called enter and is shown in figure 8.3.

The first outline of the program is

```
while read name
do       read address
         read phone
         # append to file
         . . .
done
```

The read command provided by the shell is used.

read v_1 v_2 . . .

takes one line of input from the standard input and assigns successive *words* to the variables v_1, v_2, ... If any words are left over they are assigned to the last variable. The exit status of read is 0 unless an end-of-file is encountered. Replacing the read statement by break,

read phone | | break

causes a break out of the while loop to occur if the read fails. For example, if the end-of-file is reached when reading the data or if an interrupt occurs, read will fail and break will be executed.

Each entry within the file is kept as a single record so that standard tools may be used to process the file and the outline given above assumes a single line address. A multi-line address may be converted into a single line as illustrated below where a ~ is used to separate the various sections of the address in the shell variable address. On input an address is terminated by a blank line.

```
address=
while read a
do      case $a in
        ´´)          break ;;
        *)           address="$address~$a" ;;
        esac
done
```

If this program outline were executed, the user would soon get confused, since there is no prompting. Further, there are no facilities for making corrections. The prompting is easily added to give a complete version of the enter command as shown in figure 8.3.

The prompt command used here consists of

```
echo $*\c 1>&2
```

```
date=`date`

while     prompt "name: "
          read name
do        case $name in
          ´´)          continue ;;
          q)           break ;;
          esac

          prompt "address: "
          address=   ·
          while read a
          do        case $a in
                    ´´)          # blank line ends address
                                 break ;;
                    *)           address="$address~$a" ;;
                    esac
          done

          prompt "phone: "
          read phone || break

          echo "$name① $address① $phone① $date"≫$HOME/tel
done
```

Figure 8.3 The enter command

Looking up numbers

grep is ideally suited to looking up names or numbers in the address-list as illustrated by the following tel script:

```
for i do
        grep "$i" <$HOME/tel
done
```

where $HOME/tel is the file containing the checked data. The argument to grep is quoted to prevent any enclosed metacharacters from being interpreted by the shell.

A file of the kind created here will accumulate entries that are similar, or even identical, and also will become out of date. One technique that is useful for detecting potential curiosities in the file is to sort on different fields. Exact duplicates of lines can be removed using the sort command, as in

```
sort -u <$HOME/tel >$HOME/newtel
```

Duplicate phone numbers are extracted from the file tel by the command

```
field 3 <tel | sort | uniq -d
```

where the -d option results in only one copy of each duplicated record being produced. The entire line from the original file corresponding to duplicate phone numbers may be printed by joining the output with the original tel file. The script is shown in figure 8.4.

The join input must be sorted on the fields to be joined and the file /tmp/$$1 is already appropriately sorted. However, since the tel file cannot be guaranteed to be sorted, sort is called and the output saved in /tmp/$$2.

```
field 3 <tel | sort | uniq -d >/tmp/$$1
sort -t' ⊤ ' <tel >/tmp/$$2
join -t' ⊤ ' -j1 1 -j2 3 /tmp/$$1 /tmp/$$2
rm /tmp/$$1 /tmp/$$2
```

Figure 8.4 Print duplicate phone numbers

Both sort and join require the -t' ⊤ ' option specifying that a tab is the field separator. In the script a single quote has been used to prevent this tab from being absorbed by the shell.

Another improvement that could be made to the original enter command is to check to see if numbers that are about to be added are already present. This check takes the form

```
if grep "$phone" <$HOME/tel >/dev/null
then      # the number is already present
else      # the number is missing
fi
```

The output from grep, if any, is directed to the null file, /dev/null, that is writable by everyone. Characters sent to this file are 'lost'. The exit status of grep is used to determine whether the phone number exists in the file.

A remark should be made about the efficiency of the modification just out-lined. read is built into the shell and so its use is reasonably efficient. In some ver-sions of the shell an echo or prompt command is also built-in. grep is not built into the shell and each time it is executed a new process is created. This operation is relatively expensive and may cause a noticeable reduction in the response of enter. Whether this is serious depends on the local computing environment and the size of the tel file.

8.2.2 A C language cross-reference program

The programs described in this section generate cross-references for C programs. The output is a list of the line numbers in each file where the identifiers are used. The result type is printed for function definitions. The output in figure 8.5 is the cross-reference output for the file xrefb.c from figure 8.9.

EOF	xrefb.c	25	64							
MAXW	xrefb.c	5	6	13	65					
argc	xrefb.c	10	17							
argv	xrefb.c	11								
c	xrefb.c	61	64	66	69					
cpstr( )	xrefb.c	3	36	40	43					
f1	xrefb.c	13	22	32	40	41				
f2	xrefb.c	13	23	34	36	43	44			
first	xrefb.c	14	27	28						
getchar( )	xrefb.c	64								
h	xrefb.c	1								
lastc	xrefb.c	7	46	50	63	69	72			
lastw	xrefb.c	3	6	27	28	32	34	35	48	60	65
main(argc,argv)	xrefb.c	+9								
n	xrefb.c	46	63	64						
p	xrefb.c	60	65	66	71					
printf( )	xrefb.c	18	29	35	41	44	48	52		
stdio	xrefb.c	1								
strcmp( )	xrefb.c	32	34							
strcpy( )	xrefb.c	3								
t	xrefb.c	64								
word( )	xrefb.c	25	33	42	47					
word( )/int	xrefb.c	+58								
x	xrefb.c	3								

Figure 8.5 xref **output for the file** xrefb.c

The work is divided between two programs xrefa and xrefb. The first program, xrefa, generates a list of the form

identifier ⊤ file-name ⊤ line-number

and is implemented by the lex program whose source is kept in the file xrefa.l. As shown in the shell command xref in figure 8.6, the output from xrefa is sorted and then piped into the layout program xrefb producing output of the form

identifier ⊤ file-name ⊤ line₁ line₂ ...

                    . . .

xrefb is a C program and the source is kept in the file xrefb.c. The index for this book was also partly processed by xrefb (see section 7.2). The vertically oriented output of xrefa is read by xrefb and the line numbers printed across the page.

```
xrefa $* |
   sort −ut: +0 −1 +1 −2 +2n −3 |
   xrefb
```

Figure 8.6 The xref **command**

The makefile

The makefile is shown in figure 8.7. Apart from the entries to make the programs, entries are also introduced to *clean* and *install* the system. It is assumed that the files clean and install do not exist in the source directory.

```
xref:           xrefa xrefb

xrefa:          xrefa.o
                cc −o xrefa xrefa.o −ll
xrefb:          xrefb.o
                cc −o xrefb xrefb.o

clean:;         rm xref[ab].o

install:;       cp xref xrefa xrefb /usr/local/bin

.c.o:;          cc −O −c $<
```

Figure 8.7 The makefile **for the** xref **system**

The first pass, xrefa

This section describes, briefly, the lex program for the first pass of the cross-reference. A complete description of lex is available in Lesk, 1975.

The program described here has the form

```
% options
%{
C program definitions
%}
%%
lex actions
```

The C program definitions include a definition of the function main and the lex actions consist of a pattern, as described in section 8.1, followed by an action. The action is a C program statement that is executed when the pattern matches the input. This is similar to the way an awk program works except that in lex the input is not automatically divided into records. Further, lex programs are compiled.

lex *options*

lex uses many internal tables and the %option section sets the various table sizes. The output generated by running the command

```
lex xrefa.l
```

is

```
372/500 nodes(%e),
3188/4000 positions(%p),
339/400 (%n), 21255 transitions,
54/100 packed char classes(%k),
967/1000 packed transitions(%a),
833/1000 output slots(%o)
```

and these options have been set so that sufficient space is available and are not otherwise interesting. In some cases the default lex sizes are sufficient.

The output from lex is left in the file lex.yy.c and is compiled as

```
cc lex.yy.c −ll
```

The lex *environment*

The standard input-output library is automatically provided by lex and is used in this example to open input files. Other definitions provided by lex include:

yylex( )	Invoke the lex analyzer to read the standard input file.
yyinput( )	Read a single character from the input.
yytext[ ]	The string matched by the current rule.
yyleng	The length of the string in yytext.
yylineno	Incremented for each line of input read.

The main routine provided in the definitions section of xrefa.l contains the argument handling for xrefa just like a C program. lex actions are invoked when the function yylex is called. In this example, if there are no arguments, yylex is called and the standard input is read. If arguments are provided each file is opened as the standard input by freopen, the file name remembered and yylex is called.

```
%k 100
%a 1000
%o 1000
%n 400
%e 500
%p 4000
%{
char      *filename="-";

main(argc,argv)
          int       argc;
          char      *argv[ ];
{
          register int rc=0;
          if(argc<=1) {
                    yylex( );
          }else{
                    while(argc>1) {
                              if(freopen(argv[1],"r",stdin)==NULL) {
                                        fprintf(stderr,
                                                  "xref: %s: cannot open\n",
                                                  argv[1]
                                        );
                                        rc++;
                              }else{
                                        filename=argv[1];
                                        yylineno=1;
                                        yylex( );
                              }
                              argc--; argv++;
                    }
          }
          return(rc);
} /* main */
%}
%%
"/*"      comment( );
"\""      strings( );
^[a-zA-Z_][a-zA-Z0-9 \t_]*"("[a-zA-Z0-9, ]*")""\n              fndef( );
if[ \t]*"("              ;
return[ \t]*"("          ;
while[ \t]*"("           ;
for[ \t]*"(" ;
switch[ \t]*"("          ;
auto                     ;
```

```
break              ;

. . .
[a–zA–Z_][a–zA–Z0–9_]*[ \t]*"(" {
          /* function call */
          printf("%s)\t%s\t%d\n", yytext, filename, yylineno);
          }
[a–zA–Z_][a–zA–Z0–9_]* {
          /* identifier reference */
          printf("%s\t%s\t%d\n", yytext, filename, yylineno);
          }
.                  ;
\n                 ;
```

Figure 8.8 The lex source for xrefa.l

Figure 8.8 contains lex rules for the cross-reference program. One caveat should be noted in the BUGS section of the manual page. The rule for recognizing function definitions is not exactly correct since the result type can appear on the line preceding the function name.

The lex rules are described below:

"/*" The start of a comment. The function comment is called and is defined below.

```
comment( ) {
          /* comments */
          char c;
          while(c = yyinput( )) {
                    if(c == '*' && yyinput( ) == '/')
                              break;

          }
} /* comment */
```

"\"" The opening quote of a string constant. The function strings, defined below, is called and skips characters up to the closing quote.

```
strings( ) {
          /* strings */
          char c;
          while(c = yyinput( )) {
                    if(c == '"')
                              break;
                    else if(c == '\\')
                              yyinput( );
          }
} /* strings */
```

^[a–zA–Z_][a–zA–Z0–9 \t_]*"("[a–zA–Z0–9,]*")"\n

The pattern describes an identifier at the start of a line, followed by a (, a list of identifiers and commas, a) and a newline. It is assumed to be a function definition. This rule is not strictly correct but is adequate for C programs using standard layout such as that produced by the cb command. Within a lex metacharacters, like (and) may be enclosed within double quotes to remove their special meaning. The C function fndef listed below is called and scans backwards through the text recognized by the rule looking for the end of the identifier and the result type, if any. The result type is printed after the function name and argument list.

```
fndef( )
{
            /* fn defs */
            register char *p = &yytext[yyleng];

            *--p = 0;          /* remove ) */
            while(*--p != '(');
            while(*p==' ' || *p=='\t') {
                    p--;
                    if(p<yytext) break;
            }
            while(*p!=' ' && *p!='\t') {
                    p--;
                    if(p<yytext) break;
            }
            p++;
            printf("%s", p);
            if(p !=yytext) {
                    *--p=0;
                    printf("/%s", yytext);
            }
            printf("\t%s\t+%d\n", filename, yylineno-1);
} /* fndef */
```

The remaining rules are similar to those already described. Once function definitions have been recognized, the language constructions involving parentheses are read and ignored. Any identifiers remaining that are followed by a (are treated as function calls. Identifier references are recognized last and the two rules

```
.        ;
\n       ;
```

absorb any characters that remain.

The second pass, xrefb

The second pass of the cross-reference takes the sorted output from the first pass and lays it out horizontally across the page. The program, as presented here, could easily be written as an awk script; the original program had more options to control the output format.

```
#include <stdio . h>

#define MAXW  128
char      lastw[MAXW];         /* last word read */
char      lastc;

main(argc,argv)
          int       argc;
          char      *argv[ ];
{
          char f1[MAXW], f2[MAXW];
          char first=0;

          /* args ? */
          if(argc>1) {
                    printf("unexpected argument(s)\n");
                    return(1);
          }

          f1[0]=0;
          f2[0]=0;

          while(word( ) != EOF){
                    if(lastw[0]!=first) {
                              first=lastw[0];
                              printf("\n");
                    }

                    if(strcmp(lastw, f1)==0) {
                              word( );
                              if(!strcmp(lastw, f2) == 0) {
                                        printf("\n\t%s", lastw);
                                        strcpy(f2, lastw);
                              }
                    }
                    else{
                              strcpy(f1, lastw);
                              printf("\n%s", f1);
                              word( );
                              strcpy(f2, lastw);
                              printf("\t%s", f2);
                    }
                    if(lastc != '\n'){
                              word( );
                              printf("\t%s", lastw);
                    }
                    lastc = 0;
          }
```

```
                printf("\n");
                return(0);
        } /* main */

        /* read a word from the input */
        /* result is stored in lastw */
        int word( )
        {
                register char *p = lastw;
                register int c;

                if(lastc != '\n'){
                        while((c = getchar( ))!='\t' && c!='\n' && c!=EOF) {
                                if(p < &lastw[MAXW]) {
                                        *p++ = c;
                                }
                        }
                        lastc = c;
                }
                *p++ = 0;
                return(lastc);
        } /* word */
```

Figure 8.9 The C source for xrefb.c

8.3 A tennis ladder system

This section describes the use of the UNIX system tool kit through a complete example. The programs in this section are written using standard commands with the
addition of the field described in section 8.4.

The system maintains a tennis ladder for staff members at the Murray Hill
laboratory. The ladder itself is a file containing a rank ordered list of players. Each
line of the file consists of the following fields:

- The player's identity (initials if unique).
- The numerical rank of the player.
- The player's name.
- The player's phone number.
- The player's office number.
- The number of matches won.
- The number of matches lost.
- The movement up or down the ladder since last week.
- The number of weeks the player has been inactive.

The ladder operates as follows. All matches played between Monday and
Sunday are recorded in a file. On Tuesday of each week (allowing Monday for delays in reporting matches) the ladder is updated according to the previous week's
match results. If a player beats a player higher in the ladder, the winner is moved

just above the loser. Otherwise, no movement occurs as a result of the match. However, if a player is inactive for 3 or more consecutive weeks then that player drops two places down the ladder each subsequent week. A player who is inactive for 7 weeks is dropped entirely from the ladder.

8.3.1 Organization

All files relating to this system reside in the directory $HOME/tennis or in a sub-directory of this directory. This directory is considered to be the current directory in the following description.

The commands to support and implement this system are kept in ./bin (i.e. $HOME/tennis/bin). This separation of commands and data files avoids congestion in the main directory and enables commands to be easily identified. A suitable setting of the PATH variable in the shell is:

    PATH= . :/bin:/usr/bin:./bin:$HOME/bin

A directory is created each year for use as an archive for results. It also serves as a backup in case of failure. For most of the commands that follow, the ladder file is assumed to exist and be named .ladder. When testing the system the file name was kept in the variable $ladder that was set and exported from the shell.

The remainder of this section describes the commands that implement the ladder maintenance including:

- Enter match results.
- Update the ladder weekly.
- Print the ladder.
- Determine prize winners.
- Clean up of files at the end of the season.

Command scripts

The scripts are summarized here for reference. The tree depth indicates the execution hierarchy. For example, cron calls weekly and weekly calls both run and send.

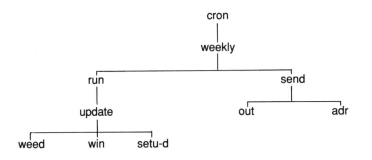

8.3.2 Entering results

Each game result consists of the identity of the winner and loser, the score and the date. Players are identified by their initials although, given a name, the initials can be looked up. Both are stored in the ladder file.

```
NL='
'

# read ladder into L_id
. readL

while     true
do        prompt 'date: '
          read D || break

          case $D in
          [0-9]*) # assume it is a date ;;
          q)       break ;;
          *)       look $D || prompt "\'$D' not found$NL"
                   continue ;;
          esac

          prompt 'winner: '
          read WP || break
          # check player is in the ladder
          eval namew\=\$L_$WP
          case $namew in
          '')      prompt "$WP not in the ladder$NL"
                   continue
          esac
          set $namew; rank1=$1; name1=$2;

          prompt 'loser: '
          read LP || break
          eval namel\=\$L_$LP
          case $namel in
          '')      prompt "$LP not in the ladder$NL"
                   continue
          esac
          set $namel; rank2=$1; name2=$2;

          prompt 'score: '
          read S || break

          prompt "$NL$D     $name1($rank1)     over $name2($rank2)"
          prompt "${NL}ok? "
          read ok
          case $ok in
          y|ok|'')  echo "$DⓉ $WPⓉ $LPⓉ $S" >>. matches  ;;
          *)        prompt "result not recorded$NL"  ;;
          esac
done
```

Figure 8.10 The record script

The program to enter results follows closely the style of the example in section 8.2.1.

The program record, is accessible from the tennis directory when the $PATH variable has been set appropriately. As shown in figure 8.10, record prompts for the following fields for each match played:

date:
winner:
loser:
score:

After the prompt, if a valid date, such as 12/7, is entered the remaining fields are requested. An end-of-file or a q will cause a break and exit. Otherwise, if the name of a player is entered, look (figure 8.11) is called to print an entry from the ladder file. If more than one entry is found by look then all such entries are printed.

Next the winner and loser are read and checked to ensure that they are on the ladder and finally the match score is requested and read. The full name and ladder position of the participants is reflected back to the user for confirmation before being added to the .matches file.

The discussion of the shell commands that read and check the player identities is deferred until after the description of the readL script.

The look *script*

look finds lines in the ladder file containing all of its arguments. In the simple case, when called with a single argument, $# is 1 and the first branch of the case statement is executed.

```
case $# in
        1)      tr "[A–Z]" "[a–z]" < .ladder | grep "$1" ;;
        0)      ;;
        *)      a="$1"; shift; look "$*" | grep "$a"
esac
```

Figure 8.11 The look script

When more than one argument is provided, as, for example, in

look bob lucky

the default branch of the case is executed. The first argument is recorded in the variable $a and look is called again with the second argument. The output from the second call of look is filtered by

... | grep "$a"

so that only lines containing both bob and lucky are printed.

The readL *script*

Certain aspects of record will be discussed further since they involve less frequently used parts of the shell. The command

    . readL

in figure 8.10 executes the commands in readL as if they were part of the file record. The effect of readL (figure 8.12) is to store information in shell variables about each player in the ladder. These variables are used later to check that players are on the ladder.

```
# read ladder into L_id
exec 3<&0 < .ladder

while read id rest
do eval L_$id="$rest"´
done

exec 0<&3 3<&-
```

Figure 8.12 The readL **script**

The body of readL consists of the while loop

```
while read id rest
do eval L_$id="$rest"´
done
```

with input being read from the file .ladder. If the first lines of the ladder file were

    hga ...
    aps ...
    ...

then, after execution of readL, the shell variables L_hga and L_aps would be set as

    L_hga=...
    L_aps=...
    ...

where the value assigned is the line from the ladder file corresponding to the player. This use of eval provides an array-like mechanism from within the shell.

The statement

    read id rest

reads the next line from the ladder and places the first word in the variable id, and the remainder of the line is placed in the variable rest.

If id is set to hga then

    eval L_$id="$rest"´

is interpreted as

    L_hga="..."

where ... is the value of the variable rest.

The exec statement of readL redirects input in the shell to allow the .ladder file to be read by the while loop. Using shell input redirection with the while loop, as in,

```
while ...
do ...
done <.ladder
```

will not work as required since a new process is created to execute the while loop when redirection (<.ladder) is present. The new process cannot return the values of shell variables to its parent.

```
exec 3<&0
```

duplicates the file descriptor 0 using the dup system call and saves it as file descriptor 3.

```
exec < . ladder
```

then redirects the standard input. These two commands can be combined as shown. The reverse operation occurs when the while loop is complete with the command

```
exec 0<&3 3<&-
```

Checking player identities

Now that the appropriate variables have been set by readL the remainder of the record script from figure 8.10 can be described.

After the winner's name has been entered it is checked to ensure that the player is on the ladder.

Names are recovered from the variables, set by readL, also using eval.

```
eval namew\=\$L_$WP
```

assigns to namew the value of the variable $L_... where ... is the value of $WP. Suppose that aps won his match, then $WP would be set to aps and this line would be interpreted as

```
namew=$L_aps
```

On the first evaluation, only $WP is interpreted by the shell. eval passes this string to the shell for interpretation causing the variable namew to be assigned the value contained in the variable

```
$L_aps
```

If aps is in the ladder namew will be set, otherwise a message is printed and the loop resumed at the beginning.

8.3.3 Weekly activities

The remainder of the work involving the ladder is left to be run in the early hours of the morning when many machines are lightly loaded and have cycles to spare. Such work is scheduled for a later time using the at command.

```
at 0300 cron
```

will copy the file cron into a system directory (/usr/spool/at) to be run at 3 a.m. The cron file for tennis is shown in figure 8.13. The first line reschedules cron to be run again the next day and

```
exec ≫cron.1 2≫cron.2
```

redirects the standard output and error output into a file, otherwise the output would be lost.

```
at 0300 cron
exec ≫cron.1  2≫cron.2

set `date`
echo $*
case $1 in
        Tue)    weekly ;;
        Sun)    date > .sunday
esac
```

Figure 8.13 The cron **script**

Each Tuesday the program weekly in figure 8.14 is run and each Sunday the output from the date command is recorded in the file .sunday. This is used later in the ladder printing program.

```
# run this week's ladder
run

# print this week's results
send
date > .lastweek
```

Figure 8.14 The weekly **script**

weekly updates the ladder by executing run (figure 8.15) and send is called to print out the ladder, one copy to each player. Lastly, the date of printing is record-ed in the file .lastweek. This file has been used in the output to indicate when the previous printing occurred. Participants can then check that all ladder print-outs have been received. The next two sections describe the ladder update and printing commands.

8.3.4 The ladder update

Having dealt with the organization of the ladder and how to schedule a weekly, daily or monthly activity, the details of updating the ladder from week-to-week are described in this section. Although this description is 'top down', in practice these high level organizational programs would be left to last when writing a set of programs of this kind.

The run *script*

The shell script run in figure 8.15 is called by the weekly cron file. It contains more organizational commands and requires little explanation.

```
set − `date`
year=$6 month=$2 day=$3
date=$month−$day

# wait for lock
trap "" 1 2 3 15
until mklock .lock
do sleep 60; done

echo $month $day weekly tennis run starting

cp .ladder $year/${date}L
cp .matches $year/${date}G
trap ´rm −f .lock; exit´ 0 1 2 3 15

# update ladder from weeks matches
update <.matches >.results

# save for printing
cp .results $year/${date}R

# empty the match file
>.matches

echo $month $day weekly tennis run ending
```

Figure 8.15 The run **script**

The command mklock (section 6.4.1) guarantees exclusive access to the file .lock. If the command fails the lock file is unavailable, otherwise the lock has been obtained. The lock may be used to prevent weekly results from being entered at the same time that the ladder update is running, although the version of enter presented earlier does not make use of this facility.

The update *script*

The updating activity is broken up into file management, kept in the run command, and the changes required to the ladder file itself that are dealt with in update (figure 8.16). Both the current ladder and the week's matches are copied into the backup directory as a safeguard against system crashes and program bugs. Also, the player identities are again checked since the win script assumes that the players are present.

```
NL='
'

# read ladder into L_id
. readL

# set u–d field to zero
setu–d

# read from match record file
while      read D WP LP S
do         eval namew\=\$L_$WP
           case $namew in
           '')       prompt "winner \`$WP\' not known$NL"
                     continue
           esac
           set $namew; rank1=$1; name1=$2;

           eval namel\=\$L_$LP
           case $namel in
           '')       prompt "loser \`$LP\' not known$NL"
                     continue
           esac
           set $namel; rank2=$1; name2=$2;

           win $WP $LP

           # generate output for results service
           echo "$DⓉ $name1($rank1)Ⓣ overⓉ $name2($rank2)Ⓣ $S"
done

# remove inactive players and penalize 3 week non players
weed
```

Figure 8.16 The update **script**

When the update of the ladder is complete the results are stored in .results and in the backup directory. In addition, the ladder manager is kept informed, by mail, of the state of the ladder update.

win is called once for each match played from within the while loop of update. Each line is read from the standard input (usually .matches) into the variables D, W, L and S. Use is again made of readL to set shell variables L_*id*. As in the record script, these variables are used to check that players are on the ladder. The output from update is a list of matches including the name of each player (rather than identity) and that player's position last week.

Field 8 of the ladder file shows the number of places up or down each player has moved since the previous week. The program setu–d (figure 8.17) sets this field to zero using an awk script. This field is used by win to record the movement up or down the ladder. Since awk is a filter, a temporary file is required to store intermediate output. When setu–d is complete this temporary file is renamed as .ladder using the mv command.

```
trap 'rm –f $tmp; exit' 0 1 2 3 15
tmp=`mktemp /tmp/tennisXXXXXX`

awk < . ladder >$tmp '
BEGIN {
          FS="      "
          OFS="     "
}
{         $8 = 0
          print
}'

trap '' 1 2 3 15
mv $tmp  . ladder
```

Figure 8.17 The setu–d **script**

The win *script*

An individual match result is recorded in the .matches file as

    date Ⓣ winner Ⓣ loser Ⓣ score

where the winner and loser correspond to the identity of the players. The win command (figure 8.18) scans the ladder using an awk script, and changes the second field containing the rank of each player. ·The number of wins or losses is incremented and the number of weeks idle is set to −1. This output is then sorted on the new rankings and the ladder file replaced with the updated version.

    The first test

    if($1=="'$1'") {

requires explanation. The first $1 represents the first field in each line as it is read from the standard input by awk. The double quotes are interpreted by awk and enclose the string passed as the first argument by the shell (the identity of the winner). The single quote belongs to the shell and ends the first part of the argument.

    awk '
    BEGIN{   . . .
          . . . '**$1**'

The bold text is interpreted by the shell. The single quote after the $1 is the resumption of the quoted argument by the shell. The $1 itself is outside the single quotes and is substituted by the shell before awk begins execution.

```
# called as: win winner loser
trap 'rm −f $tmpa; exit' 1 2 3 15
tmpa=`mktemp  . tmpaXXXXX`

awk <$ladder '
BEGIN {
        FS="       "
        OFS="      "
        W=0
        L=0
        N=1
}
{       if($1=="'$1'") {
                W = 1;
                $6 = $6 + 1;
                $9 = −1;
                if(L!=0) {
                        $2 = L;
                        N = NR;
                }
        }
        else if($1=="'$2'") {
                L = NR;
                $7 = $7 + 1;
                $9 = −1;
                if(W==0) {
                        N = NR + 1;
                        $2 = N;
                }
                else {
                        $2 = N;
                }
        }
        else {
                $2 = N;
        }
        $8 = $8 + NR − $2;
        N = N + 1;
        print
}' |
sort +1n −2 >$tmpa

trap '' 1 2 3 15
mv $tmpa $ladder
```

Figure 8.18 The win script

If win is called as

```
win hga aps
```

then the argument to awk would be

```
BEGIN{
        . . .
}
{
        if($1=="hga") {
        . . .
```

the single quotes having been stripped by the shell.

The remainder of win can be read as if it were a C program. awk takes care of string to integer conversions and the body of the awk program is executed for each line of the standard input.

The variable W is set when the winner is encountered during the scan of the file. The variable L is set to the (old) rank of the losing player and two cases are distinguished.

- *The winner is higher on the ladder than the loser.* The test

    ```
    if($1=="'$1'") {
    ```

    will succeed and L will be zero since the loser has not yet been encountered. No adjustments to the ladder are necessary.
- *The winner appears below the loser in the ladder file.* W is zero and the test W==0 succeeds. A gap is left in the numbering for the winner (N=NR+1) and the loser is assigned the next rank below. When the winner is reached L is already set to the original rank of the loser and the test L!=0 succeeds. The loser's original rank is assigned to the winner ($2=L). The remaining rankings can be left unchanged and N is reset to account for this (N=NR).

The resulting output is sorted on the new ranking field and stored in a temporary file. The last line restores the ladder from the temporary file.

Although it may seem that there is a profusion of commands, each of which does little, constructing the system in this way allows each part of the system to be tested as it is built. For example, win can be called directly from the shell and input presented interactively. Similarly, update can be run by hand once a week until the at script can be made to work.

The weed script

The last program that makes ladder changes is called weed (figure 8.19) and deals with players who have been inactive for more than 3 weeks. These players are moved down two places to encourage active participation. The top player is exempt from the 3 week rule since he is unable to challenge other players. Players who are inactive for 7 weeks are removed from the ladder.

```
: ${ladder=.ladder}
trap 'rm −f $tmp; exit' 0 1 2 3 15
tmp=`mktemp /tmp/tennisXXXXXX`

# remove inactive players and penalise 3 week non players
awk <$ladder '
BEGIN {
        OFS="Ⓣ"
        FS="Ⓣ"
}
{       $9 = $9 + 1;
        $8 = $8 + $2;
        R = 2*NR;
        if($9 >= 3 && NR!=1) R = R + 5;
        if($9 < 7 || NR==1) {
                $2 = R;
                print
        }
}' |
  sort +1n −2 |
  awk >$tmp '
  BEGIN {
        FS="Ⓣ"
        OFS="Ⓣ"
}
{       $8 = $8 − NR;
        $2 = NR
        print
}'

trap '' 1 2 3 15
mv $tmp $ladder
```

Figure 8.19 The weed script

The form of the awk scripts is, by now, familiar. The up-down movement in field 8 is maintained and the rank field is renumbered as

  2R

where R is the real rank (R=2*NR). If a player is demoted then the rank is adjusted (R=R+5). The output is then sorted on the new rankings and the rank recomputed by the second awk script.

8.3.5 Weekly ladder printing

The ladder is printed every week and addressed to each player so that the output can by fed directly into the company mail. The send script (figure 8.20) organizes the printing activity.

```
trap 'rm −f $out; exit' 0 1 2 3 15
out=`mktemp /tmp/otXXXXXX`

# generate one copy of the output
out .ladder >$out

# send to everyone
while read line
do      adr $line <$out
done <.ladder | lpr
```

Figure 8.20 The send **script**

The program out (figure 8.21) is called by send and formats the weekly ladder results. nroff is used as a formatting program with a here document providing the standard input, after substitution of shell variables. The page length for the heading is set to 6, from the default 66, since nroff fills the remainder of the page with blank lines.

```
# print the ladder and results

set `date`
year=$6 month=$2 day=$3

set − `cat .lastweek`
L_year=$6 L_month=$2 L_day=$3

# output heading
nroff ≪!
.pl 6
.ll 80
.ce 2
.nf
M U R R A Y    H I L L    T E N N I S    L A D D E R

.ce 2
Standings as of $year $month $day
(Previous Listing $L_year $L_month $L_day)

rankⓉ nameⓉ phoneⓉ roomⓉ wonⓉ lostⓉ u−dⓉ idle
!

# output ladder itself
```

```
field 2 3 4 5 6 7 8 9 <$ladder |
 sed −e ´s/∧/        /´ |
   ta="3R 5 32 42 56R 62R 68R 74C" detab

set − `cat .sunday`
S_year=$6 S_month=$2 S_day=$3

if test −s .results
then        # if results file non empty
            nroff «! − .results
.ll 80
.pl 5
.sp 2
.ce
Match results for the week ending $S_month $S_day
.sp
.tr _
.nf
.ta 5 34 39 68
!

fi
```

Figure 8.21 The out script

field selects all but the first tab separated fields and detab formats the result according to the tab setting passed as an argument. The tab inserted by sed at the
start of each line allows the first field to be right justified in nroff using the ta request.

```
(cat «! ; cat $*) | nroff
.pl 1
.nf
.ta $ta
!
```

Figure 8.22 The detab script

The text of the detab command is shown in figure 8.22.

If the results file (produced by update) is not empty then it is printed with a
heading giving the previous Sunday's date and formatted according to the tab setting.

The program adr (figure 8.23) paginates the ladder output taking its input
from the standard input. A banner is also added using the line drawing function of
nroff. The shell variable banner is set depending on whether any positional parameters have been provided. $# is set to the number of positional parameters.

```
case $# in
        0)        banner=`date` ;;
        *)        banner="$3    MH $5" ;;
esac
(cat <<!; cat) | nroff
.nf
.tr _
.ll 80
.wh 0 SP
.wh −4 EP
.de EP
.bp
..
.de SP
.sp 4
..
.SP
.ce
\l´\w´$banner´u+4\&−´
.in 70
$2
.in
.ce
$banner
.sp
.ce
\l´\w´$banner´u+4\&−´
.sp 3
!
```

Figure 8.23 The adr script

The line drawing functions in nroff are used to enclose the mailing address.

\l´\w´$adr´u+4\&−´

draws a line to enclose the mailing address ($banner).

\w´$adr´u

computes the width of the string $adr and the result is in basic units (u). To allow for an overlap on each side 4 is added (2 each side since this line is centered).

\l´...´

is the line drawing function where ... is the length computed by the previous expression. The & separates this width expression from the trailing – that would otherwise be absorbed as part of the expression.

8.3.6 The start and end of season

The initial ladder is entered into the file .initial. Each player may request a starting rank and, where possible, this is honored by ordering the initial requests. The start-up script (figure 8.24) initializes the files required to run the system and makes the backup directory. The cron file also needs to be started.

```
# create files
cat ≪! > . lastweek
– – none
!
> . results
> . matches
> . ladder

sort +0n < . initial  |
awk ´
BEGIN {
            FS="Ⓣ "
            OFS="Ⓣ "
            N = 1;
}
{       F = $1;
        $1 = $2;
        $2 = N;
        $6 = 0;
        $7 = 0;
        $8 = 0;
        $9 = 0;
        NF = 9;
        if(F != "–") {print; N=N+1;}
}
´ > . ladder
```

Figure 8.24 The startup **script**

End of season awards

Two prizes are awarded, one for the player who plays the most matches, the other for the player who wins the most matches. In both cases only two matches against the same opponent count. Two scripts are provided to determine the prize winners and each uses the atmost script, shown in figure 8.25. The command atmost produces at most two entries from the output of a command passed as the argument $1.

```
(${1?} | uniq −d ; $1 | sort −u) | sort
```

Figure 8.25 The atmost **script**

The command $1 is executed twice and is required to generate a sorted list.

```
${1?} | uniq −d
```

is executed first and generates a single line for each line occurring two or more
times.

```
$1 | sort −u
```

is executed second and generates a single line for each entry. The construction

```
( ... ) | sort
```

collects the output from the first command followed by the output form the second
and sorts the result.

The player with the most wins

The player with most wins is determined by the command most−wins shown in figure 8.26.

```
atmost list−matches |
   field 1 |
      uniq −c |
         sort +0nr
```

Figure 8.26 The most−wins **script**

The first line, atmost list−matches, generates a list of pairs of players,

```
W L
```

corresponding to matches between the players W and L, where W won the match.
The rest of the pipeline selects the field containing the winner and counts how
many times it occurs. Since the output of atmost is sorted, the first field can be
passed directly to uniq. The −c option produces

```
count winner
```

where count is the number of occurrences of winner in the input list. The final call
to sort arranges the output according to the player with the most wins as required.
The argument +0nr sorts in decreasing numerical order on the first field of the input. The list−matches script is shown in figure 8.27.

```
cd 1982; cat *G | field 2 3 | sort
```

Figure 8.27 The list–matches **script**

The player with the most matches played

This prize is for the player with the most matches played with no more than two counting against the same opponent. The command list–players (figure 8.28) generates a list of matches with the player in the first column alphabetically preceding the player in the second column. Thus, who won the match is not important, only the pair of players matters.

```
cat *G | field 2 3 |
awk 'BEGIN
{
        FS="Ⓣ "
        OFS="Ⓣ "
}
{       if($1 > $2) {
                t = $1;
                $1 = $2;
                $2 = t;
        }
        print
}' | sort
```

Figure 8.28 The list–players **script**

The output from atmost list–players is a list of the matches played by any two players with at most two against a given opponent that count. The first line of most–matches (figure 8.29) produces the list of players that needs sorting so that uniq –c can be run.

```
(atmost list–players | field 1; atmost list–players | field 2) |
  sort |
    uniq –c |
      sort +0nr
```

Figure 8.29 The most–matches **script**

8.4 Implementing the field command

The field command selects tab separated fields from its standard input and prints the result on the standard output. The manual page for the field command reads

---

NAME
  field – select fields or columns from a file.

SYNOPSIS
  field [n] ...

DESCRIPTION
  The field command copies specified, tab-separated fields from the standard input to the standard output. Fields are numbered from 1 and a field may be requested more than once.

BUGS
  The number of input or output fields may not exceed 256 and the maximum line length is 4096 characters.

The implementation of field illustrates some useful techniques. The first step is to look for a program that does something similar. Since field is a filter that copies its input to its output the cat command is a good place to start. The source for system commands is usually kept in the directory /usr/src/cmd making it easy to use one command as the starting point for another.

The program is shown in figure 8.30.

The stages in the writing of this program were simple.

- Write a program to read a line into the array L and print it out again. (This is the cat command with buffering added.)
- Add the code to record the field boundaries and print out a fixed field.
- Add the code to read the arguments and print the columns specified.
- Add the checks for exceeding the sizes of the fixed arrays.

Other options that are easy to add but have been omitted here include:

−c   Check that all input records contain the same number of fields.
−tc   Set the field separator to c.

The version presented in figure 8.30 does not check for exceeding array bounds. Also, the bounds of fv, fp, and L are fixed at compile time using the defined constants MAXF, and MAXL. A production program should check these limits or, better still, allocate the arrays dynamically. The number of output fields can be determined from the number of arguments. The number of input fields and the maximum line length are not easily found. Another solution to the fixed limits imposed in this implementation is to have options to change them. This is left as an exercise to the reader.

The limitations of this command have been documented under the BUGS section of the manual page.

```
#include <stdio . h>

#define MAXF      256
#define MAXL      4096
#define IFS       '\t'
#define OFS       '\t'

int fv[MAXF];       /* numerical equivalent of arguments */
int nf;             /* number of columns to print */
int mf;             /* number of fields in the current record */
char *fp[MAXF];     /* pointers into `L´ at field boundaries */
char L[MAXL];       /* current line buffer */

main(argc,argv)
        int argc;
        char *argv[];
{
        register char *cp;
        register char **ap;
        register int c;
        int f;

        /* read arguments into fv[. . .] */
        while (argc>1) {
                if(sscanf(argv[1], "%d", &fv[nf++]) != 1) {
                        printf("usage: field [ n ] . . .\n");
                        return(2);
                } .
                argc--; argv++;
        }

        /* read and copy input */
        nf--;
        cp = L;
        ap = fp;
        *ap++ = cp;
        while(1){
                c = getc(stdin);
                if(c=='\n' || c==EOF) {
                        int fc;
                        if(cp==L && c==EOF) break;
                        *cp++ = 0;
                        mf = ap-fp;

                        /* print this line */
                        for(fc = 0; fc <= nf; fc++) {
                                putf(fv[fc]-1);
                                if(fc != nf) putchar(OFS);
```

```
                                                }
                                                if(c == EOF) break;
                                                putchar('\n');
                                                cp = L;
                                                ap = fp;
                                                *ap++ = cp;
                                        }
                                        else if(c == IFS) {
                                                *cp++ = 0;
                                                *ap++ = cp;
                                        }
                                        else *cp++ = c;
                        }

                return(0);
        } /* main */

        /* output field n from the current line */
        putf(n)
        {
                register char *cp = fp[n];
                register char c;

                if(n<0 || n>=mf) return;
                while (c = *cp++) putchar(c);
        } /* putf */
```

Figure 8.30 The field command

Appendix 1 Commands

---

adb – absolute debugg   ADB (1)

adb [–w] [objfil [corfil]]

    adb is a general purpose debugging program. It may be used to examine files and to provide a controlled environment for the execution of UNIX programs.

    objfil is normally an executable program file, preferably containing a symbol table. Without a symbol table the symbolic features of adb cannot be used although the file can still be examined; the default for objfil is *a.out.* corfil is assumed to be a *core image* file produced after executing objfil; the default for corfil is *core.*

    Requests to adb are read from the standard input and responses are written to the standard output. If the –w flag is present then both objfil and corfil are created, if necessary, and opened for reading and writing enabling files to be modified using adb. An interrupt causes return to the next adb request and the quit signal is ignored.

---

ar – archive and library maintainer for portable archives   AR (1)

ar key [posname] afile [name] ...

    ar maintains groups of files combined into a single archive file. Its main use is to create and update library files as used by the link editor. The magic string and the file headers used by ar consist of printable ASCII characters. If an archive is composed of printable files, the entire archive is printable.

    When ar creates an archive, it creates headers in a format that is portable across all machines. The link editor, ld, makes multiple passes over libraries of object files in an efficient manner. An archive symbol table is only created and maintained by ar when there is at least one object file in the archive. The archive symbol table is in a specially named file which is always the first file in the archive. This file is never mentioned or accessible to the user. Whenever the ar(1) command is used to create or update the contents of such an archive, the symbol table is rebuilt. The s option described below will force the symbol table to be rebuilt.

    key is an optional – followed by one character from the set *drqtpmx,* optionally concatenated with one or more of *vuaibcl.* afile is the archive file. The names are constituent files in the archive file. The meanings of the key characters are:

      d   Delete the named files from the archive file.

      r   Replace the named files in the archive file. If the optional character u is used with r, then only those files with dates of modification later than the archive files are replaced. If an optional positioning character

from the set *abi* is used, then the posname argument must be present
and specifies that new files are to be placed after (a) or before (b or i)
posname. Otherwise new files are placed at the end.

q   Quickly append the named files to the end of the archive file. Option-
    al positioning characters are invalid. The command does not check
    whether the added members are already in the archive. Useful only to
    avoid quadratic behavior when creating a large archive piece-by-
    piece.

t   Print a table of contents of the archive file. If no names are given, all
    files in the archive are tabled. If names are given, only those files are
    tabled.

p   Print the named files in the archive.

m   Move the named files to the end of the archive. If a positioning char-
    acter is present, then the posname argument must be present and, as in
    r, specifies where the files are to be moved.

x   Extract the named files. If no names are given, all files in the archive
    are extracted. In neither case does x alter the archive file.

v   Give a verbose file-by-file description of the making of a new archive
    file from the old archive and the constituent files. When used with t,
    give a long listing of all information about the files. When used with
    x, precede each file with a name.

c   Suppress the message that is produced by default when afile is created.

l   Place temporary files in the local current working directory, rather
    than in the directory specified by the environment variable TMPDIR or
    in the default directory /tmp.

s   Force the regeneration of the archive symbol table even if ar(1) is not
    invoked with a command which will modify the archive contents.
    This command is useful to restore the archive symbol table after the
    strip(1) command has been used on the archive.

---

at, batch − execute commands at a later time   AT (1)

at time [date] [+ increment]
at −r job . . .
at −l [job . . .]

batch

   at and batch read commands from the standard input to be executed at a later
time. at allows you to specify when the commands should be executed, while jobs
queued with batch will execute when system load level permits. at −r removes jobs
previously scheduled with at. The −l option reports all jobs scheduled for the invoking user.
   Standard output and standard error output are mailed to the user unless they
are redirected elsewhere. The shell environment variables, current directory,
umask, and ulimit are retained when the commands are executed. Open file
descriptors, traps, and priority are lost.
   Users are permitted to use at if their name appears in the file
/usr/lib/cron/at.allow. If that file does not exist, the file /usr/lib/cron/at.deny is checked

to determine if the user should be denied access to at. If neither file exists, only the super-user is allowed to submit a job. If either file is at.deny, global usage is permitted. The allow/deny files consist of one user name per line.

The time may be specified as 1, 2, or 4 digits. One and two digit numbers are taken to be hours, four digits to be hours and minutes. The time may alternately be specified as two numbers separated by a colon, meaning hour:minute. A suffix am or pm may be appended; otherwise a 24-hour clock time is understood. The suffix zulu may be used to indicate GMT. The special names noon, midnight, now, and next are also recognized.

An optional date may be specified as either a month name followed by a day number (and possibly year number preceded by an optional comma) or a day of the week (fully spelled or abbreviated to three characters). Two special days, today and tomorrow are recognized. If no date is given, today is assumed if the given hour is greater than the current hour and tomorrow is assumed if it is less. If the given month is less than the current month (and no year is given), next year is assumed.

The optional increment is simply a number suffixed by one of the following: minutes, hours, days, weeks, months, or years. (The singular form is also accepted.)

at and batch write the job number and schedule time to standard error. batch submits a batch job. It is almost equivalent to at now, but there are some differences. For one, it goes into a different queue. For another, at now will respond with the error message too late.

at −r removes jobs previously scheduled by at or batch. The job number is the number given to you previously by the at or batch command. You can also get job numbers by typing at −l. You can only remove your own jobs unless you are the super-user.

---

awk − pattern scanning and processing language   AWK(1)

awk [−Fc] [prog] [parameters] [file ...]

awk scans each input file for lines that match any of a set of patterns specified in prog. With each pattern in prog there can be an associated action that will be performed when a line of a file matches the pattern. The set of patterns may appear literally as prog, or in a file specified as −f file. The prog string may need to be quoted to prevent interpretation by the shell.

Files are read in order; if there are no files, the standard input is read. The file name − means the standard input.

awk is described in chapter 8.

---

basename, dirname − deliver portions of pathnames   BASENAME(1)

basename string [suffix]
dirname string

basename deletes any prefix ending in / and the suffix (if present in string) from string, and prints the result on the standard output. It is normally used via command substitution within shell procedures. dirname delivers all but the last level of the pathname in string.

cal − print calendar   CAL (1)

cal [[month] year]

    cal prints a calendar for the specified year. If a month is also specified, a calendar for that month is printed. If neither is specified, a calendar for the present month is printed. year can be between 1 and 9999. The month is a number between 1 and 12. The calendar produced is that for England and her colonies.

---

calendar − reminder service   CALENDAR ( )

calendar [−]

    calendar consults the file calendar in the current directory and prints out lines that contain today's or tomorrow's date anywhere in the line. Most reasonable month-day dates such as Dec. 7, december 7, and 12/7, are recognized, but not 7 December or 7/12. If you give just a date, i.e. 1, that day in any month will do. On weekends, tomorrow extends through Monday.

    When an argument is present, calendar looks in all users' login directories for a file called calendar and sends any positive results by mail(1) to those users.

---

cat − concatenate and print files   CAT (1)

cat [−u] [−s] [−v [−t] [−e]] file ...

    cat reads each file in sequence and writes it on the standard output.

    If no input file is given, or if the argument − is encountered, cat reads from the standard input file. Output is buffered unless the −u option is specified. The −s option makes cat silent about non-existent files.

    The −v option causes non-printing characters (with the exception of tab, newline and formfeed) to be printed visibly. Control characters are printed ⌃X (control-x); the del character (octal 0177) is printed ⌃?. Non-ASCII characters (with the high bit set) are printed as M-x, where x is the character specified by the seven low order bits.

    When used with the −v option, −t causes tab to be printed as ⌃I, and −e causes a $ character to be printed at the end of each line (prior to the newline). The −t and −e options are ignored if the −v option is not specified.

---

cb − C program beautifier   CB (1)

cb [−s] [−j] [−l leng] [file ...]

    cb reads C programs either from its arguments or from the standard input and writes them on the standard output with spacing and indentation that displays the structure of the code. Under default options, cb preserves all user newlines. Under the −s flag cb produces output in the style of Kernighan and Ritchie in The C Programming Language. The −j flag causes split lines to be put back together. The −l flag causes cb to split lines that are longer than leng.

cc – C compiler   CC (1)

cc [option] ... file ...

Arguments whose names end with .c are taken to be C source programs. They are compiled, and each object program is left on the file whose name is that of the source with .o substituted for .c. The .o file is normally deleted if a single C program is compiled and loaded all at one go.

In the same way, arguments whose names end with .s are taken to be assembly source programs and are assembled, producing a .o file.

The following options are interpreted by cc. See ld(1) for link editor options and cpp(1) for more preprocessor options.

Options

- −c   Suppress the link edit phase of the compilation and force an object file to be produced even if only one program is compiled.
- −p   Arrange for the compiler to produce code that counts the number of times each routine is called; also, if link editing takes place, replace the standard startoff routine by one that automatically calls monitor(3C) at the start and arranges to write out a mon.out file at normal termination of execution of the object program. An execution profile can then be generated by use of prof(1).
- −f   Link the object program with the floating point interpreter for systems without hardware floating point.
- −g   Generate additional information needed for the use of sdb(1).
- −O   Invoke an object-code optimizer.
- −S   Compile the named C programs and leave the assembler-language output on corresponding files suffixed .s .
- −E   Run only cpp(1) on the named C programs and send the result to the standard output.
- −P   Run only cpp(1) on the named C programs and leave the result on corresponding files suffixed .i .

Other arguments are taken to be either link editor option arguments, C preprocessor option arguments, or C-compatible object programs, typically produced by an earlier cc run, or perhaps libraries of C-compatible routines. These programs, together with the results of any compilations specified, are linked (in the order given) to produce an executable program with the name a.out.

---

chmod – change mode   CHMOD (1)

chmod mode file ...

The permissions of the named files are changed according to mode, which may be absolute or symbolic. An absolute mode is an octal number constructed from the OR of the modes described in chmod(2). A symbolic mode has the form

    [who] op permission [op permission]

The who part is a combination of the letters *u* (for user's permissions), *g* (group)

and o (other). The letter a stands for *ugo,* the default if who is omitted.

op can be + to add permission to the file's mode, − to take away permission, or = to assign permission absolutely (all other bits will be reset).

permission is any combination of the letters *r* (read), *w* (write), *x* (execute), *s* (set user-id or group-id) and *t* (save text, or sticky). Letters *u*, *g*, or *o* indicate that permission is to be taken from the current mode. Omitting permission is only useful with = to take away all permissions.

Multiple symbolic modes separated by commas may be given. Operations are performed in the order specified. The letter *s* is only useful with *u* or *g* and *t* only works with *u*.

Only the owner of a file (or the super-user) may change its mode. Only the super-user may set the sticky bit. In order to set the group-id, the group of the file must correspond to your current group-id.

---

cmp − compare two files   CMP(1)

cmp [−l] [−s] file1 file2

The two files are compared. If file1 is − the standard input is read. Under default options, cmp makes no comment if the files are the same; if they differ, it announces the byte and line number at which the difference occurred. If one file is an initial subsequence of the other, that fact is noted.

Options

−l   Print the byte number (decimal) and the differing bytes (octal) for each difference.

−s   Print nothing for differing files; return codes only.

---

col − filter reverse line feeds   COL(1)

col [−bfpx]

col reads from the standard input and writes onto the standard output. It performs the line overlays implied by reverse line-feeds (ASCII code esc−7), and by forward and reverse half-line feeds (esc−9 and esc−8). col is particularly useful for filtering multi-column output made with the .rt command of nroff and output resulting from use of the tbl(1) preprocessor.

If the −b option is given, col assumes that the output device in use is not capable of backspacing. In this case, if two or more characters are to appear in the same place, only the last one read will be output.

Although col accepts half-line motions in its input, it normally does not emit them on output. Instead, text that would appear between lines is moved to the next lower full-line boundary. This treatment can be suppressed by the −f (fine) option; in this case, the output from col may contain forward half-line feeds (esc−9), but will still never contain either kind of reverse line motion.

Unless the −x option is given, col will convert white space to tabs on output wherever possible to shorten printing time.

The ASCII control characters so (\016) and si (\017) are assumed by col to start and end text in an alternate character set. The character set to which each input character belongs is remembered, and on output si and so characters are generated as appropriate to ensure that each character is printed in the correct character set.

On input, the only control characters accepted are space, backspace, tab, return, newline, si, so, vt (\013), and esc followed by 7, 8, or 9. The vt character is an alternate form of full reverse line feed, included for compatibility with some earlier programs of this type. All other non-printing characters are ignored.

Normally, col will ignore any unknown escape sequences in its input; the −p option may be used to cause col to output these sequences as regular characters, subject to overprinting from reverse line motions. The use of this option is highly discouraged unless the user is fully aware of the textual position of the escape sequences.

---

comm − select or reject lines common to two sorted files   COMM (1)

comm [− [123]] file1 file2

comm reads file1 and file2, that should be ordered lexicographically, and produces a three column output: lines only in file1; lines only in file2; and lines in both files. The file name − means the standard input.

The flags 1, 2, or 3 suppress printing of the corresponding column.

---

cp − copy   CP (1)

cp file1 file2
cp file ... directory

file1 is copied onto file2. The mode and owner of file2 are preserved if file2 already existed; otherwise, the mode of the source file is used.

In the second form, one or more files are copied into the directory with their original file names.

cp refuses to copy a file onto itself.

---

cpio − copy file archives in and out   CPIO (1)

cpio −o [acBv]

cpio −i [BcdmrtuvfsSb6] [pattern] ...

cpio −p [adlmruv] directory

cpio −o (copy out) reads the standard input to obtain a list of path names and copies those files onto the standard output together with path name and status information. Output is padded to a 512-byte boundary.

cpio −i (copy in) extracts files from the standard input, which is assumed to be the product of a previous cpio −o. Only files with names that match patterns are selected. Patterns are given in the name-generating notation of sh(1). In patterns, metacharacters ?, *, and [...] match the slash / character. Multiple patterns may be specified and if no patterns are specified, the default for patterns is * (i.e. select all files). The extracted files are conditionally created and copied into the current directory tree based upon the options described below. The permissions of the files will be those of the previous cpio −o. The owner and group of the files will be that of the current user unless the user is super-user, which causes cpio to retain the owner and group of the files of the previous cpio −o.

cpio −p (pass) reads the standard input to obtain a list of path names of files that are conditionally created and copied into the destination directory tree based upon the options described below.

Options

a	Reset access times of input files after they have been copied.
B	Input-output is to be blocked 5120 bytes to the record (does not apply to the pass option; meaningful only with data directed to or from /dev/rmt/??).
d	Directories are to be created as needed.
c	Write header information in ASCII character form for portability.
r	Interactively rename files. If the user types a null line, the file is skipped.
t	Print a table of contents of the input. No files are created.
u	Copy unconditionally (normally, an older file will not replace a newer file with the same name).
v	Verbose: causes a list of file names to be printed. When used with the t option, the table of contents looks like the output of an ls −l command (see ls(1)).
l	Whenever possible, link files rather than copying them. Usable only with the −p option.
m	Retain previous file modification time. This option is ineffective on directories that are being copied.
f	Copy in all files except those in patterns.
s	Swap bytes. Use only with the −i option.
S	Swap halfwords. Use only with the −i option.
b	Swap both bytes and halfwords. Use only with the −i option.
6	Process an old (i.e., UNIX System Sixth Edition format) file. Only useful with −i (copy in).

---

cpp − the C language preprocessor   CPP (1)

/lib/cpp [option ...] [ifile [ofile]]

cpp is the C language preprocessor which is invoked as the first pass of any C compilation using the cc(1) command. Thus the output of cpp is designed to be in a form acceptable as input to the next pass of the C compiler. As the C language evolves, cpp and the rest of the C compilation package will be modified to follow these changes. Therefore, the use of cpp other than in this framework is not suggested. The preferred way to invoke cpp is through the cc(1) command, since the functionality of cpp may someday be moved elsewhere.

cpp optionally accepts two file names as arguments. ifile and ofile are respectively the input and output for the preprocessor. The default is standard input and standard output.

Options

−P	Preprocess the input without producing the line control information

used by the next pass of the C compiler.

−C   By default, cpp strips C-style comments. If the −C option is specified, all comments (except those found on cpp directive lines) are passed along.

−U *name*

Remove any initial definition of *name*, where *name* is a reserved symbol that is predefined by the particular preprocessor.

−D *name*

−D *name=def*

Define *name* as if by a #define directive. If no =*def* is given, *name* is defined as 1. The −D option has lower precedence than the −U option. That is, if the same *name* is used in both a −U option and a −D option, the *name* will be undefined regardless of the order of the options.

−T   Preprocessor symbols are no longer restricted to eight characters. The −T option forces cpp to use only the first eight characters for distinguishing different preprocessor names. This behavior is the same as previous preprocessors with respect to the length of names and is included for backward compatibility.

−I *dir*   Change the algorithm for searching for #include files whose names do not begin with / to look in *dir* before looking in the directories on the standard list. Thus, #include files whose names are enclosed in "" will be searched for first in the directory of the file with the #include line, then in directories named in −I options, and last in directories on a standard list. For #include files whose names are enclosed in <>, the directory of the file with the #include line is not searched.

Two special names are understood by cpp. The name __LINE__ is defined as the current line number (as a decimal integer) as known by cpp, and __FILE__ is defined as the current file name (as a C string) as known by cpp. They can be used anywhere (including in macros) just as any other defined name.

All cpp directives start with lines begun by #. Any number of blanks and tabs is allowed between the # and the directive. The directives are:

#define *name token-string*

Replace subsequent instances of *name* with *token-string*.

#define *name(arg, . . ., arg) token-string*

Notice that there can be no space between *name* and the (. Replace subsequent instances of *name* followed by a (, a list of comma-separated set of tokens, and a) by *token-string*, where each occurrence of an *arg* in the *token-string* is replaced by the corresponding set of tokens in the comma-separated list. When a macro with arguments is expanded, the arguments are placed into the expanded *token-string* unchanged. After the entire *token-string* has been expanded, cpp restarts its scan for names to expand at the beginning of newly created *token-string*.

#undef *name*

The definition of *name* (if any) is forgotten from now on.

#include "*filename*"

#include <*filename*>

Read and process the contents of *filename*. When the *<filename>* no-tation is used, *filename* is only searched for in the standard places. See the −I option above for more detail.

#line *integer-constant*

Causes cpp to generate line control information for the next pass of the C compiler. *integer-constant* is the line number of the next line and *filename* is the file it comes from. If *filename* is not given, the current file name is unchanged.

#endif   Ends a section of lines begun by a test directive (#if, #ifdef, or #ifndef). Each test directive must have a matching #endif.

#ifdef *name*

The lines following will appear in the output if and only if *name* has been the subject of a previous #define without being the subject of an intervening #undef.

#ifndef *name*

The lines following will not appear in the output if and only if *name* has been the subject of a previous #define without being the subject of an intervening #undef.

#if *constant-expression*

Lines following will appear in the output if and only if the *constant-expression* evaluates to non-zero. All binary non-assignment C operators, the ?: operator, the unary −, !, and ~ operators are legal in constant-expression. The precedence of the operators is the same as defined by the C language. There is also a unary operator defined, which can be used in constant-expression in these two forms:

defined (*name*)

or

defined *name*

This allows the utility of #ifdef and #ifndef in a #if directive. Only these operators, integer constants, and names which are known by cpp should be used in *constant-expression*. In particular, the sizeof operator is not available.

#else   Reverses the notion of the test directive which matches this direc-tive. So if lines previous to this directive are ignored, the following lines will appear in the output, and vice versa.

The test directives and the possible #else directives can be nested.

---

crypt − encode/decode   CRYPT (1)

crypt [password]

crypt reads from the standard input and writes on the standard output. The password is a key that selects a particular transformation. If no password is given, crypt demands a key from the terminal and turns off printing while the key is being typed in. crypt encrypts and decrypts with the same key:

```
crypt key <clear >cipher
crypt key <cipher | pr
```

will print the clear text.

Files encrypted by crypt are compatible with those required by the editor ed in encryption mode.

The security of encrypted files depends on three factors: the fundamental method must be hard to solve; direct search of the key space must not be feasible; 'sneak paths' by which keys or clear text can become visible must be minimized.

crypt implements a one-rotor machine designed along the lines of the German Enigma, but with a 256-element rotor. Methods of attack on such machines are known, but not widely; moreover the amount of work required is likely to be large.

The transformation of a key into the internal settings of the machine is deliberately designed to be expensive, i.e. to take a substantial fraction of a second to compute. However, if keys are restricted to (say) three lower case letters, then encrypted files can be read by expending only a few minutes of machine time.

Since the key is an argument to the crypt command, it is potentially visible to users executing ps(1) or a derivative. To minimize this possibility, crypt takes care to destroy any record of the key immediately upon entry. No doubt the choice of keys and key security are the most vulnerable aspect of crypt.

---

date – print and set the date   DATE(1)

date [mmddhhmm[yy]] [+format]

If no argument is given, or if the argument begins with +, the current date and time are printed. Otherwise, the current date is set. The first mm is the month number; dd is the day number in the month; hh is the hour number (24 hour system); the second mm is the minute number; yy is the last 2 digits of the year number and is optional. The current year is the default if no year is mentioned. The system operates in GMT. date takes care of the conversion to and from local standard and daylight time.

If the argument begins with +, the output of date is under the control of the user. The format for the output is similar to that of the first argument to printf(3S). All output fields are of fixed size (zero padded if necessary). Each field descriptor is preceded by % and will be replaced in the output by its corresponding value. A single % is encoded by %%. All other characters are copied to the output without change. The string is always terminated with a newline character.

Field descriptors

n	Insert a newline character.
t	Insert a tab character.
m	Month of year from 01 to 12.
d	Day of month from 01 to 31.
y	Last 2 digits of year from 00 to 99.
D	Date as mm/dd/yy.
H	Hour from 00 to 23.
M	Minute from 00 to 59.
S	Second from 00 to 59.
T	Time as HH:MM:SS.

j	Day of year from 001 to 366.
w	Day of week where Sunday = 0.
a	Abbreviated weekday: Sun to Sat.
h	Abbreviated month: Jan to Dec.
r	Time in AM/PM notation.

---

dd – convert and copy a file   DD(1)

dd [option=value] ...

    dd copies the specified input file to the specified output with possible conversions. The standard input and output are used by default. The input and output block size may be specified to take advantage of raw physical input-output.

Options

if=	The input file name; standard input is default.
of=	The output file name; standard output is default.
ibs=n	Use an input block size n bytes (default 512).
obs=n	Use an output block size of n bytes (default 512).
bs=n	Set both input and output block size, superseding ibs and obs; also, if no conversion is specified, it is particularly efficient since no in-core copy need be done.
cbs=n	The conversion buffer size.
skip=n	Skip n input blocks before starting copy.
seek=n	Seek n blocks from beginning of output file before copying.
count=n	Copy only n input blocks.
conv=ascii	Convert EBCDIC to ASCII.
ebcdic	Convert ASCII to EBCDIC.
lcase	Map alphabetics to lower case.
ucase	Map alphabetics to upper case.
swab	Swap every pair of bytes.
noerror	Do not stop processing on an error.
sync	Pad every input block to ibs.
...,...	Several comma-separated conversions.

    Where sizes are specified, a number of bytes is expected. A number may end with k, b, or w to specify multiplication by 1024, 512, or 2, respectively; a pair of numbers may be separated by x to indicate a product.

    cbs is used only if ascii or ebcdic conversion is specified. In the former case cbs characters are placed into the conversion buffer, converted to ASCII, and trailing blanks trimmed and newline added before sending the line to the output. In the latter case ASCII characters are read into the conversion buffer, converted to EBCDIC, and spaces added to make up an output block of size cbs.

    After completion, dd reports the number of whole and partial input and output blocks.

deroff – remove nroff, troff, tbl and eqn constructs   DEROFF (1)

deroff [−w] file ...

deroff reads each file and removes all nroff and troff request lines, backslash constructions, macro definitions, eqn constructs (between .EQ and .EN lines or between delimiters), and table descriptions and writes the remainder on the standard output. deroff follows chains of included files (.so and .nx requests); if a file has already been included, a .so is ignored and a .nx terminates execution. If no input file is given, deroff reads from the standard input file.

If the −w flag is given, the output is a word list, one word (string of letters, digits, and apostrophes, beginning with a letter; apostrophes are removed) per line, and all other characters ignored. Otherwise, the output follows the original.

---

df – disk free   DF (1)

df filesystem

df prints the number of free blocks available on the specified filesystem, e.g. /dev/rp0a. If no file system is specified, the free space on all of the normally mounted file systems is printed.

The reported numbers are in file system block units. On some systems each filesystem block is 1024 bytes long, twice the size of the blocks reported by du(1) or ls(1) with the −s option.

---

diction, explain – print wordy sentences; thesaurus for diction   DICTION (1)

diction [−ml] [−mm] [−n] [−f pfile] file ...
explain

diction finds all sentences in a document that contain phrases from a data base of bad or wordy diction. Each phrase is bracketed with [ ]. Formatting header files should be included as part of the input. The default macro package is −ms. The −mm option uses the −mm macro library. The flag −ml causes deroff to skip lists and should be used if the document contains many lists of non-sentences. The user may supply a pattern file to be used in addition to the default file with −f pfile. If the flag −n is also supplied the default file will be suppressed.

explain is an interactive thesaurus for the phrases found by diction.

---

diff – differential file comparator   DIFF (1)

diff [option] file1 file2

diff lists the lines that must be changed in the files to bring them into agreement. Except in rare circumstances, diff finds a smallest sufficient set of file differences. If file1 or file2 is a −, the standard input is used.

There are several options for output format; the default output format contains lines of these forms:

n1 a *n3,n4*
n1,n2 d *n3*
n1,n2 c *n3,n4*

These lines resemble ed commands to convert file1 into file2. The numbers after the letters pertain to file2. By exchanging a for d and reading backward one may ascertain equally how to convert file2 into file1. As in ed, identical pairs where *n1=n2* or *n3=n4* are abbreviated as a single number.

Following each of these lines come all the lines that are affected in the first file flagged by <, then all the lines that are affected in the second file flagged by >.

Except for −b, which may be given with any of the others, the options are mutually exclusive.

Options

    −e   Produce a script of a, c and d commands for the editor ed, that will re-create file2 from file1.

    −f   Produce a script similar to that produced by −e, although not useful with ed, in the opposite order.

    −h   Do a fast, half-hearted job. It works when changed stretches are short and well separated, and on files of unlimited length.

    −b   Trailing blanks (spaces and tabs) are ignored, and other strings of blanks compare equal.

---

du − summarize disk usage   DU (1)

du [−s] [−a] [−r] [name ...]

    du gives the number of blocks contained in all files and (recursively) directories within each specified directory or file name. If name is missing, the current directory is used.

    The optional argument −s causes only the grand total to be given. The optional argument −a causes an entry to be generated for each file. Absence of either causes an entry to be generated for each directory only.

    du is normally silent about unreadable directories or files that cannot be opened. The −r option causes du to generate messages in such instances.

    A file which has two or more links to it is only counted once.

---

echo − echo arguments   ECHO (1)

echo [arg] ...

    echo writes its arguments separated by blanks and terminated by a newline on the standard output. It also understands C-like escape conventions:

    \b   backspace.
    \c   Print line without newline.
    \f   formfeed.
    \n   newline.
    \r   return.
    \t   tab.
    \v   vertical tab .

\\   \.

\n   The 8-bit character whose ASCII code is the octal number *n*. *n* consists
           of up to 3 digits and starts with a 0.

---

ed – text editor   ED(1)

ed [–] [name]

ed is the standard text editor.

If a name argument is given, ed simulates an e command (see below) on the
named file; the file is read into the ed buffer so that it can be edited. The optional
– suppresses the printing of explanatory output and should be used when the standard input is an editor script.

If an interrupt signal is sent, ed prints a ? and returns to its request level.

Some size limitations: 512 characters per line, 256 characters per global request list, 64 characters per file name and, on mini computers, 128K characters in
the temporary file. The limit on the number of lines depends on the memory available.

When reading a file, ed discards ASCII nul characters and all characters after
the last newline. It refuses to read files containing non-printing characters.

---

eqn, neqn – typeset mathematics   EQN(1)

eqn [file] ...

eqn is a troff(1) preprocessor for typesetting mathematics. neqn provides similar facilities with output suitable for terminals.

Input is read from the specified file(s), and if no files are specified, eqn and
neqn read from the standard input.

---

expr – evaluate arguments as an expression   EXPR(1)

expr arg ...

The arguments are taken as an expression. After evaluation, the result is written on the standard output. Terms of the expression must be separated by blanks.
Note that 0 is returned to indicate a zero value, rather than the null string. Strings
containing blanks or other special characters should be quoted. Integer-valued arguments may be preceded by a unary minus sign. Internally, integers are treated as
32-bit, 2's complement numbers.

The operators and keywords are listed below. The list is in order of increasing precedence, with equal precedence operators grouped within { } symbols.

expr | expr   Return the first expr if it is neither null nor 0; otherwise return
               the second expr.

expr & expr   Return the first expr if neither expr is null or 0; otherwise return
               0.

expr { =, >, >=, <, <=, != } expr
               Return the result of an integer comparison if both arguments
               are integers; otherwise return the result of a lexical comparison.

expr { +, − } expr
> Addition or subtraction of integer-valued arguments.

expr { *, /, % } expr
> Multiplication, division, or remainder of the integer-valued arguments.

expr : expr   The matching operator : compares the first argument with the second argument which must be a regular expression. Regular expression syntax is the same as that of ed(1), except that all patterns are anchored at the beginning of the string. Therefore, ∧ is not a special character in that context. Normally, the matching operator returns the number of characters matched (0 on failure). Alternatively, the (...) pattern symbols can be used to return a portion of the first argument.

---

f77 − Fortran 77 compiler   F77 (1)

f77 [option ...] file ...

f77 accepts several types of file arguments.

Arguments whose names end with .f are taken to be Fortran 77 source programs; they are compiled and each object program is left in the current directory in a file whose name is that of the source, with .o substituted for .f.

Arguments whose names end with .r or .e are taken to be ratfor or efl source programs, respectively. These are first transformed by the appropriate preprocessor, then compiled by f77, producing .o files.

In the same way, arguments whose names end with .c or .s are taken to be C or assembly source programs and are compiled or assembled, producing .o files.

Options

The following options have the same meaning as in cc(1). See ld(1) for link editor options.

−c   Suppress link editing and produce .o files for each source file.

−p   Prepare object files for profiling (see prof(1)).

−O   Invoke an object-code optimizer.

−S   Compile the named programs and leave the assembler-language output in corresponding files whose names are suffixed with .s. (No .o files are created.)

−o file   Name the final output file *file,* instead of *a.out.*

−f   In systems without floating point hardware, use a version of f77 that handles floating point constants and links the object program with the floating point interpreter.

−g   Generate additional information needed for the use of sdb(1).

The following options are peculiar to f77.

−onetrip
> Compile DO loops that are performed at least once if reached. (Fortran 77 DO loops are not performed at all if the upper limit is smaller

than the lower limit.)

-1   Same as −onetrip.

-66 Suppress extensions which enhance Fortran 66 compatibility.

-C   Generate code for runtime subscript range-checking.

-U   Do not fold cases. f77 is normally a no-case language (i.e., a is equal to A). The −U option causes f77 to treat upper and lower cases to be separate.

-u   Make the default type of a variable *undefined*, rather than using the default Fortran rules.

-v   Verbose mode. Provide diagnostics for each process during compilation.

-w   Suppress all warning messages. If the option is −w66, only Fortran 66 compatibility warnings are suppressed.

-F   Apply efl and ratfor preprocessor to relevant files, put the result in files whose names have their suffix changed to .f. (No .o files are created.)

-m   Apply the m4 preprocessor to each efl or ratfor source file.

-E   The remaining characters in the argument are used as an efl flag argument whenever processing a .e file.

-N[qxscnl] *nnn*
     Change size of table [qxscnl] to *nnn*. The compiler will provide a diagnostic when a table overflows. The tables and corresponding default values for *nnn* are:

q   150 (equivalences),

x   200 (common blocks, subroutine and function names),

s   401 (statement numbers),

s   201 (symbol table),

c   20 (depth of loops or if-then-elses),

n   401 (variable names and common block names),

l   125 (labels for computers and assigned gotos and the number of alternate returns).

-R   The remaining characters in the argument are used as a ratfor flag argument whenever processing a .r file.

Other arguments are taken to be either link editor option arguments or f77-compilable object programs (typically produced by an earlier run), or libraries of f77-compilable routines. These programs, together with the results of any compilations specified, are linked (in the order given) to produce an executable program with the default name *a.out.*

---

find − find files   FIND(1)

find pathname-list expression

find recursively descends the directory hierarchy for each pathname in the pathname-list (i.e. one or more path names) seeking files that match the Boolean expression. In the descriptions, the argument n is used as a decimal integer where +n means more than n, −n means less than n and n means exactly n.

-name *file*   True if *file* matches the current file name.

−perm *onum*	True if the file permission flages exactly match the octal number *onum* (see chmod(1)). If *onum* is prefixed by a minus sign, more flag bits (017777, see stat(2)) become significant and the flags are compared.
−type *c*	True if the type of the file is *c*, where *c* is b, c, d, p, or f for block special file, character special file, directory, fifo (named pipe), or plain file respectively.
−links *n*	True if the file has *n* links.
−user *name*	True if the file belongs to the user *name*. If *name* is numeric and does not appear as a login name in the /etc/passwd file, it is taken as a user-id.
−group *name*	True if the file belongs to the group *name*. If *name* is numeric and does not appear in the /etc/group file, it is taken as a group-id.
−size *n*[c]	True if the file is *n* blocks long (512 bytes per block). If *n* is followed by a c, the size is in characters.
−atime *n*	True if the file has been accessed in *n*days. The access time of directories in pathname-list is changed by find itself.
−mtime *n*	True if the file has been modified in *n* days.
−ctime *n*	True if the file has been changed in *n* days.
−exec *cmd*;	True if the executed *cmd* returns a zero value as exit statut. A command argument { } is replaced by the current pathname.
−ok *cmd*;	Like −exec except that the generated command line is printed with a question mark first, and is executed only if the user responds by typing y.
−print	Always true; causes the current pathname to be printed.
−cpio *device*	Always true; write the current file on *device* in cpio format (5120-byte records).
−newer *file*	True if the current file has been modified more recently than the argument *file*.
−depth	Always true; causes descent of the directory hierarchy to be done so that all entries in a directory are acted on before the directory itself. This can be useful when find is used with cpio(1) to transfer files that are contained in directories without write permission.
(expression)	True if the parenthesized expression is true (parentheses are special to the shell and must be escaped).

The primaries may be combined using the following operators (in order of decreasing precedence):

!p   True if p is false, and false if p is true.

p1 p2 True if both p1 and p2 are true, and false otherwise.

p −o pTrue if either p1 or p2 is true, and false otherwise.

---

grep, egrep, fgrep – search a file for a pattern   GREP (1)

grep [option ...] expression [file] ...
egrep [option ...] expression [file] ...
fgrep [option ...] [strings] [file] ...

Commands of the grep family search the input files (standard input default) for lines matching a pattern. Normally, each line found is copied to the standard output. grep patterns are limited regular expressions in the style of ed(1); it uses a compact non-deterministic algorithm. egrep patterns are full regular expressions; it uses a fast deterministic algorithm that sometimes needs exponential space. fgrep patterns are fixed strings; it is fast and compact.

Options

　　　　−v   All lines but those matching are printed.
　　　　−x   (Exact) only lines matched in their entirety are printed (fgrep only).
　　　　−c   Only a count of matching lines is printed.
　　　　−i   Ignore upper/lower case distinction during comparisons.
　　　　−l   Only the names of files with matching lines are listed (once), separated by newlines.
　　　　−n   Each line is preceded by its relative line number in the file.
　　　　−b   Each line is preceded by the block number on which it was found. This is sometimes useful in locating disk block numbers by context.
　　　　−s   The error messages produced for nonexistent or unreadable files are suppressed (grep only).
　　−e *expression*
　　　　　　Same as a simple *expression* argument, but useful when the expression begins with a − (does not work with grep).
　　−f *file*   The regular expression (egrep) or strings list (fgrep) is taken from the file.

In all cases, the file name is output if there is more than one input file. The characters $, *, [, ⌃, |, (,), and \ need to be quoted in a command argument since they are also meaningful to the shell.

fgrep searches for lines that contain one of the strings separated by newlines.

egrep accepts extended regular expressions as described in chapter 8.

---

join − relational database operator   JOIN (1)

join [options] ... file1 file2

join forms, on the standard output, a join of the two relations specified by the lines of file1 and file2. If file1 is −, the standard input is used.

file1 and file2 must be sorted lexicographically on the fields on which they are to be joined, normally the first in each line.

There is one line in the output for each pair of lines in file1 and file2 that have identical join fields. The output line normally consists of the common field, then the rest of the line from file1, then the rest of the line from file2.

Fields are normally separated by white space. Multiple separators count as one, and leading separators are discarded.

Options

-a *n*   In addition to the normal output, produce a line for each unpairable line in file *n,* where *n* is 1 or 2.

-e *s*   Replace empty output fields by string *s.*

-j *n m*   Join on the *m-th* field of file *n.* If *n* is missing, use the *m-th* field in each file.

-o *list*   Each output line comprises the fields specified in *list,* each element of which has the form n.m, where n is a file number and m is a field number.

-t *c*   Use character *c* as separator (tab character). Every appearance of *c* in a line is significant.

---

kill – terminate a process   KILL (1)

kill [−signo] pid ...

kill sends signal 15 (terminate) to the specified processes. This will normally kill processes that do not catch or ignore the signal. The process number of each asynchronous process started with & is reported by the shell (unless more than one process is started in a pipeline, in which case the number of the last process in the pipeline is reported). Process numbers can also be found by using ps(1).

The details of the kill command are described in kill(2). For example, if process number 0 is specified, all processes in the process group are signaled.

A process may only be killed by the user who created it or the super-user.

If a signal number preceded by – is given as first argument, that signal is sent instead of terminate (see signal(2)).

---

ld – link editor for common object files   LD (1)

ld [option] ... filename ...

The ld command combines several object files into one, performs relocation, resolves external symbols, and supports symbol table information for symbolic debugging. In the simplest case, the names of several object programs are given, and ld combines them, producing an object module that can either be executed or used as input for a subsequent ld run. The output of ld is left in *a.out.* By default this file is executable if no errors occurred during the load. If any input file, filename, is not an object file, ld assumes it is either an archive library or a text file containing link editor directives.

If any argument is a library, it is searched exactly once at the point it is encountered in the argument list. Only those routines defining an unresolved external reference are loaded. The library (archive) symbol table is searched sequentially with as many passes as are necessary to resolve external references which can be satisfied by library members. Thus, the ordering of library members is unimportant.

Options

-e *sym* Set the default entry point address for the output file to be that of the symbol *sym*.

-f *fill*   Set the default *fill* pattern for holes within an output section as well as initialized bss sections. The argument *fill* is a two-byte constant.

-l *x*   Search a library lib *x* .a, where *x* is up to seven characters. A library is searched when its name is encountered, so the placement of a -l is significant. By default, libraries are located in /lib and /usr/lib/.

-m   Produce a map or listing of the input-output sections on the standard output.

-o *file* Produce an output object file by the name *file*. The name of the default object file is *a.out*.

-r   Retain relocation entries in the output object file. Relocation entries must be saved if the output file is to become an input file in a subsequent ld run. The link editor will not complain about unresolved references, and the output file will not be executed.

-s   Strip line number entries and symbol table information from the output object file.

-t   Turn off the warning about multiply-defined symbols that are not the same size.

-u *name*

Enter *name* as an undefined symbol in the symbol table. This is useful for loading entirely from a library, since initially the symbol table is empty and an unresolved reference is needed to force the loading of the first routine.

-x   Do not preserve local (non-global) symbols in the output symbol table; enter external and static symbols only. This option saves some space in the output file.

-z   Do not bind anything to address zero. This option will allow runtime detection of null pointers.

-L *dir* Change the algorithm of searching for lib *x* .a to look in *dir* before looking in /lib and /usr/lib. This option is effective only if it precedes the -l option on the command line.

-M   Output a message for each multiply-defined external definition. However, if the objects being loaded include debugging information, extraneous output is produced (see the -g option in cc(1)).

-N   Put the data section immediately following the text in the output file.

-V   Output a message giving information about the version of ld being used.

-VS *n* Use *n* as a decimal version stamp identifying the *a.out* file that is produced. The version stamp is stored in the optional header.

lex – generate programs for simple lexical tasks   LEX(1)

lex [option] [file] ...

lex generates programs to be used in simple lexical analysis of text.

The input files (standard input default) contain strings and expressions to be searched for, and C text to be executed when strings are found.

−r	Indicates ratfor actions.
−c	Indicates C actions and is the default.
−t	Causes the lex.yy.c program to be written instead to standard output.
−v	Provides a one-line summary of statistics.
−n	Will not print out the − summary.

Multiple files are treated as a single file. If no files are specified, standard input is used.

---

lint – a C program checker   LINT(1)

lint [option] ... file ...

lint attempts to detect features of the C program files that are likely to be bugs, non-portable, or wasteful. It also checks type usage more strictly than the compilers. Among the things that are currently detected are unreachable statements, loops not entered at the top, automatic variables declared and not used, and logical expressions whose value is constant. Moreover, the usage of functions is checked to find functions that return values in some places and not in others, functions called with varying numbers or types of arguments, and functions whose values are not used or whose values are used but none returned.

Arguments whose names end with .c are taken to be C source files. Arguments whose names end with .ln are taken to be the result of an earlier invocation of lint with either the −c or the −o option used. The .ln files are analogous to .o (object) files that are produced by the cc(1) command when given a .c file as input.

lint will take all the .c, .ln, and llib−l x.ln (specified by −l x) files and process them in their command line order. By default, lint appends the standard C lint library (llib−lc.ln) to the end of the list of files. However, if the −p option is used, the portable C lint library (llib−port.ln) is appended instead. When the −c option is not used, the second pass of lint checks this list of files for mutual compatibility. When the −c option is used, the .ln and the llib−l x.ln files are ignored.

Any number of lint options may be used, in any order, intermixed with filename arguments.

Options

−a	Suppress complaints about assignments of long values to variables that are not long.
−b	Suppress complaints about break statements that cannot be reached. (Programs produced by lex or yacc will often result in many such complaints.)
−h	Do not apply heuristic tests that attempt to intuit bugs, improve style, and reduce waste.

−u   Suppress complaints about functions and external variables used and not defined, or defined and not used. (This option is suitable for running lint on a subset of files of a larger program.)

−v   Suppress complaints about unused arguments in functions.

−x   Do not report variables referred to by external declarations but never used.

−l x Include additional lint library llib−l x.ln. For example, you can include a lint version of the Math Library llib−lm.ln by inserting −lm on the command line. This argument does not suppress the default use of llib−lc.ln. These lint libraries must be in the assumed directory. This option can be used to reference local lint libraries and is useful in the development of multi-file projects.

−n   Do not check compatibility against either the standard or the portable lint library.

−p   Attempt to check portability to other dialects (IBM and GCOS) of C. Along with stricter checking, this option causes all non-external names to be truncated to eight characters and all external names to be truncated to six characters and one case.

−c   Produce a .ln file for every .c file on the command line. These .ln files are the product of lint's first pass only, and are not checked for inter-function compatibility.

−o lib Cause lint to create a lint library with the name llib−l*lib*.ln. The −c option nullifies any use of the −o option. The lint library produced is the input that is given to lint's second pass. The −o option simply causes this file to be saved in the named lint library. To produce a llib−l*lib*.ln without extraneous messages, use of the −x option is suggested. The −v option is useful if the source file(s) for the lint library are just external interfaces (for example, the way the file llib−lc is written). These option settings are also available through the use of lint comments (see below).

The −D, −U, and −I options of cpp(1) and the −g and −O options of cc(1) are also recognized as separate arguments. The −g and −O options are ignored, but, by recognizing these options, lint's behavior is closer to that of the cc(1) command. The preprocessor symbol lint is defined to allow certain questionable code to be altered or removed for lint. Therefore, the symbol lint should be thought of as a reserved word for all code that is planned to be checked by lint.

Certain conventional comments in the C source will change the behavior of lint.

/*NOTREACHED*/
    At appropriate points stops comments about unreachable code.
/*VARARGS n */
    Suppresses the usual checking for variable numbers of arguments in the following function declaration. The data types of the first n arguments are checked; a missing n is taken to be 0.
/*ARGSUSED*/
    Turns on the −v option for the next function.
/*LINTLIBRARY*/

At the beginning of a file shuts off complaints about unused functions and function arguments in this file. This is equivalent to using the −v and −x options.

lint produces its first output on a per-source-file basis. Complaints regarding included files are collected and printed after all source files have been processed. Finally, if the −c option is not used, information gathered from all input files is collected and checked for consistency. At this point, if it is not clear whether a complaint stems from a given source file or from one of its included files, the source file name will be printed followed by a question mark.

The behavior of the −c and the −o options allows for incremental use of lint on a set of C source files. Generally, one invokes lint once for each source file with the −c option. Each of these invocations produces a .ln file which corresponds to the .c file, and prints all messages that are about just that source file. After all the source files have been separately run through lint, it is invoked once more (without the −c option), listing all the .ln files with the needed −l*x* options. This will print all the inter-file inconsistencies. This scheme works well with make(1); it allows make to be used to lint only the source files that have been modified since the last time the set of source files were linted.

---

ln − link files   LN(1)

ln [−f] file1 [file2 ...] target

file1 is linked to target. file1 and target cannot be the same. If target is a directory, then one or more files are linked to that directory. If target is a file, its contents are destroyed.

If ln determines that the mode of target forbids writing, it will print the mode (see chmod(2)), ask for a response, and read the standard input for one line; if the line begins with y, the link is made, if permissible; if not, the command exits. No questions are asked and the ln is done when the −f option is used or if the standard input is not a terminal. It is forbidden to link to a directory or to link across file systems. If file1 is a file and target is a link to another file with links, the other links remain and target becomes a new file.

---

login − sign on   LOGIN(1)

login [name]

The login command is used at the beginning of each terminal session and allows you to identify yourself to the system. It may be invoked as a command or by the system when a connection is first established. Also, it is invoked by the system when a previous user has terminated the initial shell.

If login is invoked as a command it must replace the initial command interpreter. This is accomplished by typing

    exec login

from the initial shell.

login asks for your user name (if not supplied as an argument), and, if appropriate, your password. Echoing is turned off (where possible) during the typing of your password, so it will not appear on the written record of the session.

At some installations, an option may be invoked that will require you to enter a second password. This will occur only for dial-up connections, and will be prompted by the message dialup password:. Both passwords are required for a successful login.

If you do not complete the login successfully within a certain period of time (typically one minute), you are disconnected.

After a successful login, accounting files are updated, the shell procedure /etc/profile is executed, the message-of-the-day, if any, is printed, the user-id, the group-id, the working directory, and the command interpreter (usually sh(1)) is initialized, and the file .profile in the working directory is executed, if it exists. These specifications are found in the /etc/passwd file entry for the user. The name of the command interpreter is − followed by the last component of the interpreter's pathname (i.e., −sh). If this field in the password file is empty, then the default command interpreter, /bin/sh is used.

login initializes the environment with information specifying home directory, command interpreter, shell, mail location and timezone specification.

---

lorder − find ordering relation for an object library   LORDER(1)

lorder file ...

The input is one or more object or library archive files (see ar(1)). The standard output is a list of pairs of object file names, such that the first file of the pair refers to external identifiers defined in the second. The output may be processed by tsort(1) to find an ordering of a library suitable for one-pass access by ld(1). Note that the link editor ld is capable of multiple passes over an archive and does not require that lorder be used when building an archive. lorder may, however, provide for a slightly more efficient access of the archive during the link edit process.

---

ls − list contents of directory   LS(1)

ls [option] name ...

For each directory argument, ls lists the contents of the directory; for each file argument, ls repeats its name and any other information requested. The output is sorted alphabetically by default. When no argument is given, the current directory is listed. When several arguments are given, the arguments are first sorted appropriately, but file arguments appear before directories and their contents.

There are three major listing formats. The default format is to list one entry per line, the −C and −x options enable multi-column formats, and the −m option enables stream output format in which files are listed across the page, separated by commas. The −C, −x, and m options use an environment variable, COLUMNS, to determine the number of character positions available on one output line. If this variable is not set, the number of columns is based on the environment variable TERM. If this information cannot be obtained, 80 columns are assumed.

Options

    −R   Recursively list sub-directories encountered.

    −a   List all entries; usually entries whose names begin with a. are not listed.

−d	If an argument is a directory, list only its name (not its contents); often used with −l to get the status of a directory.
−C	Multi-column output with entries sorted down the columns.
−x	Multi-column output with entries sorted across the page.
−m	Stream output format.
−l	List in long format, giving mode, number of links, owner, group, size in bytes, and time of last modification for each file. If the file is a special file, the size field will contain the major and minor device numbers rather than a size.
−n	The same as −l, except that the numeric user-id and group-id are printed, rather than the associated character strings.
−o	The same as −l, except that the group is not printed.
−g	The same as −l, except that the owner is not printed.
−r	Reverse the order of sort to get reverse alphabetic or oldest first as appropriate.
−t	Sort by time modified (latest first) instead of by name.
−u	Use time of last access instead of last modification for sorting (with the −t option) or printing (with the −l option).
−c	Use time of last modification of the i-node (file created, mode changed, etc.) for sorting (−t) or printing (−l).
−p	Put a slash (/) after each file name if that file is a directory
−F	Put a slash (/) after each file name if that file is a directory and put an asterisk (*) after each file name if that file is executable.
−b	Print non-graphic characters in the octal \ddd notation.
−q	Force printing of non-graphic characters in file names as the character (?).
−i	For each file, print the i-number in the first column of the report.
−s	Give size in blocks, including indirect blocks, for each entry. When the sizes of the files in a directory are listed, a total count of blocks, including indirect blocks, is printed.
−f	Force each argument to be interpreted as a directory and list the name found in each slot. This option turns off −l, −t, −s, and −r, and turns on −a; the order is the order in which entries appear in the directory.

---

mail − send mail to users   MAIL (1)

mail [−epqr] [−f file]

mail [−t] persons

mail without arguments prints a user's mail, message-by-message, in last-in, first-out order. For each message, the user is prompted with a ?, to determine the disposition of the message and a line is read from the standard input as follows.

Requests

return	Go on to next message.
d	Delete message and go on to next message.
p	Print message again.

−   Go back to previous message.

s [*file*] . . .Save message in the named *file* (mbox is default).

w [*file*] . . .

Save message, without its header, in the named *file* (mbox is default).

m [*person*] . . .

Mail the message to the named *person* (yourself is default).

q   Put undeleted mail back in the mailfile and stop.

end-of-file Same as q.

x   Put all mail back in the mailfile unchanged and stop.

! *cmd*   Escape to the shell to execute cmd.

*   Print a command summary.

The optional arguments alter the printing of the mail:

−e   Do not print mail. An exit value of 0 is returned if the user has mail; otherwise, an exit value of 1 is returned.

−p   Print all mail without prompting for disposition.

−q   Terminate mail after interrupts. Normally an interrupt only causes the termination of the message being printed.

−r   Printed messages to be in first-in, first-out order.

−f *file* Use *file* (e.g. mbox) instead of the default mailfile.

When persons are named, mail takes the standard input up to an end-of-file (or up to a line consisting of just a .) and adds it to each person's mailfile. The message is preceded by the sender's name and a postmark. Lines that look like postmarks in the message (i.e. From ...) are preceded with a >. The −t option causes the message to be preceded by all persons the mail is sent to. A person is usually a user name recognized by login(1). If a person being sent mail is not recognized, or if mail is interrupted during input, the file dead.letter will be saved to allow editing and resending. Note that this is regarded as a temporary file in that it is recreated every time needed, erasing the previous contents of dead.letter.

To denote a recipient on a remote system, prefix *person* by the system name and exclamation mark (see uucp(1)). Everything after the first exclamation mark in *persons* is interpreted by the remote system. In particular, if *persons* contains additional exclamation marks, it can denote a sequence of machines through which the message is to be sent on the way to its ultimate destination. mail will not use uucp if the remote system is the local system name.

The mailfile may be manipulated in two ways to alter the function of mail. The other permissions of the file may be read-write, read-only, or neither read nor write to allow different levels of privacy. If changed to other than the default, the file will be preserved even when empty to perpetuate the desired permissions. The file may also contain the first line:

Forward to *person*

which will cause all mail sent to the owner of the mailfile to be forwarded to person. This is especially useful to forward all of a person's mail to one machine in a multiple machine environment. In order for forwarding to work properly the mailfile should have mail as group-id, and the group permission should be read-write.

When a user logs in, the presence of mail, if any, is indicated. Also, notification is made if new mail arrives while using mail.

make – maintain, update, and regenerate groups of programs   MAKE (1)

make [–f makefile] [option] ... [name] ...

Options

   –f *makefile*

> Description file name. *makefile* is assumed to be the name of a description file. A file name of – denotes the standard input. The contents of *makefile* override the built-in rules if they are present.

   –p   Print out the complete set of macro definitions and target descriptions.

   –i   Ignore error codes returned by invoked commands. This mode is entered if the fake target name .IGNORE appears in the description file.

   –k   Abandon work on the current entry, but continue on other branches that do not depend on that entry.

   –s   Silent mode. Do not print command lines before executing. This mode is also entered if the fake target name .SILENT appears in the description file.

   –r   Do not use the built-in rules.

   –n   No execute mode. Print commands, but do not execute them. Even lines beginning with an @ are printed.

   –b   Compatibility mode for old makefiles.

   –e   Environment variables override assignments within makefiles.

   –m   Print a memory map showing text, data, and stack. This option is a no-operation on systems without the getu system call.

   –t   Touch the target files (causing them to be up-to-date) rather than issue the usual commands.

   –d   Debug mode. Print out detailed information on files and times examined.

   –q   Question. The make command returns a zero or non-zero status code depending on whether the target file is or is not up-to-date.

   .DEFAULT

> If a file must be made but there are no explicit commands or relevant built-in rules, the commands associated with the name .DEFAULT are used if it exists.

   .PRECIOUS

> Dependents of this target will not be removed when quit or interrupt signals are received.

   .SILENT

> Same effect as the –s option.

   .IGNORE

> Same effect as the –i option.

    make executes commands in makefile to update one or more target names. name is typically a program. If no –f option is present, makefile, Makefile, s.makefile, and s.Makefile are tried in order. If makefile is –, the standard input is taken. More than one – makefile argument pair may appear.

    make updates a target only if its dependents are newer than the target. All prerequisite files of a target are added recursively to the list of targets. Missing files are deemed to be out of date.

makefile contains a sequence of entries that specify dependencies. The first line of an entry is a blank-separated, non-null list of targets, then a :, then a (possibly null) list of prerequisite files or dependencies. Text following a ; and all following lines that begin with a tab are shell commands to be executed to update the target. The first line that does not begin with a tab or # begins a new dependency or macro definition. Shell commands may be continued across lines with the \return sequence. Everything printed by make (except the initial tab) is passed directly to the shell as is. # and newline delimit comments.

Command lines are executed one at a time, each by its own shell. The first one or two characters in a command can be the following: −, @, −@, or @−. If @ is present, printing of the command is suppressed. If − is present, make ignores an error. A line is printed when it is executed unless the −s option is present, or the entry .SILENT: is in makefile, or unless the initial character sequence contains @. The −n option specifies printing without execution; however, if the command line has the string $(MAKE) in it, the line is always executed (see discussion of the MAKEFLAGS macro under Environment). The −t (touch) option updates the modified date of a file without executing any commands.

Commands returning non-zero status normally terminate make. If the −i option is present, or the entry .IGNORE: appears in makefile, or the initial character sequence of the command contains − the error is ignored. If the −k option is present, work is abandoned on the current entry, but continues on other branches that do not depend on that entry.

The −b option allows old makefiles (those written for the old version of make) to run without errors. The difference between the old version of make and this version is that this version requires all dependency lines to have a (possibly null or implicit) command associated with them. The previous version of make assumed, if no command was specified explicitly, that the command was null.

Interrupt and quit cause the target to be deleted unless the target is a dependent of the special name .PRECIOUS.

Environment

The environment is read by make. All variables are assumed to be macro definitions and processed as such. The environment variables are processed before any makefile and after the internal rules; thus, macro assignments in a makefile override environment variables. The −e option causes the environment to override the macro assignments in a makefile.

The MAKEFLAGS environment variable is processed by make as containing any legal input option (except −f, −p, and −d) defined for the command line. Further, upon invocation, make invents the variable if it is not in the environment, puts the current options into it, and passes it on to invocations of commands. Thus, MAKEFLAGS always contains the current input options. This proves very useful for super-makes. In fact, as noted above, when the −n option is used, the command $(MAKE) is executed anyway; hence, one can perform a make −n recursively on a whole software system to see what would have been executed.

Macros

Entries of the form string1 = string2 are macro definitions. string2 is defined as all characters up to a comment character or an unescaped return. Subsequent appearances of $(string1[:subst1 =[subst2]]) are replaced by string2. The parentheses are optional if a single character macro name is used and there is no substitute sequence. The optional :subst1 = subst2 is a substitute sequence. If it is specified, all non-overlapping occurrences of subst1 in the named macro are replaced by subst2. Strings (for the purposes of this type of substitution) are delimited by blank, tab, or newline, and beginnings of lines.

Internal macros

There are five internally maintained strings that are useful for writing rules for building targets.

$*   The file name part of the current dependent with the suffix deleted. It is evaluated only for inference rules.

$@   The full target name of the current target. It is evaluated only for explicitly named dependencies.

$<   The $< string is only evaluated for inference rules or the .DEFAULT rule. It is the module which is out of date with respect to the target (i.e. the manufactured dependent file name). Thus, in the .c.o rule, the $< macro would evaluate to the .c file.

$?   The $? macro is evaluated when explicit rules from the makefile are evaluated. It is the list of prerequisites that are out of date with respect to the target; essentially, those modules which must be rebuilt.

$%   The $% macro is only evaluated when the target is an archive library member of the form lib(file.o). In this case, $@ evaluates to lib and $% evaluates to the library member, file.o.

Four of the five macros can have alternative forms. When an upper case D or F is appended to any of the four macros, the meaning is changed to directory part for D and file part for F. Thus, $(@D) refers to the directory part of the string $@. If there is no directory part, ./ is generated. The only macro excluded from this alternative form is $?.

Suffixes

Certain names (for instance, those ending with .o) have inferable prerequisites such as .c, .s. If no update commands for such a file appear in makefile, and if an inferable prerequisite exists, that prerequisite is compiled to make the target. In this case, make has inference rules which allow building files from other files by examining the suffixes and determining an appropriate inference rule to use. The default inference rules are:

```
.c .c~ .sh .sh~ .c.o .c~.o .c~.c .s.o .s~.o .y.o .y~.o
.l.o .l~.o
.y.c .y~.c .l.c .c.a .c~.a .s~.a .h~.h
```

The internal rules for make are contained in the source file rules.c for the make program. These rules can be locally modified.

A ~ in the above rules refers to an SCCS file. Thus, the rule .c~.o would transform an SCCS C source file into an object file (.o). Because the s. of the SCCS files is a prefix, it is incompatible with the make view of a suffix. Hence, the tilde is a way of changing any file reference into an SCCS file reference.

A rule with only one suffix (i.e. .c:) is the definition of how to build x from x.c. In effect, the other suffix is null. This is useful for building targets from only one source file (e.g. shell procedures, simple C programs).

Additional suffixes are given as the dependency list for .SUFFIXES. Order is significant; the first possible name for which both a file and a rule exist is inferred as a prerequisite. The default list is:

    .o .c .y .l .s

Multiple suffix lists accumulate; .SUFFIXES: with no dependencies clears the list of suffixes.

Inference rules

Certain macros are used by the default inference rules to permit the inclusion of optional matter in any resulting commands. For example, CFLAGS, LFLAGS, and YFLAGS are used for compiler options to cc(1), lex(1), and yacc(1), respectively.

The inference of prerequisites can be controlled. The rule to create a file with suffix .o from a file with suffix .c is specified as an entry with .c.o: as the target and no dependents. Shell commands associated with the target define the rule for making a .o file from a .c file. Any target that has no slashes in it and starts with a dot is identified as a rule and not a true target.

Libraries

If a target or dependency name contains parentheses, it is assumed to be an archive library, the string within parentheses referring to a member within the library. Thus lib(file.o) and $(LIB)(file.o) both refer to an archive library which contains file.o. (This assumes the LIB macro has been previously defined.) The expression $(LIB)(file1.o file2.o) is not legal. Rules pertaining to archive libraries have the form .XX.a where the XX is the suffix from which the archive member is to be made. An unfortunate byproduct of the current implementation requires the XX to be different from the suffix of the archive member. Thus, one cannot have lib(file.o) depend upon file.o explicitly.

---

man − print entries in this manual   MAN (1)

man [option] ... [section] title ...

man locates and prints the entry of this manual named title in the specified section. (For historical reasons, the word page is often used as a synonym for entry in this context.) The title is entered in lower case. The section number may not have a letter suffix. If no section is specified, the whole manual is searched for title and all occurrences of it are printed.

Options

    −T *term*   Print the entry as appropriate for terminal type *term*. The default value of *term* is 450.

    −w   Print on the standard output only the pathnames of the entries, relative to /usr/catman, or to the current directory for −d option.

−d   Search the current directory rather than /usr/catman; requires the full file name, e.g., cu.1c, rather than just cu.

−c   Invoke col(1); col(1) is invoked automatically by man unless *term* is one of 300, 300s, 450, 37, 4000a, 382, 4014, tek, 1620, and X.

man examines the environment variable TERM and attempts to select options that adapt the output to the terminal being used. The −T *term* option overrides the value of $TERM; in particular, one should use −T *lp* when sending the output of man to a line printer.

section may be changed before each title.

---

mesg − permit or deny messages   MESG(1)

mesg [n] [y]

mesg with argument n forbids messages via write(1) by revoking non-user write permission on the user's terminal. mesg with argument y reinstates permission. Without arguments, mesg reports the current state without changing it.

---

mkdir − make a directory   MKDIR(1)

mkdir dirname ...

mkdir creates specified directories in mode 777 (possibly altered by umask(1)). Standard entries, ., for the directory itself, and .., for its parent, are made automatically.

mkdir requires write permission in the parent directory.

---

mv − move files   MV(1)

mv [−f] file1 [file2 ...] target

file1 is moved to target. file1 and target cannot be the same. If target is a directory, then one or more files are moved to that directory. If target is an existing file, its contents are replaced.

If mv determines that the mode of target forbids writing, it will print the mode (see chmod(2)), ask for a response, and read the standard input for one line; if the line begins with y, the mv occurs, if permissible; if not, the command exits. No questions are asked and the mv is done when the −f option is used or if the standard input is not a terminal.

mv will allow file1 to be a directory, in which case the directory rename will occur only if the two directories have the same parent; file1 is renamed target. If file1 is a file and target is a link to another file with links, the other links remain and target becomes a new file.

newgrp — log in to a new group   NEWGRP (1)

newgrp [−] [group]

newgrp changes a user's group identification. The user remains logged in and the current directory is unchanged, but calculations of access permissions to files are performed with respect to the new real and effective group-id's. newgrp always gives the user a new shell, replacing the current shell regardless of whether it terminated successfully or due to an error condition (e.g. unknown group).

Exported variables retain their values after invoking newgrp; however, all unexported variables are either reset to their default value or set to null. System variables (such as PS1, PS2, PATH, MAIL, and HOME), unless exported by the system or explicitly exported by the user, are reset to default values. For example, a user has a primary prompt string (PS1) other than $ (default) and has not exported PS1. After an invocation of newgrp, successful or not, their PS1 will now be set to the default prompt string $.

With no arguments, newgrp changes the group identification back to the group specified in the user's password file entry.

If the first argument to newgrp is a −, the environment is changed to what would be expected if the user actually logged in again.

A password is demanded if the group has a password and the user does not, or if the group has a password and the user is not listed in /etc/group as being a member of that group.

---

nice — run a command at low priority   NICE (1)

nice [− number] command [argument] ...

nice executes command with low scheduling priority. If the number argument is present, the priority is incremented (higher numbers mean lower priorities) by that amount up to a limit of 20. The default number is 10.

The super-user may run commands with priority higher than normal by using a negative priority, e.g. −−10.

---

nm — print name list of common object file   NM (1)

nm [option] filename ...

The nm command displays the symbol table of each common object file filename. filename may be a relocatable or absolute common object file, or it may be an archive of relocatable or absolute common object files.

Options may be used in any order, either singly or in combination, and may appear anywhere in the command line. For each symbol, the following information will be printed:

Name   The name of the symbol.
Value Its value expressed as an offset or an address depending on its storage class.
Class Its storage class.

Type   Its type and derived type. If the symbol is an instance of a structure or of a union then the structure or union tag will be given following the type. If the symbol is an array, then the array dimensions will be given following the type. The object file must have been compiled with the −g option of the cc(1) command for this information to appear.

Size   Its size in bytes, if available. The object file must have been compiled with the −g option of the cc(1) command for this information to appear.

Line   The source line number at which it is defined, if available. Note that the object file must have been compiled with the −g option of the cc(1) command for this information to appear.

Section For storage classes static and external, the object file section containing the symbol.

Options

−o   Print the value and size of a symbol in octal instead of decimal.

−x   Print the value and size of a symbol in hexadecimal instead of decimal.

−h   Do not display the output header data.

−v   Sort external symbols by value before they are printed.

−n   Sort external symbols by name before they are printed.

−e   Print only external and static symbols.

−f   Produce full output. Print redundant symbols (.text, .data, and .bss), normally suppressed.

−u   Print undefined symbols only.

−V   Print the version of the nm command executing on the standard error output.

−T   By default, nm prints the entire name of the symbols listed. Since object files can have symbol names with an arbitrary number of characters, a name that is longer than the width of the column set aside for names will overflow its column, forcing every column after the name to be misaligned. The −T option causes nm to truncate every name which would otherwise overflow its column and place an asterisk as the last character in the displayed name to mark it as truncated.

---

nohup − run a command immune to hangups and quits   NOHUP (1)

nohup command [arguments]

nohup executes command with hangups and quits ignored. If output is not redirected by the user, both standard output and standard error are sent to nohup.out. If nohup.out is not writable in the current directory, output is redirected to $HOME/nohup.out.

It is frequently desirable to apply nohup to pipelines or lists of commands. This can be done only by placing pipelines and command lists in a single shell procedure.

od – octal dump   OD(1)

od [option] [file] [[+] offset[.][b]]

od prints file in one or more formats as selected by the first argument. If the first argument is missing, –o is default.

Options

-b   Interpret bytes in octal.
-c   Interpret bytes in ASCII. Certain non-graphic characters appear as C escapes: null=\0, backspace=\b, formfeed=\f, newline=\n, return=\r, tab=\t; others appear as 3-digit octal numbers.
-d   Interpret words in unsigned decimal.
-o   Interpret words in octal.
-s   Interpret 16-bit words in signed decimal.
-x   Interpret words in hexadecimal.

The file argument specifies which file is to be dumped. If no file argument is specified, the standard input is used.

The offset argument specifies the offset in the file where printing is to commence. This argument is normally interpreted as a byte count. If . is appended, the offset is interpreted in decimal. If b is appended, the offset is interpreted in blocks of 512 bytes. If the file argument is omitted, the offset argument must be preceded by +.

Printing continues until end-of-file.

passwd – change login password   PASSWD(1)

passwd [name]

This command changes or installs a password associated with the login name.

Ordinary users may change only the password which corresponds to their login name.

passwd prompts ordinary users for their old password, if any. It then prompts for the new password twice. The first time the new password is entered passwd checks to see if the old password has aged sufficiently. If aging is insufficient the new password is rejected and passwd terminates.

Assuming aging is sufficient, a check is made to insure that the new password meets construction requirements. When the new password is entered a second time the two copies of the new password are compared.

Passwords must be constructed to meet the following requirements:

- Each password must have at least six characters. Only the first eight characters are significant.
- Each password must contain at least two alphabetic characters and at least one numeric or special character. In this case, alphabetic means upper and lower case letters.
- Each password must differ from the user's login name and any reverse or circular shift of that login name. For comparison purposes, an upper case letter and its corresponding lower case letter are equivalent.

● New passwords must differ from the old by at least three characters. For comparison purposes, an upper case letter and its corresponding lower case letter are equivalent.

---

pr – print files   PR(1)

pr [option] ... [file] ...

pr prints the named files on the standard output. If file is –, or if no files are specified, the standard input is assumed. By default, the listing is separated into pages, each headed by the page number, a date and time, and the name of the file.

By default, columns are of equal width, separated by at least one space; lines which do not fit are truncated. If the –s option is used, lines are not truncated and columns are separated by the separation character.

If the standard output is associated with a terminal, error messages are withheld until pr has completed printing. The options below may appear singly or be combined in any order.

Options

+*n*	Begin printing with page *n* (default is 1).
–*n*	Produce *n*-column output (default is 1). The options –e and –i are assumed for multi-column output.
–a	Print multi-column output across the page.
–m	Merge and print all files simultaneously, one per column (overrides the – *n*, and –a options).
–d	Double-space the output.
–e *cn*	Expand input tabs to character positions *n*+1, 2 * *n*+1, 3 * *n*+1, etc. If *n* is 0 or is omitted, default tab settings at every eighth position are assumed. tabs in the input are expanded into the appropriate number of spaces. If *c* (any non-digit character) is given, it is treated as the input tab character (default for *c* is a tab).
–i *cn*	In output, replace white space wherever possible by inserting tabs to character positions *n*+1, 2 * *n*+1, 3 * *n*+1, etc. If *n* is 0 or is omitted, default tab settings at every eighth position are assumed. If *c* (any non-digit character) is given, it is treated as the output tab character (default for *c* is a tab).
–n *cn*	Provide *n*-digit line numbering (default for *n* is 5). The number occupies the first *n*+1 character positions of each column of normal output or each line of –m output. If *c* (any non-digit character) is given, it is appended to the line number to separate it from whatever follows (default for *c* is a tab).
–w *n*	Set the width of a line to *n* character positions (default is 72 for equal-width multi-column output, no limit otherwise).
–o *n*	Offset each line by *n* character positions (default is 0). The number of character positions per line is the sum of the width and offset.
–l *n*	Set the length of a page to *n* lines (default is 66).
–h	Use the next argument as the header to be printed instead of the file name.
–p	Pause before beginning each page if the output is directed to a ter-

minal (pr will ring the bell at the terminal and wait for a carriage return).

–f   Use formfeed for new pages (default is to use a sequence of
linefeeds). Pause before beginning the first page if the standard output is associated with a terminal.

–r   Print no diagnostic reports on failure to open files.

–t   Print neither the five-line identifying header nor the five-line trailer
normally supplied for each page. Quit printing after the last line of
each file without spacing to the end of the page.

–s c   Separate columns by the single character c instead of by the appropriate number of spaces (default for c is a tab).

---

prof – display profile data   PROF (1)

prof [option] [–m mdata] [prog]

    prof interprets a profile file produced by the monitor(3C) function. The symbol
table in the object file prog (a.out by default) is read and correlated with a profile
file (mon.out by default). For each external text symbol the percentage of time
spent executing between the address of that symbol and the address of the next is
printed, together with the number of times that function was called and the average
number of milliseconds per call.

Options

The mutually exclusive options t, c, a, and n determine the type of sorting of the
output lines.

–t   Sort by decreasing percentage of total time (default).

–c   Sort by decreasing number of calls.

–a   Sort by increasing symbol address.

–n   Sort lexically by symbol name.

The mutually exclusive options o and x specify the printing of the address of
each symbol monitored.

–o   Print each symbol address (in octal) along with the symbol name.

–x   Print each symbol address (in hexadecimal) along with the symbol
name.

The following options may be used in any combination.

–g   Include non-global symbols (static functions).

–z   Include all symbols in the profile range (see monitor(3C)), even if associated with zero number of calls and zero time.

–h   Suppress the heading normally printed on the report.

–s   Print a summary of several of the monitoring parameters and statistics
on the standard error output.

–m mdata
    Use file mdata instead of mon.out as the input profile file.

    A program creates a profile file if it has been compiled with the –p option of
cc(1). This option to the cc command arranges for calls to monitor(3C) at the be-

ginning and end of execution. It is the call to monitor at the end of execution that causes a profile file to be written. The number of calls to a function is tallied if the −p option was used when the file containing the function was compiled.

The name of the file created by a profiled program is controlled by the environment variable PROFDIR. If PROFDIR does not exist, *mon.out* is produced in the current directory when the program terminates. If PROFDIR is the null string no profiling output is produced. Otherwise, if PROFDIR is set, $PROFDIR/pid.progname is produced, where progname consists of argv[0] with any path prefix removed, and pid is the program's process-id.

---

ps − report process status   PS(1)

ps [option] ...

ps prints information about active processes. Without option, information is printed about processes associated with the current terminal. The output consists of a short listing containing only the process-id, terminal identifier, cumulative execution time, and the command name. Otherwise, the information that is displayed is controlled by the selection of options.

Options using lists as arguments can have the list specified in one of two forms: a list of identifiers separated from one another by a comma, or a list of identifiers enclosed in double quotes and separated from one another by a comma and/or one or more spaces.

Options

-e   Print information about all processes.

-d   Print information about all processes, except process group leaders.

-a   Print information about all processes, except process group leaders and processes not associated with a terminal.

-f   Generate a full listing. (See below for meaning of columns in a full listing.)

-l   Generate a long listing. See below.

-c *core*Use the file *core* in place of /dev/mem.

-s *swap*
      Use the file *swap* in place of /dev/swap. This is useful when examining a *corefile;* a *swapdev* of /dev/null will cause the user block to be zeroed out.

-n *namelist*
      The argument will be taken as the name of an alternative system *namelist* file in place of /unix.

-t *termlist*
      Restrict listing to data about the processes associated with the terminals given in *termlist.* Terminal identifiers may be specified in one of two forms: the device's file name (e.g. tty04) or if the device's file name starts with tty, just the digit identifier (e.g. 04).

-p *proclist*
      Restrict listing to data about processes whose process-id numbers are given in *proclist.*

-u *uidlist*

Restrict listing to data about processes whose user-id numbers or login names are given in *uidlist*. In the listing, the numerical user-id will be printed unless the −f option is used, in which case the login name will be printed.

−g *grplist*

Restrict listing to data about processes whose process group leaders are given in *grplist*.

The column headings and the meaning of the columns in a ps listing are given below.

F	Flags (octal and additive) associated with the process:
	0 swapped;
	1 in core;
	2 system process;
	4 locked-in core (e.g. for physical input-output);
	10 being swapped;
	20 being traced by another process;
	40 another tracing flag.
S	The state of the process:
	0 non-existent;
	1 sleeping;
	W waiting;
	R running;
	I intermediate;
	Z terminated;
	T stopped;
	X growing.
UID	The user-id number of the process owner; the login name is printed under the −f option.
PID	The process-id of the process.
PPID	The process-id of the parent process.
C	Processor utilization for scheduling.
PRI	The priority of the process; higher numbers mean lower priority.
NI	Nice value; used in priority computation.
ADDR	The memory address of the process if resident; otherwise, the disk address.
SZ	The size in blocks of the core image of the process.
WCHAN	
	The event for which the process is waiting or sleeping; if blank, the process is running.
STIME	Starting time of the process.
TTY	The controlling terminal for the process.
TIME	The cumulative execution time for the process.
CMD	The command name; the full command name and its arguments are printed under the −f option.

A process that has exited and has a parent, but has not yet been waited for by the parent, is marked <defunct>.

Under the −f option, ps tries to determine the command name and arguments given when the process was created by examining memory or the swap area. Failing this, the command name, as it would appear without the –f option, is printed in square brackets.

---

ptx – permuted index   PTX (1)

ptx [option] ... [input [output]]

ptx generates the file output that can be processed with a text formatter to produce a permuted index of file input (standard input and output default). It has three phases: the first does the permutation, generating one line for each keyword in an input line. The keyword is rotated to the front. The permuted file is then sorted. Finally, the sorted lines are rotated so the keyword comes at the middle of each line. ptx output is in the form:

.xx "tail" "before keyword" "keyword and after" "head"

where .xx is assumed to be an nroff or troff(1) macro provided by the user. The before keyword and keyword and after fields incorporate as much of the line as will fit around the keyword when it is printed. tail and head, at least one of which is always the empty string, are wrapped-around pieces small enough to fit in the unused space at the opposite end of the line.

Options

–f   Fold upper and lower case letters for sorting.

–t   Prepare the output for the phototypesetter.

–w *n*   Use the next argument, *n,* as the length of the output line. The default line length is 82 characters for nroff and 100 for troff.

–g *n*   Use the next argument, *n,* as the number of characters that ptx will reserve in its calculations for each gap among the four parts of the line as finally printed. The default gap is 3.

–o *only* Use as keywords only the words given in the *only* file.

–i *ign* Do not use as keywords any words given in the *ign* file. If the –i and –o options are missing, use /usr/lib/eign as the *ignore* file.

–b *break*
        Use the characters in the *break* file to separate words. tab, newline, and space characters are always used as *break* characters.

–r   Take any leading non-blank characters of each input line to be a reference identifier (as to a page or chapter), separate from the text of the line. Attach that identifier as a 5th field on each output line.

---

pwd – working directory name   PWD (1)

pwd

pwd prints the pathname of the working (current) directory.

rm, rmdir − remove files or directories   RM (1)

rm [−fri] file . . .

rmdir dir . . .

   rm removes the entries for one or more files from a directory. If an entry was
the last link to the file, the file is destroyed. Removal of a file requires write permission in its directory, but neither read nor write permission on the file itself.
   If a file has no write permission and the standard input is a terminal, its permissions are printed and a line is read from the standard input. If that line begins
with y the file is deleted, otherwise the file remains. No questions are asked when
the −f option is given or if the standard input is not a terminal.
   If a designated file is a directory, an error comment is printed unless the optional argument −r has been used. In that case, rm recursively deletes the entire
contents of the specified directory, and the directory itself.
   If the −i (interactive) option is in effect, rm asks whether to delete each file,
and, under −r, whether to examine each directory.
   rmdir removes entries for the named directories, which must be empty.

---

sdb − symbolic debugger   SDB (1)

sdb [objfil [corfil [directory]]]

   sdb is a symbolic debugger that can be used with C and f77 programs. It may
be used to examine files and to provide a controlled environment for execution.
   objfil is an executable program file that has been compiled with the −g (debug)
option; the default for objfil is *a.out.* corfil is assumed to be a core image file produced after executing objfil; the default for corfil is *core.* The core file need not be
present.
   At any time there is a current line and current file. If corfil exists then they are
initially set to the line and file containing the source statement at which the process
terminated or stopped. Otherwise, they are set to the first line in *main.* The
current line and file may be changed with the source file examination requests.
   Names of variables are written just as they are in C or f77. Variables local to
a procedure may be accessed using the form procedure:variable. If no procedure
name is given, the procedure containing the current line is used by default. It is
also possible to refer to structure members as variable.member, pointers to structure
members as variable−>member and array elements as variable[number]. Combinations of these forms may also be used.
   It is also possible to specify a variable by its address. All forms of integer
constants that are valid in C may be used, so that addresses may be input in
decimal, octal, or hexadecimal.
   Line numbers in the source program are referred to as filename:number or
procedure:number. In either case the number is relative to the beginning of the file.
If no procedure or file name is given, the current file is used by default. If no
number is given, the first line of the named procedure or file is used.

Data examination requests

t   Print a stack trace (the names of the most recently called functions) for the terminated or stopped program.

T   Print the top line of the stack trace.

variable/*clm*

Print the value of variable according to length *l* and format *m*. A numeric count *c* indicates that a region of memory, beginning at the address implied by the variable, is to be displayed. If *l* and *m* are omitted, sdb chooses a length and format suitable for the variable's type as declared in the program. The length specifiers are:

    b   One byte.
    h   Two bytes (half word).
    ' l   Four bytes (long word).
    numberString length for formats s and a (see below).

Legal values for *m* are:

    c   Character.
    d   Decimal.
    u   Decimal, unsigned.
    o   Octal.
    x   Hexadecimal.
    f   32-bit single precision floating point.
    g   64-bit double precision floating point.
    s   Assume variable is a string pointer and print characters until a null character is reached.
    a   Print characters starting at the variable's address until a null character is reached.
    p   A pointer to procedure.
    i   Disassemble machine-language instruction with addresses printed numerically and symbolically.
    I   Disassemble machine-language instruction with addresses printed only numerically.

The length specifiers are only effective with the formats c, d, u, o, and x. If one of these formats is specified and any of c, l, and m, are omitted, the length defaults to the word length of the host machine; 4 for the VAX 11/780. The last variable may be redisplayed with the request . / .

The shell metacharacters * and ? may be used within procedure and variable names, providing a limited form of pattern matching. If no procedure name is given, both variables local to the current procedure and global (common for f77) variables are matched; while if a procedure name is specified then only variables local to that procedure are matched. To match only global variables (or blank common for f77) the form :pattern is used. The name of a common block may be specified instead of a procedure name for f77 programs.

variable= *lm*

linenumber= *lm*

number= *lm*
> Print the address of the variable, line number, or the value of the number, in the specified format. If no format is given, then lx is used. The last variant of this request provides a convenient way to convert between decimal, octal, and hexadecimal.

variable ! value
> Set the variable to the given value. The value may be a number, character constant, or a variable. If the variable is of type float or double, the value may also be a floating constant.

Source files requests

e procedure
e filename.c
e directory
e directory filename.c
> Set the current file to the file containing the named procedure or the named filename. Set the current line to the first line in the named procedure or file. All source files are assumed to be in directory. The default for directory is the working directory. If no procedure or file name is given, the current procedure and file names are reported.

/regular expression/
> Search forward from the current line for a line containing a string matching the regular expression as in section 8.1. The trailing / may be elided.

?regular expression?
> Search backward from the current line for a line containing a string matching the regular expression. The trailing ? may be elided.

p
> Print the current line.

z
> Print the current line followed by the next 9 lines. Set the current line to the last line printed.

^D
> Scroll. Print the next 10 lines. Set the current line to the last line printed.

w
> Window. Print the 10 lines around the current line.

numberSet the current line to the given line number. Print the new current line.

count + Advance the current line by *count* lines. Print the new current line.

count – Retreat the current line by *count* lines. Print the new current line.

Execution control requests

count r *args*

count RRun the program with the given arguments. The r request with no arguments reuses the previous arguments to the program while the R request runs the program with no arguments. An argument beginning with < or > causes redirection for the standard input or output respectively. If *count* is given, it specifies the number of breakpoints to be ignored.

linenumber c *count*
linenumber C *count*

Continue after a breakpoint or interrupt. If *count* is given, it specifies the number of breakpoints to be ignored. C continues with the signal that caused the program to stop and c ignores it. If a linenumber is specified then a temporary breakpoint is placed at the line and execution is continued. The breakpoint is deleted when the command finishes.

count s Single step. Run the program through *count* lines. If no count is given then the program is run for one line.

count S Single step, but step through subroutine calls.

k   Kill the debugged program.

procedure(arg1, arg2, . . .)

procedure(arg1, arg2, . . .)/*m*

Execute the named procedure with the given arguments. Arguments can be integer, character or string constants or names of variables accessible from the current procedure. The second form causes the value returned by the procedure to be printed according to format *m*. If no format is given, the default is d.

linenumber b *requests*

Set a breakpoint at the given line. If a procedure name without a line number is given (e.g. proc:), a breakpoint is placed at the first line in the procedure even if it was not compiled with the debug flag. If no *linenumber* is given, a breakpoint is placed at the current line. If no requests are given then execution stops just before the breakpoint and control is returned to sdb. Otherwise the requests are executed when the breakpoint is encountered and execution continues. Multiple requests are separated by ; .

linenumber d

Delete a breakpoint at the given line. If no *linenumber* is given then the breakpoints are deleted interactively. Each breakpoint location is printed and a line is read from the standard input. If the line begins with a y or d then the breakpoint is deleted.

B   Print a list of the currently active breakpoints.

D   Delete all breakpoints.

l   Print the last executed line.

linenumber a

Announce. If *linenumber* is of the form proc:number, the request effectively executes a linenumber b l. If *linenumber* is of the form proc:, the request executed is proc: b T.

Miscellaneous requests

! *cmd*   The command is interpreted by sh(1).

return   If the previous request printed a source line then advance the current line by 1 line and print the new current line. If the previous request displayed a core location then display the next core location.

"   Print the given string.

q   Exit the debugger.

---

sed − stream editor   SED (1)

sed [−n] [−e script] [−f sfile] [file] ...

    sed copies the named files (standard input default) to the standard output, edit-
ed according to a script of requests. The −f option causes the script to be taken
from file sfile; these options accumulate. If there is just one −e option and no −f,
the flag −e may be omitted. The −n option suppresses the default output.

    A script consists of editing requests, one per line, of the following form:

    [address [, address]] function [arguments]

In normal operation sed cyclically copies a line of input into a *pattern space* (unless
there is something left after a D request), applies in sequence all requests whose *addresses* select that pattern space, and at the end of the script copies the pattern
space to the standard output (except under the −n flag) and deletes the pattern
space.

    An *address* is either a decimal number that counts input lines cumulatively
across files, a $ that addresses the last line of input, or a context address, /regular
expression/, as described in section 8.1 modified thus:

- The escape sequence \n matches a newline embedded in the pattern space.
- A . matches any character except the terminal newline of the pattern
  space.

A request line with no addresses selects every pattern space.

    A request line with one address selects each pattern space that matches the ad-
dress.

    A request line with two addresses selects the inclusive range from the first
pattern space that matches the first address through the next pattern space that
matches the second. (If the second address is a number less than or equal to the
line number first selected, only one line is selected.) Thereafter the process is repeated, looking again for the first address.

    Editing requests can be applied only to non-selected pattern spaces by use of
the negation function ! (below).

    An argument denoted *text* consists of one or more lines, all but the last of
which end with \ to hide the newline. \ in text is treated like \ in the replacement
string of an s request, and may be used to protect initial blanks and tabs against the
stripping that is done on every script line.

    An argument denoted *rfile* or *wfile* must terminate the request line and must be
preceded by exactly one blank. Each *wfile* is created before processing begins.
There can be at most 10 distinct *wfile* arguments.

    a\   Append.
    text Place *text* on the output before reading the next input line.
    b *label* Branch to the : request bearing the *label*. If *label* is empty, branch to the
           end of the script.
    c\   Change.
    text Delete the pattern space. With 0 or 1 address or at the end of a 2-
           address range, place *text* on the output. Start the next cycle.

d   Delete the pattern space. Start the next cycle.

D   Delete the initial segment of the pattern space through the first newline.
        Start the next cycle.

g   Replace the contents of the pattern space by the contents of the hold
        space.

G   Append the contents of the hold space to the pattern space.

h   Replace the contents of the hold space by the contents of the pattern
        space.

H   Append the contents of the pattern space to the hold space.

i\   Insert.

text Place *text* on the standard output.

l   List the pattern space on the standard output in an unambiguous form.
        Non-printing characters are spelled in two-digit ASCII and long lines
        are folded.

n   Copy the pattern space to the standard output. Replace the pattern
        space with the next line of input.

N   Append the next line of input to the pattern space with an embedded
        newline. (The current line number changes.)

p   Print. Copy the pattern space to the standard output.

P   Copy the initial segment of the pattern space through the first newline
        to the standard output.

q   Quit. Branch to the end of the script. Do not start a new cycle.

r *rfile* Read the contents of *rfile*. Place them on the output before reading the
        next input line.

s / *regular expression*/ *replacement*/ *flags*

        Substitute the *replacement* string for instances of the *regular expression*
        in the pattern space. As in the editor ed any character may be used in-
        stead of /. *flags* is zero or more of

        n   *n* = 1, ... 512. Substitute for all non-overlapping instances
                of the regular expression rather than just the first one.

        g   Global. Substitute for all non-overlapping instances of
                the *regular expression* rather than just the first one.

        p   Print the pattern space if a replacement was made.

        w *file* Write. Append the pattern space to *file* if a replacement
                was made.

t *label* Test. Branch to the : request bearing the *label* if any substitutions have
        been made since the most recent reading of an input line or execution
        of a t. If *label* is empty, branch to the end of the script.

w *file* Write. Append the pattern space to *file*.

x   Exchange the contents of the pattern and hold spaces.

y /*string1*/*string2*/

        Transform. Replace all occurrences of characters in *string1* with the
        corresponding character in *string2*. The lengths of *string1* and *string2*
        must be equal.

! *function*

        Apply the *function* (or group, if *function* is {...}) only to lines not select-
        ed by the address(es).

: *label* This request does nothing; it defines a *label* for b and t requests to branch to.

=   Place the current line number on the standard output as a line.

{   Execute the following requests through a matching } only when the pattern space is selected.

        An empty request is ignored.

\#   If a # appears as the first character on the first line of a script file, then that entire line is treated as a comment, with one exception. If the character after the # is an n then the default output will be suppressed. The rest of the line after #n is also ignored. A script file must contain at least one non-comment line.

---

sh – command language   SH(1)

sh [options] [args] ...

If the shell is invoked through exec(2) and the first character of argument zero is –, commands are initially read from /etc/profile and from $HOME/.profile, if such files exist. Thereafter, commands are read as described below, which is also the case when the shell is invoked as /bin/sh. The flags below are interpreted by the shell on invocation only. Unless the –c or –s flag is specified, the first argument is assumed to be the name of a file containing commands, and the remaining arguments are passed as positional parameters to that command file.

Options

    –c *string*   Commands are read from *string.*

    –s   If the –s flag is present or if no arguments remain commands are read from the standard input. Any remaining arguments specify the positional parameters. Shell output (except for Special Commands) is written to file descriptor 2.

    –i   If the –i flag is present or if the shell input and output are attached to a terminal, this shell is interactive. In this case the terminate signal is ignored (so that kill 0 does not kill an interactive shell) and the interrupt signal is caught and ignored (so that wait is interruptible). In all cases, the quit signal is ignored by the shell.

    –r   If the –r flag is present the shell is a restricted shell.

---

size – print section sizes of common object files   SIZE(1)

size [–o] [–x] [–V] files

The size command produces section size information for each section in the common object files. The size of the text, data and bss (uninitialized data) sections are printed along with the total size of the object file. If an archive file is input to the size command the information for all archive members is displayed.

Numbers will be printed in decimal unless either the –o or the –x option is used, in which case they will be printed in octal or in hexadecimal, respectively.

The –V flag will supply the version information on the size command.

sleep − suspend execution for an interval   SLEEP(1)

sleep time

   sleep suspends execution for time seconds. It is used to execute a command
after a certain amount of time.

---

sort − sort and/or merge files   SORT(1)

sort [options] [+pos1 [−pos2]] [file] ...

   sort sorts lines of all the named files together and writes the result on the standard output. The standard input is read if − is used as a file name or no input files
are named.
   Comparisons are based on one or more sort keys extracted from each line of
input. By default, there is one sort key, the entire input line, and ordering is lexicographic.

Options

−c   Check that the input file is sorted according to the ordering rules; give
        no output unless the file is not sorted.
−m   Merge only, the input files are already sorted.
−u   Unique: suppress all but one in each set of lines having equal keys.
−o *output*
        The argument given is the name of an output file to use instead of the
        standard output. This file may be the same as one of the inputs. There
        may be optional blanks between −o and output.
−y *kmem*
        The amount of main memory used by the sort has a large impact on its
        performance. Sorting a small file in a large amount of memory is a
        waste. If this option is omitted, sort begins using a system default
        memory size, and continues to use more space as needed. If this op-
        tion is presented with a value, *kmem,* sort will start using that number
        of kilobytes of memory, unless the administrative minimum or max-
        imum is violated, in which case the corresponding extremum will be
        used. Thus, −y0 is guaranteed to start with minimum memory. By
        convention, −y (with no argument) starts with maximum memory.
−z *recsz*
        The size of the longest line read is recorded in the sort phase so buffers
        can be allocated during the merge phase. If the sort phase is omitted
        via the −c or −m options, a system default size will be used. Lines
        longer than the buffer size will cause sort to terminate abnormally.
        Supplying the actual number of bytes in the longest line to be merged
        (or some larger value) will prevent abnormal termination.

The following options override the default ordering rules.

−d   Dictionary order: only letters, digits and blanks (spaces and tabs) are
        significant in comparisons.
−f   Fold lower case letters into upper case.

−i   Ignore characters outside the ASCII range 040-0176 in non-numeric comparisons.

−M   Compare as months. The first three non-blank characters of the field are folded to upper case and compared so that jan < feb < ... < dec. Invalid fields compare low to jan. The −M option implies the −b option (see below).

−n   An initial numeric string, consisting of optional blanks, optional minus sign, and zero or more digits with optional decimal point, is sorted by arithmetic value. The −n option implies the −b option (see below).

−r   Reverse the sense of comparisons. When ordering options appear before restricted sort key specifications, the requested ordering rules are applied globally to all sort keys. When attached to a specific sort key (described below), the specified ordering options override all global ordering options for that key. The notation +pos1 −pos2 restricts a sort key to one beginning at pos1 and ending at pos2. The characters at positions pos1 and pos2 are included in the sort key (provided that pos2 does not precede pos1). A missing −pos2 means the end of the line.

Specifying pos1 and pos2 involves the notion of a field, a minimal sequence of characters followed by a field separator or a newline. By default, the first blank (space or tab) of a sequence of blanks acts as the field separator. All blanks in a sequence of blanks are considered to be part of the next field; for example, all blanks at the beginning of a line are considered to be part of the first field. The treatment of field separators can be altered using the following options:

−t x   Use x as the field separator character; x is not considered to be part of a field (although it may be included in a sort key). Each occurrence of x is significant (e.g. xx delimits an empty field).

−b   Ignore leading blanks when determining the starting and ending positions of a restricted sort key. If the −b option is specified before the first +pos1 argument, it will be applied to all +pos1 arguments. Otherwise, the b flag may be attached independently to each +pos1 or −pos2 argument (see below). pos1 and pos2 each have the form $m.n$ optionally followed by one or more of the flags bdfinr. A starting position specified by +$m.n$ is interpreted to mean the n+1st character in the m+1st field. A missing .n means .0, indicating the first character of the m+1st field. If the b flag is in effect, n is counted from the first non-blank in the m+1st field; +m.0b refers to the first non-blank character in the m+1st field. A last position specified by −$m.n$ is interpreted to mean the nth character (including separators) after the last character of the mth field. A missing .n means .0, indicating the last character of the mth field. If the b flag is in effect n is counted from the last leading blank in the m+1st field; −m.1b refers to the first non-blank in the m+1st field. Note that the −b option is only effective when restricted sort key specifications are in effect.

When there are multiple sort keys, later keys are compared only after all earlier keys compare equal. Lines that otherwise compare equal are ordered with all bytes significant.

spell − find spelling errors   SPELL (1)

spell [option] ... [+local_file] [file] ...

spell collects words from the named files and looks them up in a spelling list. Words that neither occur among nor are derivable (by applying certain inflections, prefixes, and/or suffixes) from words in the spelling list are printed on the standard output. If no files are named, words are collected from the standard input.

spell ignores most troff(1), tbl(1), and eqn(1) constructions.

Under the −v option, all words not literally in the spelling list are printed, and plausible derivations from the words in the spelling list are indicated.

Under the −b option, British spelling is checked. Besides preferring centre, colour, programme, speciality, travelled, etc., this option insists upon −ise in words like standardise, Fowler and the OED to the contrary notwithstanding.

Under the −x option, every plausible stem is printed with = for each word.

By default, spell (like deroff(1)) follows chains of included files (.so and .nx troff(1) requests), unless the names of such included files begin with /usr/lib. Under the −l option, spell will follow the chains of all included files. Under the −i option, spell will ignore all chains of included files.

Under the +local_file option, words found in local_file are removed from the output. local_file is the name of a user-provided file that contains a sorted list of words, one per line. With this option, the user can specify a set of words that are correct spellings (in addition to the standard spelling list) for each job.

The spelling list is based on many sources, and while more haphazard than an ordinary dictionary, is also more effective with respect to proper names and popular technical words. Coverage of the specialized vocabularies of biology, medicine, and chemistry is light.

Pertinent auxiliary files may be specified by name arguments, indicated below with their default settings. Copies of all output are accumulated in the history file. The stop list filters out misspellings (e.g. thier=thy−y+ier) that would otherwise pass.

---

strip − strip symbol and line number information   STRIP (1)

strip [option] name ...

The strip command strips the symbol table and line number information from common object files, including archives. Once this has been done, no symbolic debugging access will be available for that file; therefore, this command is normally run only on production modules that have been debugged and tested.

Options

−l   Strip line number information only; do not strip any symbol table information.

−x   Do not strip static or external symbol information.

−r   Reset the relocation indexes into the symbol table.

−V   Print the version of the strip command executing on the standard error output.

If there are any relocation entries in the object file and any symbol table information is to be stripped, strip will complain and terminate without stripping name unless the −r flag is used.

If the strip command is executed on a common archive file the archive symbol table will be removed. The archive symbol table must be restored by executing the ar(1) command with the s option before the archive can be link-edited by the ld(1) command. strip will instruct the user with appropriate warning messages when this situation arises.

---

stty − set the options for a terminal   STTY(1)

stty [−a] [−g] [option ...]

stty sets certain terminal input-output options for the device that is the current standard input; without arguments, it reports the settings of certain options; with the −a option, it reports all of the option settings; with the −g option, it reports current settings in a form that can be used as an argument to another stty command. Detailed information about the modes listed in the first five groups below may be found in ioctl(2). Options in the last group are implemented using options in the previous groups. Note that many combinations of options make no sense, but no sanity checking is performed.

Options

The options listed with a [−] are switches. The meaning of the − option is indicated in the text in square brackets.

[−]parenb	Enable [disable] parity generation and detection.
[−]parodd	Select odd [even] parity.
cs5 cs6 cs7 cs8	
	Select character size (see ioctl(2)).
0	Hang up phone line immediately.
50 75 110 134 150 200 300 600 1200 1800 2400 4800 9600 exta extb	
	Set terminal baud rate to the number given, if possible. (All speeds are not supported by all hardware interfaces.)
[−]hupcl	[Do not] hang up modem connection on last close.
[−]hup	Same as −hupcl.
[−]cstopb	Use two [one] stop bits per character.
[−]cread	Enable [disable] the receiver.
[−]clocal	Assume a line without [with] modem control.
[−]loblk	[Do not] block output from a non-current layer.
[−]ignbrk	[Do not] ignore break on input.
[−]brkint	[Do not] signal interrupt on break.
[−]ignpar	[Do not] ignore parity errors.
[−]parmrk	[Do not] mark parity errors (see ioctl(2)).
[−]inpck	Enable [disable] input parity checking.
[−]istrip	[Do not] strip input characters to seven bits.
[−]inlcr	[Do not] map NL to CR on input.
[−]igncr	[Do not] ignore CR on input.
[−]icrnl	[Do not] map CR to NL on input.
[−]iuclc	[Do not] map upper case alphabetics to lower case on input.

[−]ixon	Enable [disable] start/stop output control. Output is stopped by sending an ASCII DC3 and started by sending an ASCII DC1.
[−]ixany	Allow any character [only DC1] to restart output.
[−]ixoff	Request that the system [not] send start/stop characters when the input queue is nearly empty/full.
[−]opost	[Do not] post-process output (ignore all other output modes).
[−]olcuc	[Do not] map lower case alphabetics to upper case on output.
[−]onlcr	[Do not] map NL to CR-NL on output.
[−]ocrnl	[Do not] map CR to NL on output.
[−]onocr	Do [not] output CRs at column zero.
[−]onlret	On the terminal NL does [not] perform the CR function.
[−]ofill	Use timing [fill characters] for delays.
[−]ofdel	Fill characters are nuls [dels].
cr0 cr1 cr2 cr3	
	Select style of delay for carriage returns (see ioctl(2)).
nl0 nl1	Select style of delay for line feeds (see ioctl(2)).
tab0 tab1 tab2 tab3	
	Select style of delay for horizontal tabs (see ioctl(2).
bs0 bs1	Select style of delay for backspaces (see ioctl(2)).
ff0 ff1	Select style of delay for form feeds (see ioctl(2)).
vt0 vt1	Select style of delay for vertical tabs (see ioctl(2)).
[−]isig	Enable [disable] the checking of characters against the special control characters intr, quit, and swtch.
[−]icanon	Enable [disable] canonical input (erase and kill processing).
[−]xcase	Canonical [unprocessed] upper/lower case presentation.
[−]echo	[Do not] echo back every character typed.
[−]echoe	[Do not] echo erase character as a backspace-space-backspace string. Note: this mode will erase the erased character on many CRT terminals; however, it does not keep track of column position and, as a result, may be confusing on escaped characters, tabs, and backspaces.
[−]echok	[Do not] echo NL after kill character.
[−]echonl	[Do not] echo NL.
[−]noflsh	Enable [disable] flush after intr, quit, or swtch.
[−]stwrap	Enable [disable] truncation of lines longer than 79 characters on a synchronous line.
[−]stflush	Enable [disable] flush on a synchronous line after every write(2).
[−]stappl	Use application [line] mode on a synchronous line.
control-character c	
	Set control-character to c, where control-character is erase, kill, intr, quit, swtch, eof, ctab, min, or time (ctab is used with −stappl; min and time are used with −icanon; see ioctl(2)). If c is preceded by ∧, then the value used is the corresponding control character (e.g. ∧d is ctrl-d); ∧? is interpreted as del and ∧ − is interpreted as undefined.
line i	Set line discipline to i (0 < i < 127).
evenp or parity	
	Enable parenb and cs7.

oddp	Enable parenb, cs7, and parodd.
—parity, —evenp, or —oddp	
	Disable parenb, and set cs8.
raw	Enable raw input and output (no erase, kill, intr, quit, swtch, eot, or output post-processing).
—raw or cooked	
	Disable raw input and output (no erase, kill, intr, quit, swtch, eot, or output post-processing).
nl	Unset icrnl, onlcr.
[—]nl	Set icrnl, onlcr. In addition —nl unsets inlcr, igncr, ocrnl, and onlret.
lcase	Set xcase, iuclc, and olcuc.
[—]lcase	Unset xcase, iuclc, and olcuc.
LCASE	Same as lcase.
[—]LCASE	Same as —lcase.
tabs	Preserve tabs when printing.
[—]tabs or tab3	
	Expand tabs to spaces when printing.
ek	Reset erase and kill characters back to normal # and .
sane	Reset all modes to some reasonable values.
term	Set all modes suitable for the terminal type term, where term is one of tty33, tty37, vt05, tn300, ti700, or tek.

---

style — analyze surface characteristics of a document   STYLE(1)

style [—ml] [—mm] [option ...] file ...

   style analyzes the surface characteristics of the writing style of a document. It reports on readability, sentence length and structure, word length and usage, verb type, and sentence openers. Because style runs deroff before looking at the text, formatting header files should be included as part of the input. The default macro package —ms may be overridden with the option —mm. The option —ml, that causes deroff to skip lists, should be used if the document contains many lists of non-sentences.

Options

—a	Print all sentences with their length and readability index.
—e	Print all sentences that begin with an expletive.
—p	Print all sentences that contain a passive verb.
—l n	Print all sentences longer than n.
—r n	Print all sentences whose readability index is greater than n.
—P	Print parts of speech of the words in the document.

tabs − set tabs on a terminal   TABS (1)

tabs [tabspec] [+mn] [−Ttype]

    tabs sets the tab stops on the user's terminal according to the tab specification
tabspec, after clearing any previous settings. Tab and margin setting is performed
via the standard output. The user's terminal must have remotely-settable hardware
tabs.

    Four types of tab specification are accepted for tabspec: canned, repetitive, ar-
bitrary, and file. If no tabspec is given, the default value is −8. The lowest column
number is 1. Note that for tabs, column 1 always refers to the leftmost column on a
terminal, even one whose column markers begin at 0, e.g. the DASI 300, DASI
300s, and DASI 450.

Options

    −code Gives the name of one of a set of canned tabs. The legal codes and
          their meanings are as follows:

              −a   1,10,16,36,72. Assembler, IBM S/370, first format.
              −a2   1,10,16,40,72. Assembler, IBM S/370, second format.
              −c   1,8,12,16,20,55 5. COBOL, normal format.
              −c2   1,6,10,14,49. COBOL compact format (columns 1−6 om-
                      itted). Using this code, the first typed character
                      corresponds to card column 7, one space gets you to
                      column 8, and a tab reaches column 12. Files using this
                      tab setup should include a format specification as follows:

                      <:t −c2 m6 s66 d:>

              −c3   1,6,10,14,18,22,26,30,34,38,42,46,50,54,58,62,67.
                      COBOL compact format (columns 1−6 omitted), with
                      more tabs than −c2. This is the recommended format for
                      COBOL. The appropriate format specification is

                      <:t −c3 m6 s66 d:>

              −f   1,7,11,15,19,23. FORTRAN.
              −p   1,5,9,13,17,21,25,29,33,37,41,45,49,53,57,61. PL/I.
              −s   1,10,55. SNOBOL.
              −u   1,12,20,44. UNIVAC 1100 Assembler.

    In addition to these 'canned' formats, three other types exist:

             −n   A repetitive specification requests tabs at columns n+1,
                      2*n+1, etc. Of particular importance is the value −8.
                      This represents the UNIX system 'standard' tab setting,
                      and is the most likely tab setting to be found at a terminal.
                      It is required for use with the nroff −h option for high-
                      speed output. Another special case is the value −0, imply-
                      ing no tabs at all.
        n1,n2,...

                      The arbitrary format permits the user to type any chosen

set of numbers, separated by commas, in ascending order. Up to 40 numbers are allowed. If any number (except the first one) is preceded by a +, it is taken as an increment to be added to the previous value.

−−*file*   If the name of the file is given, tabs reads the first line of the file, searching for a format specification. If it finds one there, it sets the tab stops according to it, otherwise it sets them as −8. This type of specification may be used to make sure that a tabbed file is printed with correct tab settings.

Any of the following may be used also; if a given flag occurs more than once, the last value given takes effect:

−T*type*   tabs usually needs to know the type of terminal in order to set tabs and always needs to know the type to set margins. If no −T flag is supplied, tabs searches for the $TERM value in the environment. If no type can be found, tabs tries a sequence that will work for many terminals.

+m*n*   The margin argument may be used for some terminals. It causes all tabs to be moved over *n* columns by making column *n*+1 the left margin. If +m is given without a value of *n*, the value assumed is 10. The normal (leftmost) margin on most terminals is obtained by +m0. The margin for most terminals is reset only when the +m flag is given explicitly.

---

tail – deliver the last part of a file   TAIL (1)

tail [±number [lbc] [f]] [file]

tail copies the named file to the standard output beginning at a designated place. If no file is named, the standard input is used.

Copying begins at distance +number from the beginning, or −number from the end of the input (if number is null, the value 10 is assumed). number is counted in units of lines, blocks, or characters, according to the appended option l, b, or c. When no units are specified, counting is by lines.

With the −f (follow) option, if the input file is not a pipe, the program will not terminate after the line of the input file has been copied, but will enter an endless loop, wherein it sleeps for a second and then attempts to read and copy further records from the input file. Thus it may be used to monitor the growth of a file that is being written by some other process.

tar – tape file archiver   TAR (1)

tar [key] [file] . . .

    tar saves and restores files on magnetic tape. Its actions are controlled by the key argument. The key is a string of characters containing at most one function letter and possibly one or more function modifiers. Other arguments to the command are files (or directory names) specifying which files are to be dumped or restored. In all cases, appearance of a directory name refers to the files and (recursively), sub-directories of that directory.

    The function portion of the key is specified by one of the following letters:

r
: The named files are written on the end of the tape. The c function implies this function.

x
: The named files are extracted from the tape. If a named file matches a directory whose contents had been written onto the tape, this directory is (recursively) extracted. If a named file on tape does not exist on the system, the file is created with the same mode as the one on tape except that the set-user-id and set-group-id bits are not set unless you are super-user. If the files exist, their modes are not changed except for the bits described above. The owner, group, and modification time are restored (if possible). If no files argument is given, the entire content of the tape is extracted. Note that if several files with the same name are on the tape, the last one overwrites all earlier ones.

t
: The names of all the files on the tape are listed.

u
: The named files are added to the tape if they are not already there, or have been modified since last written on that tape.

c
: Create a new tape; writing begins at the beginning of the tape, instead of after the last file. This command implies the r function.

    The following characters may be used in addition to the letter that selects the desired function.

#s
: Where # is a tape drive number (0,. . .,7), and s is the density (l – low (800 bpi), m – medium (1600 bpi), or h – high (6250 bpi)). This modifier selects the drive on which the tape is mounted. The default is 0m.

v
: Normally, tar does its work silently. The v (verbose) option causes it to type the name of each file it treats, preceded by the function letter. With the t function, v gives more information about the tape entries than just the name.

w
: Causes tar to print the action to be taken, followed by the name of the file, and then wait for the user's confirmation. If a word beginning with y is given, the action is performed. Any other input means no.

f	Causes tar to use the next argument as the name of the archive instead of /dev/mt/??. If the name of the file is −, tar writes to the standard output or reads from the standard input, whichever is appropriate. Thus, tar can be used as the head or tail of a pipeline.
b	Causes tar to use the next argument as the blocking factor for tape records. The default is 1, the maximum is 20. This option should only be used with raw magnetic tape archives (see f above). The block size is determined automatically when reading tapes (key letters x and t).
l	Tells tar to complain if it cannot resolve all of the links to the files being dumped. If l is not specified, no error messages are printed.
m	Tells tar not to restore the modification times. The modification time of the file will be the time of extraction.
o	Causes extracted files to take on the user and group identifier of the user running the program rather than those on the tape.

---

tbl – format tables for nroff or troff   TBL (1)

tbl [files] . . .

---

tbl is a preprocessor for formatting tables for nroff or troff(1). The input files are copied to the standard output, except for lines between .TS and .TE command lines, that are assumed to describes tables and are reformatted.

If no arguments are given, tbl reads the standard input, so it may be used as a filter. When it is used with eqn or neqn the tbl command should be first, to minimize the volume of data passed through pipes.

---

test – condition evaluation command   TEST (1)

test expr
[expr]

---

test evaluates the expression expr and, if its value is true, returns a zero exit status; otherwise, a non-zero (false) exit status is returned; test also returns a non-zero exit status if there are no arguments. The following primitives are used to construct expr:

−r file	True if file exists and is readable.
−w file	True if file exists and is writable.
−x file	True if file exists and is executable.
−f file	True if file exists and is a regular file.
−d file	True if file exists and is a directory.
−c file	True if file exists and is a character special file.

−b file	True if file exists and is a block special file.
−p file	True if file exists and is a named pipe (fifo).
−u file	True if file exists and its set-user-id bit is set.
−g file	True if file exists and its set-group-id bit is set.
−k file	True if file exists and its sticky bit is set.
−s file	True if file exists and has a size greater than zero.
−t [fildes]	True if the open file whose file descriptor number is fildes (1 by default) is associated with a terminal device.
−z s1	True if the length of string s1 is zero.
−n s1	True if the length of the string s1 is non-zero.
s1 = s2	True if strings s1 and s2 are identical.
s1 != s2	True if strings s1 and s2 are not identical.
s1	True if s1 is not the null string.
n1 −eq n2	True if the integers n1 and n2 are algebraically equal. Any of the comparisons −ne, −gt, −ge, −lt, and −le may be used in place of −eq.

These primaries may be combined with the following operators:

!	Unary negation operator.
−a	Binary and operator.
−o	BInary or operator (−a has higher precedence than −o).
(expr)	Parentheses are for grouping.

All the operators and flags are separate arguments to test.

---

time – time a command   TIME (1)

time command

command is executed; after it is complete, time prints the elapsed time during the command, the time spent in the system, and the time spent in execution of the command. Times are reported in seconds and are printed on standard error output.

---

touch – update access and modification times of a file   TOUCH (1)

touch [−amc] [mmddhhmm[yy]] file . . .

touch causes the access and modification times of each argument to be updated. The file name is created if it does not exist. If no time is specified (see date(1)) the current time is used. The −a and −m options cause touch to update only the access or modification times respectively (default is −am). The −c option silently prevents touch from creating the file if it did not previously exist.

The return code from touch is the number of files for which the times could not be successfully modified (including files that did not exist and were not created).

tr – translates characters   TR (1)

tr [−cds] [string1 [string2]]

tr copies the standard input to the standard output with substitution or deletion of selected characters. Input characters found in string1 are mapped into the corresponding characters of string2.

Options

Any combination of the options −cds may be used:

−c   Complements the set of characters in string1 with respect to the universe of characters whose ASCII codes are 001 through 377 octal.

−d   Deletes all input characters in string1.

−s   Squeezes all strings of repeated output characters that are in string2 to single characters.

The following abbreviation conventions may be used to introduce ranges of characters or repeated characters into the strings:

[a-z]   Stands for the string of characters whose ASCII codes run from character a to character z, inclusive.

[a*n]   Stands for n repetitions of a. If the first digit of n is 0, n is considered octal; otherwise, n is taken to be decimal. A zero or missing n is taken to be huge; this facility is useful for padding string2.

The escape character \ may be used to remove special meaning from any character in a string. In addition, \ followed by 1, 2, or 3 octal digits stands for the character whose ASCII code is given by those digits.

troff, nroff – text formatting and typesetting   TROFF (1)

troff [option . . .] [file] . . .

nroff [option . . .] [file] . . .

troff formats text in the named files for printing on a phototypesetter; nroff for typewriter-like devices.

If no file argument is present, the standard input is read. An argument consisting of a − is taken as a file name corresponding to the standard input.

Options

The options may appear in any order so long as they appear before the files.

−o list Print only pages whose page numbers appear in the comma-separated list of numbers and ranges. A range $n-m$ means pages n

through *m*; an initial −*n* means from the beginning to page *n*; and a final *n*− means from *n* to the end.

−n *p*   Number first generated page *p*.

−s *n*   Stop every *n* pages. nroff will halt prior to every *n* pages (default *n*=1) to allow paper loading or changing, and will resume on receipt of a newline. troff will stop the phototypesetter every n pages, produce a trailer to allow changing cassettes, and resume when the typesetter's start button is pressed.

−m *name*
     Prepend the macro file /usr/lib/tmac/tmac.*name* to the input files.

−ra *n*   Set register a (one-character) to *n*.

−i   Read standard input after the input files are exhausted.

nroff only

−T name
     Prepare output for specified terminal. Known names are *37* for the (default) Teletype Corporation Model 37 terminal, *tn300* for the GE TermiNet 300 (or any terminal without half-line capability), *300S* for the DASI-300S, *300* for the DASI-300, and *450* for the DASI-450 (Diablo Hiterm).

−e   Produce equally-spaced words in adjusted lines, using full terminal resolution.

−h   Use output tabs during horizontal spacing to speed output and reduce output character count. Tab settings are assumed to be every 8 nominal character widths.

troff only

−t   Direct output to the standard output instead of the phototypesetter.

−f   Refrain from feeding out paper and stopping the phototypesetter at the end of the run.

−w   Wait until the phototypesetter is available, if currently busy.

−b   Report whether the phototypesetter is busy or available. No text processing is done.

−a   Send a printable ASCII approximation of the results to the standard output.

−p n   Print all characters in point size *n* while retaining all precribed spacings and motions, to reduce phototypesetter elapsed time.

---

tsort – topological sort   TSORT (1)

tsort [file]

   tsort produces on the standard output a totally ordered list of items
consistent with a partial ordering of items mentioned in the input file. If no file is
specified, the standard input is understood.
   The input consists of pairs of items (non-empty strings) separated by
blanks. Pairs of different items indicate ordering. Pairs of identical items
indicate presence, but not ordering.

---

uniq – report repeated lines in a file   UNIQ (1)

uniq [−udc [+ n] [− n]] [input [output]]

   uniq reads the input file comparing adjacent lines. In the normal case, the
second and succeeding copies of repeated lines are removed; the remainder is
written on the output file. Repeated lines must be adjacent in order to be found;
see sort(1). If the −u flag is used, the lines that are not repeated in the original
file are output. The −d option specifies that one copy of the repeated lines is to
be written. The normal mode of output is the union of the −u and −d mode
outputs.
   The −c option supersedes −u and −d and generates an output report in
default style but with each line preceded by a count of the number of times it
occurred.
   The n arguments specify skipping an initial portion of each line in the
comparison:

   − n   The first n field together with any blanks before each are ignored.
            A field is defined as a string of non-blank characters separated by
            white space from its neighbors.
   + n   The first n characters are ignored. Fields are skipped before
            characters.

---

units – conversion program   UNITS (1)

units

   units converts quantities expressed in various standard scales to their
equivalents in other scales. It works interactively in this fashion.:

                You have: *inch*
                You want: *cm*
                     * 2.54000e+00
                     / 3.93701e−01

A quantity is specified as a multiplicative combination of units optionally
preceded by a numeric multiplier. Powers are indicated by suffixed positive
integers, division by the usual sign:

You have: *15 pounds forcelin2*
You want: *atm*
    * 1.02069e+00
    / 9.79730e−01

units only does multiplicative scale changes. Thus it can convert Kelvin to Rankine, but not Centigrade to Fahrenheit. Most familiar units, abbreviations, and metric prefixes are recognized, together with a generous leavening of exotica and a few constants of nature including:

pi	Ratio of circumference to diameter
c	Speed of light.
e	Charge on an electron.
g	Acceleration of gravity.
force	same as g.
mole	Avogadro's number.
water	Pressure head per unit height of water.
au	Astronomical unit.

pound is not a unit of mass, lb is. Compound names are run together, e.g. lightyear. British units that differ from their US counterparts are prefixed thus: brgallon. Currency is denoted belgiumfranc, britainpound, . . .

For a complete list of units, cat/usr/lib/unitttab.

---

uucp – unix to unix copy   UUCP (1)

uucp [option] . . . source-file . . . destination-file

uucp copies files named by the source-file arguments to the destination-file argument. A file name may be a pathname on your machine, or may have the form

system-name!pathname

where system-name is taken from a list of system-names which uucp knows about. Shell metacharacters ?* [ ] appearing in the pathname part will be expanded on the appropriate system.

Pathnames may be one of the following.

- A full pathname.
- A pathname preceded by ~user; where user is a login-name on the specified system and is replaced by that user's login directory.
- Anything else is prefixed by the current directory.

If the result is an erroneous pathname for the remote system the copy will fail. If the destination-file is a directory, the last part of the source-file name is used. If a simple ~user destination is inaccessible to uucp, data is copied to a spool directory and the user is notified by mail(1).

uucp preserves execute permissions across the transmission and gives 0666 read and write permissions (see chmod(2)).

Options

−d	Make all necessary directories for the file copy.
−c	Use the source file when copying out rather than copying the file to the spool directory.
−C	Copy the source file to the spool directory.
−f	Do not make intermediate directories for the file copy.
−m	Send mail to the requester when the copy is complete.
−n	Notify the user on the remote system that a file was sent.
−e *sys*	Send the uucp command to *sys* to be executed there.
−r	Queue job but do not start the file transfer process. By default a file transfer process is started each time uucp is evoked.
−j	Control writing of the uucp job number to standard output.

---

vi – screen oriented (visual) display editor   VI (1)

vi [−t tag] [+request] [−l] [−wn] [−R] name . . .

vi (visual) is the display oriented text editor described in chapter 3. The name argument indicates files to be edited.

Options

−t *tag*	Edit the file containing *tag* and position the editor at its definition.
−r *x*	Recover file *x* following a system crash or terminal hangup.
−l	lisp mode; indents appropriately for lisp code. The () {} [[and]] commands in vi and open are modified to have meaning for lisp.
−w *n*	Set the initial window size to *n*.
−R	Read only mode. The readonly flag is set, preventing accidental overwriting of the file.
+ *request*	Execute *request* before reading requests from the terminal; useful for initial positioning of the file. The default is to start at the last line of the document.

---

wc – word count   WC(1)

wc [−lwc] [file] . . .

wc counts lines, words, and characters in the named files, or in the standard input if no names appear. It also keeps a total count for all named files. A word is a maximal string of characters delimited by a blank, tab, or newline.

The options l, w, and c may be used in any combinations to specify that a subset of lines, words, and characters are to be reported. The default is −lwc.

When files are specified on the command line, they will be printed along with the counts.

---

who – who is on the system   WHO(1)

who [option] [file]

who am i

who am I

who can list the user's name, terminal line, login time, elapsed time since activity occurred on the line, and the process-id of the command interpreter (shell) for each current user. It examines the /etc/utmp file to obtain its information. If file is given, that file is examined. Usually, file will be /etc/wtmp, which contains a history of all the logins since the file was last created.

who with the am i or am I option identifies the invoking user.

Except for the default −s option, the general format for output entries is:

name [state] line time activity pid [comment] [exit]

With options, who can list logins, logoffs, reboots, and changes to the system clock, as well as other processes spawned by the init process.

Options

−u   List on those users who are currently logged in. The name is the user's login name. The line is the name of the line as found in the directory /dev. The time is the time that the user logged in. The activity is the number of hours and minutes since activity last occurred on that particular line. A . indicates that the terminal has seen activity in the last minute and is therefore current. If more than twenty-four hours have elapsed or the line has not been used since boot time, the entry is marked old. This field is useful when trying to determine whether a person is working at the terminal or not. The pid is the process-id of the user's shell. The comment is the comment field associated with this line as found in /etc/inittab. This can contain information about where the terminal is located, the telephone number of the dataset, type of terminal if hard-wired, etc.

−T   This option is the same as the −u option, except that the state of the terminal line is printed. The state describes whether someone else can write to that terminal. A + appears if the terminal is writable by anyone; a − appears if it is not. The super-user can write to all lines having a + or a − in the state field. If a bad line is encountered, a ? is printed.

−I   List only those lines on which the system is waiting for someone to login. The name field is LOGIN in such cases. Other fields are the same as for user entries except that the state field does not exist.

-H   Print column headings above the regular output.

-d   This is a quick who, displaying only the names and the number of users currently logged on. When this option is used, all other options are ignored.

-p   List any other process which is currently active and has been previously spawned by init. The name field is the name of the program executed by init as found in /etc/inittab. The state, line, and activity fields have no meaning. The comment field shows the id field of the line from /etc/inittab that spawned this process.

-d   Display all processes that have expired and not been respawned by init. The exit field appears for dead processes and contains the termination and exit values (as returned by wait(2)), of the dead process. This can be useful in determining why a process terminated.

-b   Indicate the time and date of the last reboot.

-r   Indicate the current run-level of the init process.

-t   Indicate the last change to the system clock (via the date(1) command).

-a   Process /etc/utmp or the named file with all options turned on.

-s   This option is the default and lists only the name, line, and time fields.

---

write – write to another user   WRITE(1)

write user [line]

write copies lines from your terminal to that of another user. When first called, it sends the message:

Message from yourname (tty??) [date] . . .

to the person you want to talk to. When it has successfully completed the connection, it also sends two bells to your own terminal to indicate that what you are typing is being sent.

The recipient of the message should write back at this point. Communication continues until an end-of-file is read from the terminal, an interrupt is sent, or the recipient has executed "mesg n". At that point write writes EOT on the other terminal and exits.

If you want to write to a user who is logged in more than once, the line argument may be used to indicate which line or terminal to send to (e.g., tty00); otherwise, the first writable instance of the user found in /etc/utmp is assumed and the following message posted:

user is logged on more than one place.
You are connected to "terminal".
Other locations are:

terminal

Permission to write may be denied or granted by use of the mesg(1) command. Writing to others is normally allowed by default. Certain commands, in particular nroff(1) and pr(1) disallow messages in order to prevent interference with their output. However, if the user has super-user permissions, messages can be forced onto a write-inhibited terminal.

If the character ! is found at the beginning of a line, write calls the shell to execute the rest of the line as a command.

The following protocol is suggested for using write: when you first write to another user, wait for a response before starting to send. Each person should end a message with a distinctive signal (i.e. (o) for over) so that the other person knows when to reply. The signal (oo) (for over and out) is suggested when the conversation is to be terminated.

---

yacc – yet another compiler-compiler   YACC(1)

yacc [−vdlt] grammar

yacc converts a context-free grammar into a set of tables for a simple automaton which executes an LR(1) parsing algorithm. The grammar may be ambiguous; specified precedence rules are used to break ambiguities.

The output file, y.tab.c, must be compiled by the C compiler to produce a program yyparse. This program must be loaded with the lexical analyzer program, yylex, as well as main and yyerror, an error handling routine. These routines must be supplied by the user; lex(1) is useful for creating lexical analyzers usable by yacc.

If the −v flag is given, the file y.output is prepared, which contains a description of the parsing tables and a report on conflicts generated by ambiguities in the grammer.

If the −d flag is used, the file y.tab.h is generated, with the #define statements that associate the yacc-assigned token codes with the user-declared token names. This allows source files other than y.tab.c to access the token codes.

If the −l flag is given, the code produced in y.tab.c will not contain any #line constructs. This should only be used after the grammar and the associated actions are fully debugged.

Runtime debugging code is always generated in y.tab.c under conditional compilation control. By default, this code is not included when y.tab.c is compiled. However, when the −t option is used, this debugging code will be compiled by default. Independent of whether the −t option was used, the runtime debugging code is under the control of YYDEBUG, a preprocessor symbol. If YYDEBUG has a non-zero value, then the debugging code is included. If its value is zero, then the code will not be included. The size and execution time of a program produced without the runtime debugging code will be smaller and slightly faster.

Appendix 2 **System Calls**

---

access – determine accessibility of a file ACCESS(2)

```
int access(name, mode)
char *name;
int mode;
```

      access checks the file name for accessibility according to mode, using the real user-id in place of the effective user-id and the real group-id in place of the effective group-id. mode is 04 (read), 02 (write), 01 (execute), 00 (check existence of file), or a combination thereof.

      access returns 0 if successful, −1 otherwise.

---

alarm – set a process alarm clock ALARM(2)

```
unsigned alarm(seconds)
unsigned seconds;
```

      alarm instructs the alarm clock of the calling process to send the signal SIGALRM to the calling process in a number of real time seconds specified by the argument.

      alarm requests are not stacked; successive calls reset the alarm clock of the calling process.

      If the argument is 0, any previously made alarm request is canceled.

      The return value is the amount of time remaining in the previously called alarm clock.

---

brk, sbrk – change data segment space allocation BRK(2)

```
int brk(addr)
char *addr;

char *sbrk(incr)
int incr;
```

      brk and sbrk are used to change dynamically the amount of space allocated for the calling process's data segment; see exec(2). The change is made by resetting the process's break value and allocating the appropriate amount of space. The break value is the address of the first location beyond the end of the data segment. The amount of allocated space increases as the break value increases. The newly allocated space is set to zero.

      brk sets the break value to addr and changes the allocated space accordingly.

sbrk adds incr bytes to the break value and changes the allocated space accordingly. incr can be negative, in which case the amount of allocated space is decreased.

brk and sbrk will fail without making any change in the allocated space if the space being requested exceeds the system-imposed maximum defined by ulimit(2).

If successful, brk returns a value of 0 and sbrk returns the old break value. Otherwise, −1 is returned.

---

chdir − change working directory   CHDIR (2)

```
int chdir(dirname)
char *dirname;
```

chdir causes the directory dirname to become the current working directory. chdir returns 0 if successful, −1 otherwise.

---

chmod − change mode of file   CHMOD (2)

```
int chmod(name, mode)
char *name;
int mode;
```

name points to the pathname of a file. chmod sets the access permission portion of the named file's mode according to the bit pattern contained in mode.

Access permission bits are interpreted as follows:

04000	Set user-id on execution.
02000	Set group-id on execution.
01000	Save text image after execution.
00400	Read by owner.
00200	Write by owner.
00100	Execute (search if a directory) by owner.
00070	Read, write, execute (search) by group.
00007	Read, write, execute (search) by others.

The *effective-user-id* of the process must match the owner of the file or be super-user to change the mode of a file.

If the *effective-user-id* of the process is not super-user, mode bit 01000 (save text image on execution) is cleared.

If the *effective-user-id* of the process is not super-user and the *effective-group-id* of the process does not match the group-id of the file, mode bit 02000 *(set group-id* on execution) is cleared.

If an executable file is prepared for sharing then mode bit 01000 prevents the system from abandoning the swap-space image of the program-text portion of the file when its last user terminates. Thus, when the next user of the file executes it, the text need not be read from the file system but can simply be swapped in, saving time.

chmod returns 0 if successful, −1 otherwise.

close – close a file descriptor   CLOSE (2)

int close(fildes)
int fildes;

>   close closes the file descriptor indicated by fildes.
>   close returns 0 if successful, −1 otherwise.

---

creat – create a new file or rewrite an existing one   CREAT (2)

int creat(name, mode)
char *name;
int mode;

>   creat creates a new ordinary file or prepares to rewrite an existing file called name.
>   If the file exists, the length is truncated to 0 and the mode and owner are unchanged. Otherwise, the file's owner-id is set to the effective user-id of the process and the group-id of the file is set to the effective group-id. The low-order 12 bits of the file mode are set to the value of mode with all bits set in the process's file mode creation mask cleared. The 'save text image after execution bit' of the mode is cleared.
>   Upon successful completion, the file descriptor is returned and the file is open for writing, even if the mode does not permit writing. The file pointer is set to the beginning of the file. The file descriptor is set to remain open across exec system calls (see fcntl(2)). No process may have more than 20 files open simultaneously. A new file may be created with a mode that forbids writing.
>   creat returns the file descriptor if successful, −1 otherwise.

---

dup – duplicate an open file descriptor   DUP (2)

int dup(fildes)
int fildes;

>   dup returns a new file descriptor having the same open file, file pointer, and access mode as fildes.
>   The new file descriptor is set to remain open across exec system calls. See fcntl(2).
>   The file descriptor returned is the lowest one available.
>   dup returns the file descriptor if successful, −1 otherwise.

---

errno – system call error numbers   ERRNO (2)

#include <errno.h>

Most system calls have one or more error returns. An error condition is indicated by an otherwise impossible returned value. This is almost always −1; the individual descriptions specify the details. An error number is also made available in the external variable errno. errno is not cleared on successful calls, so it should be tested only after an error has been indicated.

The following is a complete list of the error numbers and their names as defined in <errno.h>.

1 EPERM Not owner

Typically indicates an attempt to modify a file in some way forbidden except to its owner or super-user. It is also returned for attempts by ordinary users to do things allowed only to the super-user.

2 ENOENT No such file or directory

Occurs when a file name does not exist, or when one of the directories in a pathname does not exist.

3 ESRCH No such process

No process can be found corresponding to that specified by pid in kill.

4 EINTR Interrupted system call

An asynchronous signal (such as interrupt or quit), which the user has elected to catch, occurred during a system call. If execution is resumed after processing the signal, it will appear as if the interrupted system call returned this error condition.

5 EIO input-output error

Some physical input-output error has occurred. This error may in some cases occur on a call following the one to which it actually applies.

6 ENXIO No such device or address

Input-output on a special file refers to a subdevice which does not exist, or beyond the limits of the device. It may also occur when, for example, a tape drive is not on-line or no disk pack is loaded on a drive.

7 E2BIG Arg list too long

An argument list longer than 5120 bytes is presented to a member of the exec family.

8 ENOEXEC Exec format error

A request is made to execute a file which, although it has the appropriate permissions, does not start with a valid magic number.

9 EBADF Bad file number

Either a file descriptor refers to no open file, or a read (respectively, write) request is made to a file which is open only for writing (respectively, reading).

10 ECHILD No child processes

A wait was executed by a process that had no existing or unwaited-for child processes.

11 EAGAIN No more processes

A fork failed because the system's process table is full or the user is not allowed to create any more processes.

12 ENOMEM Not enough space

During an exec, brk, or sbrk, a program asks for more space than the system is able to supply. This is not a temporary condition; the maximum space size is a system parameter. The error may also occur if the arrangement of text, data, and stack segments requires too many segmentation registers, or if there is not enough swap space during a fork.

13 EACCES Permission denied

> An attempt was made to access a file in a way forbidden by the protection system.

14 EFAULT Bad address

> The system encountered a hardware fault in attempting to use an argument of a system call.

15 ENOTBLK Block device required

> A non-block file was mentioned where a block device was required, e.g. in mount.

16 EBUSY Device or resource busy

> An attempt was made to mount a device that was already mounted or an attempt was made to dismount a device on which there is an active file (open file, current directory, mounted-on file, active text segment). It will also occur if an attempt is made to enable accounting when it is already enabled. The device or resource is currently unavailable.

17 EEXIST File exists

> An existing file was mentioned in an inappropriate context, e.g. link.

18 EXDEV Cross-device link

> A link to a file on another device was attempted.

19 ENODEV No such device

> An attempt was made to apply an inappropriate system call to a device; e.g. read a write-only device.

20 ENOTDIR Not a directory

> A non-directory was specified where a directory is required, for example in a path prefix or as an argument to chdir(2).

21 EISDIR Is a directory

> An attempt was made to write on a directory.

22 EINVAL Invalid argument

> Some invalid argument, e.g. dismounting a non-mounted device; mentioning an undefined signal in signal, or kill; reading or writing a file for which lseek has generated a negative pointer. Also set by the math functions described in section 3M of the manual.

23 ENFILE File table overflow

> The system file table is full, and temporarily no more opens can be accepted.

24 EMFILE Too many open files

> No process may have more than 20 file descriptors open at a time.

25 ENOTTY Not a character device

> Use of ioctl (2) on a file that is not a special character device.

26 ETXTBSY Text file busy

> An attempt was made to execute a pure-procedure program that is currently open for writing. Also an attempt to open for writing a pure-procedure program that is being executed.

27 EFBIG File too large

> The size of a file exceeded the maximum file size (1 082 201 088 bytes) or ULIMIT; see ulimit(2).

28 ENOSPC No space left on device

> During a write to an ordinary file, there is no free space left on the

device.

29 ESPIPE Illegal seek

An lseek was issued to a pipe.

30 EROFS Read-only file system

An attempt to modify a file or directory was made on a device mounted read-only.

31 EMLINK Too many links

An attempt to make more than the maximum number of links (1000) to a file.

32 EPIPE Broken pipe

A write on a pipe for which there is no process to read the data. This condition normally generates a signal; the error is returned if the signal is ignored.

33 EDOM Math argument

The argument of a function in the math package (3M) is out of the domain of the function.

34 ERANGE Result too large

The value of a function in the math package (3M) is not representable within machine precision.

35 ENOMSG No message of desired type

An attempt was made to receive a message of a type that does not exist on the specified message queue.

36 EIDRM Identifier Removed

This error is returned to processes that resume execution due to the removal of an identifier from the file system's name space.

45 EDEADLK Deadlock

A deadlock situation was detected and avoided.

Definitions

process-id

Each active process in the system is uniquely identified by a positive integer called a process-id. The range of the process-id is from 1 to 30 000.

parent process-id

A new process is created by a currently active process; see fork(2). The parent process-id of a process is the process-id of its creator.

process group-id

Each active process is a member of a process group that is identified by a positive integer called the process group-id. The process-id of the group leader is used to identify the process group. This grouping permits the signaling of related processes; see kill(2).

tty group-id

Each active process can be a member of a terminal group that is identified by a positive integer called the tty group-id. This grouping is used to terminate a group of related processes upon termination of one of the processes in the group; see exit(2) and signal(2).

real user-id and real group-id

Each user allowed on the system is identified by a positive integer called a real user-id. Each user is also a member of a group. The group is identified by a positive integer called the real group-id.

An active process has a real user-id and real group-id that are set to the real user-id and real group-id, respectively, of the user responsible for the creation of the process.

effective user-id and effective group-id

An active process has an effective user-id and an effective group-id that are used to determine file access permissions. The effective user-id and effective group-id are equal to the process's real user-id and real group-id respectively, unless the process or one of its ancestors evolved from a file that had the set-user-id bit or set-group-id bit set; see exec(2).

super-user

A process is recognized as a super-user process and is granted special privileges if its effective user-id is 0.

special processes

The processes with a process-id of 0 and a process-id of 1 are special processes and are referred to as proc0 and proc1. proc0 is the scheduler. proc1 is the initialization process (init). proc1 is the ancestor of every other process in the system and is used to control the process structure.

file descriptor

A file descriptor is a small integer used as a handle for input-output on a file. The value of a file descriptor is from 0 to 19. A process may have no more than 20 file descriptors (0–19) open simultaneously. A file descriptor is returned by system calls such as open(2), or pipe(2). The file descriptor is used as an argument by calls such as read(2), write(2), ioctl(2), and close(2).

file name

Names consisting of 1 to 14 characters may be used to name an ordinary file, special file or directory. Characters may be selected from the set of all character values excluding \0 (null) and the ASCII code for /.

It is generally unwise to use *, ?, [, or] as part of file names because of the special meaning attached to these characters by the shell. Although permitted, it is advisable to avoid the use of unprintable characters in file names.

path name and path prefix

A pathname is a null-terminated character string starting with an optional slash (/), followed by zero or more directory names separated by slashes, optionally followed by a file name.

More precisely, a pathname is a null-terminated character string constructed as follows:

```
<path-name>::=<file-name> | <path-prefix><file-name> | /
<path-prefix>::=<rtprefix> | /<rtprefix>
<rtprefix>::=<dirname>/ | <rtprefix><dirname>/
```

where <file-name> is a string of 1 to 14 characters other than the ASCII slash and null, and <dirname> is a string of 1 to 14 characters (other than the ASCII slash and null) that names a directory.

If a pathname begins with a slash, the path search begins at the root directory. Otherwise, the search begins from the current working directory.

A slash by itself names the root directory.

Unless specifically stated otherwise, the null pathname is treated as if it named a non-existent file.

directory

> Directory entries are called links. By convention, a directory contains at least two links, . and .., referring to the directory itself and its parent directory respectively.

root directory and current working directory

> Each process has associated with it a root directory and a current working directory for resolving pathname searches. The root directory of a process need not be the root directory of the root file system.

file access permissions

> Read, write, and execute/search permissions on a file are granted to a process if one or more of the following are true:

- The effective user-id of the process is super-user.
- The effective user-id of the process matches the user-id of the owner of the file and the appropriate access bit of the 'owner' portion (0700) of the file mode is set.
- The effective user-id of the process does not match the user-id of the owner of the file, and the effective group-id of the process matches the group of the file and the appropriate access bit of the 'group' portion (070) of the file mode is set.
- The effective user-id of the process does not match the user-id of the owner of the file, and the effective group-id of the process does not match the group-id of the file, and the appropriate access bit of the 'other' portion (07) of the file mode is set.

Otherwise, the corresponding permissions are denied.

---

execl, execv, execle, execve, execlp, execvp – execute a file   EXEC(2)

```
int execl(name, arg0, arg1, ..., argn, 0)
char *name, *arg0, *arg1, ..., *argn;

int execv(name, argv)
char *name, *argv[];
```

exec in all its forms transforms the calling process into a new process. The new process is constructed from an ordinary, executable file (the *new process file*). This file consists of a header, a text segment, and a data segment. The data segment contains an initialized portion and an uninitialized portion (bss). There can be no return from a successful exec because the calling process is overlaid by the new process.

name points to a pathname that identifies the new process file.

argv is an array of character pointers to null-terminated strings. These strings constitute the argument list available to the new process. By convention, argv must have at least one member, and it must point to a string that is the same as name (or its last component). argv is terminated by a null pointer.

envp is a pointer to an array of strings that constitute the environment of the process. Each string consists of a name, an =, and a null-terminated string value. The array of pointers is terminated by a null pointer.

The C runtime start-off routine places a copy of envp in the global cell environ, which is used by execv and execl to pass the environment to any subprograms executed by the current program. The exec routines use lower-level routines as follows to pass an environment explicitly:

```
execve(file, argv, environ);
execle(file, arg0, arg1, ..., argn, 0, environ);
```

execlp and execvp are called with same arguments as execl and execv, but duplicate the shell's actions in searching for an executable file in a list of directories. The directory list is obtained from the environment.

File descriptors open in the calling process remain open in the new process, except for those whose close-on-exec flag is set (see fcntl(2)). For those file descriptors that remain open, the file pointer is unchanged.

Signals set to terminate the calling process will be set to terminate the new process. Signals set to be ignored by the calling process will be set to be ignored by the new process. Signals set to be caught by the calling process will be set to terminate new process (see signal(2)).

If the *set user-id* mode bit of the new process file is set (see chmod(2)), exec sets the *effective-user-id* of the new process to the owner-id of the new process file. Similarly, if the *set-group-id* mode bit of the new process file is set, the *effective-group-id* of the new process is set to the group-id of the new process file. The *real-user-id* and *real-group-id* of the new process remain the same as those of the calling process.

Profiling is disabled for the new process; see profil(2).

The new process also inherits the following attributes from the calling process:

- Nice value (see nice(2)).
- Process-id.
- Parent process-id.
- Process group-id.
- tty group-id (see exit(2) and signal(2)).
- Trace flag.
- Time left until an alarm clock signal (see alarm(2)).
- Current working directory.
- Root directory.
- File mode creation mask (see umask(2)).
- File size limit (see ulimit(2)).
- utime, stime, cutime, and cstime (see times(2)).

If exec returns to the calling process an error has occurred; the return value will be −1 and errno will be set.

exit − terminate process   EXIT (2)

```
void exit(status)
int status;
```

```
void _exit(status)
int status;
```

exit terminates the calling process with the following consequences:

- All of the file descriptors open in the calling process are closed.
- If the parent process of the calling process is executing a wait, it is notified of the calling process's termination and the low order eight bits (i.e. bits 0377) of status are made available to it; see wait(2).
- If the parent process of the calling process is not executing a wait, the calling process is transformed into a zombie process. A zombie process is a process that only occupies a slot in the process table. It has no other space allocated either in user or kernel space. The process table slot that it occupies is partially overlaid with time accounting information (see <sys/proc.h>). to be used by times.
- The parent process-id of all of the calling process's existing child processes and zombie processes is set to 1. This means the initialization process inherits each of these processes.
- An accounting record is written on the accounting file if the system's accounting routine is enabled.
- If the process-id, tty group-id, and process group-id of the calling process are equal, the SIGHUP signal is sent to each process that has a process group-id equal to that of the calling process.

The C function exit may cause cleanup actions before the process exits. The function _exit circumvents all cleanup.

---

fcntl − file control   FCNTL (2)

`#include <fcntl.h>`

```
int fcntl(fildes, cmd, arg)
int fildes, cmd, arg;
```

fcntl provides for control over open files. fildes is an open file descriptor obtained from a creat, open, dup, fcntl, or pipe system call.

The commands available are:

F_DUPFD   Return the lowest numbered available file descriptor greater than or equal to arg. The file descriptor has the same open file (or pipe) as the original fiie, the same file pointer as the original fiie (i.e. both file descriptors share one file pointer), the same access mode (read, write or read/write), and the same file status flags (i.e. both file descriptors share the same file status flags).
The close-on-exec flag associated with the new file descriptor is set to remain open across exec(2) system calls.

F_GETFD   Get the close-on-exec flag associated with the file descriptor
            fildes. If the low-order bit is 0 the file will remain open across
            exec, otherwise the file will be closed upon execution of exec.

F_SETFD   Set the close-on-exec flag associated with fildes to the low-order
            bit of arg (0 or 1 as above).

F_GETFL   Get file status flags.

F_SETFL   Set file status flags to arg. Only certain flags can be set.

F_GETLK   Get the first lock which blocks the lock description given by the
            variable of type struct flock pointed to by arg. The information re-
            trieved overwrites the information passed to fcntl in the flock
            structure. If no lock is found that would prevent this lock from
            being created, then the structure is passed back unchanged except
            for the lock type which will be set to F_UNLCK.

F_SETLK   Set or clear a file segment lock according to the variable of type
            struct flock pointed to by arg. The cmd F_SETLK is used to estab-
            lish read (F_RDLCK) and write (F_WRLCK) locks, as well as re-
            move either type of lock (F_UNLCK). If a read or write lock can-
            not be set, fcntl will return immediately with an error value of −1.

F_SETLKW   This cmd is the same as F_SETLK except that if a read or write
            lock is blocked by other locks, the process will sleep until the
            segment is free to be locked.

A read lock prevents any process from write locking the protected area. More
than one read lock may exist for a given segment of a file at a given time. The file
descriptor on which a read lock is being placed must have been opened with read
access.

A write lock prevents any process from read locking or write locking the protected area. Only one write lock may exist for a given segment of a file at a given
time. The file descriptor on which a write lock is being placed must have been
opened with write access.

The structure flock describes the type (l_type), starting offset (l_whence), relative offset (l_start), size (l_len), and process-id (l_pid) of the segment of the file to be
affected. The process-id field is only used with the F_GETLK cmd to return the
value for a block in lock. Locks may start and extend beyond the current end of a
file, but may not be negative relative to the beginning of the file. A lock may be
set to always extend to the end of file by setting l_len to zero (0). If such a lock
also has l_start set to zero (0), the whole file will be locked. Changing or unlock-
ing a segment from the middle of a larger locked segment leaves two smaller segments for either end. Locking a segment that is already locked by the calling process causes the old lock type to be removed and the new lock type to take effect.
All locks associated with a file for a given process are removed when a file
descriptor for that file is closed by that process or the process holding that file
descriptor terminates. Locks are not inherited by a child process in a fork(2) system call.

Upon successful completion, the value returned depends on cmd as follows:

F_DUPFD   A new file descriptor.

F_GETFD   Value of flag (only the low-order bit is defined).

F_SETFD   Value other than −1.

F_GETFL	Value of file flags.
F_SETFL	Value other than −1.
F_GETLK	Value other than −1.
F_SETLK	Value other than −1.
F_SETLKW	Value other than −1.

Otherwise, a value of −1 is returned and errno is set to indicate the error.

---

fork − create a new process   FORK(2)

int fork( )

fork causes creation of a new process. The new process (child process) is an exact copy of the calling process (parent process). This means the child process inherits the following attributes from the parent process:

- Environment.
- Close-on-exec flag (see exec(2)).
- Signal handling settings (i.e. SIG_DFL, SIG_ING, function address).
- Set-user-id mode bit.
- Set-group-id mode bit.
- Profiling on/off status.
- Nice value (see nice(2)).
- Process group-id.
- tty group-id (see exit(2) and signal(2)).
- Trace flag (used by debuggers).
- Time left until an alarm clock signal (see alarm(2)).
- Current working directory.
- Root directory.
- File mode creation mask (see umask(2)).
- File size limit (see ulimit(2)).

The child process differs from the parent process in the following ways:

- The child process has a unique process-id.
- The child process has a different parent process-id (i.e. the process-id of the parent process).
- The child process has its own copy of the parent's file descriptors. Each of the child's file descriptors shares a common file pointer with the corresponding file descriptor of the parent.
- The child process's utime, stime, cutime, and cstime are set to 0. The time left until an alarm clock signal is reset to 0.

Upon successful completion, fork returns a value of 0 to the child process and returns the process-id of the child process to the parent process. Otherwise, a value of −1 is returned to the parent process, no child process is created, and errno is set.

getuid, geteuid, getgid, getegid – get user-id and group-id   GETUID(2)

```
unsigned short getuid( )
unsigned short geteuid( )
unsigned short getgid( )
unsigned short getegid( )
```

getuid returns the real user-id of the current process, geteuid the effective user-id. The real user-id identifies the person who is logged in, in contradistinction to the effective user-id, that determines the access permission at the moment. It is thus useful to programs using the *set user-id* mode, to find out who invoked them.

getgid returns the real group-id, getegid the effective group-id.

---

ioctl – control device   IOCTL(2)

```
ioctl(fildes, request, arg)
int fildes, request;
```

ioctl performs a variety of functions on character special files (devices).

Several ioctl(2) system calls apply to terminal files. The primary calls use the following structure, defined in <termio.h>:

```
#define NCC8
struct termio {
            unsigned short    c_iflag;          /* input modes */
            unsigned short    c_oflag;          /* output modes */
            unsigned short    c_cflag;          /* control modes */
            unsigned short    c_lflag;          /* local modes */
            char              c_line;           /* line discipline */
            unsigned char     c_cc[ NCC ];      /* control chars */
};
```

The special control characters are defined by the array c_cc. The relative positions and initial values for each function are as follows:

0	VINTR	DEL
1	VQUIT	FS
2	VERASE	#
3	VKILL	@
4	VEOF	EOT
5	VEOL	NUL
6	reserved	
7	SWTCH	NUL

The c_flag field describes the basic terminal input control.

IGNBRK	0000000	Ignore break condition.
BRKINT	0000000	Signal interrupt on break.
IGNPAR	0000000	Ignore characters with parity errors.
PARMRK	0000000	Mark parity errors.
INPCK	0000000	Enable input parity check.

ISTRIP	0000000	Strip character.
INLCR	0000000	Map NL to CR on input.
IGNCR	0000000	Ignore CR.
ICRNL	0000000	Map CR to NL on input.
IRCLC	0000000	Map upper case to lower case on input.
IXON	0000000	Enable start/stop output control.
IXANY	0000000	Enable any character to restart output.
IXOFF	0000000	Enable start/stop input control.

If IGNBRK is set, the break condition (a character framing error with data all zeros) is ignored, that is, not put on the input queue and therefore not read by any process. Otherwise, if BRKINT is set, the break condition will generate an interrupt signal and flush both the input and output queues. If IGNPAR is set, characters with other framing and parity errors are ignored.

If PARMRK is set, a character with a framing or parity error which is not ignored is read as the three-character sequence 0377, 0, X where X is the data of the character received in error. To avoid ambiguity in this case, if ISTRIP is set, a valid character of 0377 is read as 0377, 0377. If PARMRK is not set, a framing or parity error which is not ignored is read as the character NUL (0).

If INPCK is set, input parity checking is enabled, otherwise it is disabled. This allows output parity generation without input parity errors.

If ISTRIP is set, valid input characters are first stripped to 7 bits, otherwise all 8 bits are processed.

If INLCR is set, a received NL character is translated into a CR character. If IGNCR is set, a received CR character is ignored (not read). Otherwise, if ICRNL is set, a received CR character is translated into a NL character.

If IUCLC is set, a received upper case alphabetic character is translated into the corresponding lower case character.

If IXON is set, start/stop output control is enabled. A received *stop* character will suspend output and a received *start* character will restart ouptut. All start/stop characters are ignored and not read. If IXANY is set, any input character will restart suspended output.

If IXOFF is set, the system will transmit start/stop characters when the input queue is nearly empty or full respectively.

The initial input control value is all-bits-clear.

The c_oflag field specifies the system treatment of output.

OPOST	0000001	Post-process output.
OLCUC	0000002	Map lower case to upper case on output.
ONLCR	0000004	Map NL to CR-NL on output.
OCRNL	0000010	Map CR to NL on output.
ONOCR	0000020	No CR output at column 0.
ONLRET	0000040	NL performs CL function.
OFILL	0000100	Use fill characters for delay.
OFDEL	0000200	Fill is DEL, else NUL.
NLDLY	0000400	Select newline delays.
	NL0	0
	NL1	0000400
CRDLY	0003000	Select carriage return delays.

	CR0	0
	CR1	0001000
	CR2	0002000
	CR3	0003000
TABDLY	0014000	Select horizontal tab delays.
	TAB0	0
	TAB1	0004000
	TAB2	0010000
	TAB3	0014000 Expand tabs to spaces.
BSDLY	0020000	Select backspace delays.
	BS0	0
	BS1	0020000
VTDLY	0040000	Select vertical tab delays.
	VT0	0
	VT1	0040000
FFDLY	0100000	Select form feed delays.
	FF0	0
	FF1	0100000

If OPOST is set, output characters are post-processed as indicated by the remaining flags, otherwise characters are transmitted without change.

If OLCUC is set, a lower case alphabetic character is transmitted as the corresponding upper case character. This function is often used in conjunction with IUCLC.

If ONCLR is set, the NL character is transmitted as the CR-NL character pair. If OCRNL is set, no CR character is transmitted when at column 0. If ONLRET is set, the NL character is assumed to do the carriage return function; the column pointer will be set to zero, and the delays specified for CR will be used. Otherwise, the NL character is assumed to do just the line feed function; the column pointer will remain unchanged. The column pointer is also set to 0 if the CR character is actually transmitted.

The delay bits specify how long transmission stops to allow for mechanical or other movement when certain characters are sent to the terminal. In all cases a value of 0 indicates no delay. If OFILL is set, fill characters will be transmitted for delay instead of a timed delay. This is useful for high baud rate terminals which need only a minimal delay. If OFDEL is set, the fill character is DEL, otherwise NUL.

If a form feed or vertical tab delay is specified, it lasts for about 2 seconds.

Newline delay lasts about 0.10 seconds. If ONLRET is set, the carriage return delays are used instead of the newline delays. If OFILL is set, two fill characters will be transmitted.

Carriage return delay type 1 is dependent on the current column position, type 2 is about 0.10 seconds, and type 3 is about 0.15 seconds. If OFILL is set, delay type 1 transmits two fill characters, and type 2 four fill characters.

Horizontal tab delay type 1 is dependent on the current column position. Type 2 is about 0.10 seconds. Type 3 specifies that tabs are to be expanded into spaces. If OFILL is set, two fill characters will be transmitted for any delay.

Backspace delay lasts about 0.05 seconds. If OFILL is set, one fill character will be transmitted.

The actual delays depend on line speed and system load. The initial output control value is all bits clear.

The c_cflag field describes the hardware control of the terminal:

CBAUD	0000017 Baud rate.		
	B0	0	Hang up
	B50	0000001	50 baud
	B75	0000002	75 baud
	B110	0000003	110 baud
	B134	0000004	134.5 baud
	B150	0000005	150 baud
	B200	0000006	200 baud
	B300	0000007	300 baud
	B600	0000010	600 baud
	B1200	0000011	1200 baud
	B1800	0000012	1800 baud
	B2400	0000013	2400 baud
	B4800	0000014	4800 baud
	B9600	0000015	9600 baud
EXTA	0000016	External A	
EXTB	0000017	External B	
CSIZE	0000060	Character size.	
	CS5	0	5 bits
	CS6	0000020	6 bits
	CS7	0000040	7 bits
	CS8	0000060	8 bits
CSTOPB	0000100	Send two stop bits, else one.	
CREAD	0000200	Enable receiver.	
PARENB	0000400	Parity enable.	
PARODD	0001000	Odd parity, else even.	
HUPCL	0002000	Hang up on last close.	
CLOCAL	0004000	Local line, else dial-up.	
LOBLK	0010000	Block layer output.	

The CBAUD bits specify the baud rate. The zero baud rate, B0, is used to hang up the connection. If B0 is specified, the data-terminal-ready signal will not be asserted. Normally, this will disconnect the line. For any particular hardware, impossible speed changes are ignored.

The CSIZE bits specify the character size in bits for both transmission and reception. This size does not include the parity bit, if any. If CSTOPB is set, two stop bits are used, otherwise one stop bit. For example, at 110 baud, two stops bits are required.

If PARENB is set, parity generation and detection is enabled and a parity bit is added to each character. If parity is enabled, the PARODD flag specifies odd parity if set, otherwise even parity is used.

If CREAD is set, the receiver is enabled. Otherwise no characters will be received.

If HUPCL is set, the line will be disconnected when the last process with the line open closes it or terminates. That is, the data-terminal-ready signal will not be asserted.

If CLOCAL is set, the line is assumed to be a local, direct connection with no modem control. Otherwise modem control is assumed.

If LOBLK is set, the output of a job control layer will be blocked when it is not the current layer. Otherwise the output generated by that layer will be multiplexed onto the current layer.

The initial hardware control value after open is B300, CS8, CREAD, HUPCL.

The c_lflag field of the argument structure is used by the line discipline to control terminal functions. The basic line discipline (0) provides the following:

ISIG	0000001	Enable signals.
ICANON	0000002	Canonical input (erase and kill processing).
XCASE	0000004	Canonical upper/lower presentation.
ECHO	0000010	Enable echo.
ECHOE	0000020	Echo erase character as BS-SP-BS.
ECHOK	0000040	Echo NL after kill character.
ECHONL	0000100	Echo NL.
NOFLSH	0000200	Disable flush after interrupt or quit.

If ISIG is set, each input character is checked against the special control characters INTR, SWTCH, and QUIT. If an input character matches one of these control characters, the function associated with that character is performed. If ISIG is not set, no checking is done. Thus these special input functions are possible only if ISIG is set. These functions may be disabled individually by changing the value of the control character to an unlikely or impossible value (e.g. 0377).

If ICANON is set, canonical processing is enabled. This enables the erase and kill edit functions, and the assembly of input characters into lines delimited by NL, EOF, and EOL. If ICANON is not set, read requests are satisfied directly from the input queue. A read will not be satisfied until at least MIN have been received or the timeout value TIME has expired between characters. This allows fast bursts of input to be read efficiently while still allowing single character input. The MIN and TIME values are stored in the position for the EOF and EOL characters, respectively. The time value represents tenths of seconds.

If XCASE is set, and if ICANON is set, an upper case letter is accepted on input by preceding it with a \ character, and is output preceded by a \ character. In this mode, the following escape sequences are generated on output and accepted on input:

for:	use:
`	\'
|	\!
~	\^
{	\(
}	\)
\	\\

For example, A is input as \a, \n as \\n, and \N as \\\n.

If ECHO is set, characters are echoed as received.

When ICANON is set, the following echo functions are possible. If ECHO and

ECHOE are set, the erase character is echoed as ASCII BS SP BS, which will clear the last character from a CRT screen. If ECHOE is set and ECHO is not set, the erase character is echoed as ASCII SP BS. If ECHOK is set, the NL character will be echoed after the kill character to emphasize that the line will be deleted. Note that an escape character preceding the erase or kill character removes any special function. If ECHONL is set, the NL character will be echoed even if ECHO is not set. This is useful for terminals set to local echo (so-called half duplex). Unless escaped, the EOF character is not echoed. Because EOT is the default EOF character, this prevents terminals that respond to EOT from hanging up.

If NOFLSH is set, the normal flush of the input and output queues associated with the quit, switch, and interrupt characters will not be done.

The initial line-discipline control value is all bits clear.

The primary ioctl(2) system calls have the form:

```
ioctl(fildes, command, arg)
struct termio *arg;
```

The commands using this form are:

TCGETA Get the parameters associated with the terminal and store in the termio structure referenced by arg.

TCSETA Set the parameters associated with the terminal from the structure referenced by arg. The change is immediate.

TCSETAW
  Wait for the output to drain before setting the new parameters. This form should be used when changing parameters that will affect output.

TCSETAF Wait for the output to drain, then flush the input queue and set the new parameters.

Additional ioctl(2) calls have the form:

```
ioctl(fildes, command, arg)
int arg;
```

The commands using this form are:

TCSBRK Wait for the output to drain. If arg is 0, then send a break (zero bits for 0.25 seconds).

TCXONC Start/stop control. If arg is 0, suspend output; if 1, restart suspended output.

TCFLSH If arg is 0, flush the input queue; if 1, flush the output queue; if 2, flush both the input and output queues.

If an error has occurred, a value of −1 is returned and errno is set.

kill – send a signal to a process or a group of processes   KILL(2)

```
int kill(pid, sig)
int pid, sig;
```

kill sends a signal to a process or a group of processes. The process or group of processes to which the signal is to be sent is specified by pid. The signal that is to be sent is specified by sig and is either one from the list given in signal(2), or 0. If sig is 0 (the null signal), error checking is performed but no signal is actually sent. This can be used to check the validity of pid.

The real or effective user-id of the sending process must match the real or effective user-id of the receiving process, unless the effective user-id of the sending process is super-user.

The processes with a process-id of 0 and a process-id of 1 are special processes and will be referred to below as proc0 and proc1, respectively.

If pid is greater than zero, sig will be sent to the process whose process-id is equal to pid. pid may equal 1.

If pid is 0, sig will be sent to all processes excluding proc0 and proc1 whose process group-id is equal to the process group-id of the sender.

If pid is −1 and the effective user-id of the sender is not super-user, sig will be sent to all processes excluding proc0 and proc1 whose real user-id is equal to the effective user-id of the sender.

If pid is −1 and the effective user-id of the sender is super-user, sig will be sent to all processes excluding proc0 and proc1.

If pid is negative but not −1, sig will be sent to all processes whose process group-id is equal to the absolute value of pid.

kill returns 0 if successful, −1 otherwise.

---

link – link to a file   LINK(2)

```
int link(name1, name2)
char *name1, *name2;
```

name1 points to a pathname naming an existing file. name2 points to a pathname naming the new directory entry to be created. link creates a new directory entry for the existing file.

link returns 0 if successful, −1 otherwise.

---

lseek – move read/write file pointer   LSEEK(2)

```
long lseek(fildes, offset, whence)
int fildes;
long offset;
int whence;
```

lseek sets the file pointer associated with fildes according to whence.

0   The pointer is set to offset bytes.
1   The pointer is set to its current location plus offset.

2   The pointer is set to the size of the file plus offset.

lseek returns the file pointer value if successful, −1 otherwise.

---

nice − change priority of a process   NICE (2)

```
int nice(incr)
int incr;
```

nice adds the value of incr to the nice value of the calling process. A process's nice value is a positive number for which a more positive value results in lower CPU priority.

A maximum nice value of 39 and a minimum nice value of 0 are imposed by the system. Requests for values above or below these limits result in the nice value being set to the corresponding limit.

nice returns the new nice value minus 20 if successful, −1 otherwise.

---

open − open for reading or writing   OPEN (2)

```
#include <fcntl.h>
int open(name, oflag [ , mode ] )
char *name;
int oflag, mode;
```

open opens a file descriptor for the file name and sets the file status flags according to the value of oflag. oflag values are constructed by combining flags from the following list with a logical OR. Only one of the first three flags below may be used:

O_RDONLY   Open for reading only.
O_WRONLY   Open for writing only.
O_RDWR   Open for reading and writing.
O_NDELAY   This flag may affect subsequent reads and writes. See read(2) and write(2). When opening a fifo with O_RDONLY or O_WRONLY set, if O_NDELAY is set, an open for reading-only will return without delay, and open for writing-only will return an error if no process currently has the file open for reading. If O_NDELAY is clear, an open for reading-only will block until a process opens the file for writing, and open for writing-only will block until a process opens the file for reading. When opening a file associated with a communication line, if O_NDELAY is set, the open will return without waiting for carrier, and if O_NDELAY is clear, the open will block until carrier is present.
O_APPEND   If set, the file pointer will be set to the end of the file prior to each write.
O_CREAT   If the file exists, this flag has no effect. Otherwise, the owner-id of the file is set to the effective user-id of the process, the group-id of the file is set to the effective group-id of the process, and the low-order 9 bits of the file mode are set to the

value of mode which is modified (see creat(2)) so that all bits set in the file mode creation mask of the process are cleared (see umask(2)), and the 'save text image after execution bit' of the mode is cleared (see chmod(2)).

O_TRUNC   If the file exists, its length is truncated to 0 and the mode and owner are unchanged.

O_EXCL   If O_EXCL and O_CREAT are set, open will fail if the file exists.

The file pointer used to mark the current position within the file is set to the beginning of the file.

The new file descriptor is set to remain open across exec system calls (see fcntl(2)).

open returns the file descriptor if successful, −1 otherwise.

---

pause − suspend process until signal   PAUSE (2)

pause( )

pause suspends the calling process until it receives a signal. The signal must be one that is not currently set to be ignored by the calling process.

If the signal causes termination of the calling process, pause will not return.

If the signal is caught by the calling process and control is returned from the signal-catching function (see signal(2)), the calling process resumes execution from the point of suspension; with a return value of −1 from pause and errno set to EINTR.

---

pipe − create an interprocess channel   PIPE (2)

int pipe(fildes)
int fildes[2];

pipe creates an input-output mechanism called a pipe and returns two file descriptors, fildes[0] and fildes[1]. fildes[0] is opened for reading and fildes[1] is opened for writing.

Up to 5120 bytes of data are buffered by the pipe before the writing process is blocked. A read only file descriptor fildes[0] accesses the data written to fildes[1] on a first-in-first-out (fifo) basis.

pipe returns 0 if successful, −1 otherwise.

---

profil − execution time profile   PROFIL (2)

void profil(buff, bufsiz, offset, scale)
char *buff;
int bufsiz, offset, scale;

buff points to an area of memory whose length (in bytes) is given by bufsiz. After this call, the user's program counter (pc) is examined each clock tick (1/60 second); offset is subtracted from it, and the result multiplied by scale. If the resulting number corresponds to a word inside buff, that word is incremented.

The scale is interpreted as an unsigned, fixed-point fraction with binary point at the left: 0177777 (octal) gives a 1-1 mapping of pc values to words in buff; 077777 (octal) maps each pair of instruction words together. 02(octal) maps all instructions onto the beginning of buff (producing a non-interrupting core clock).

Profiling is turned off by giving a scale of 0 or 1. It is rendered ineffective by giving a bufsiz of 0. Profiling is turned off when an exec is executed, but remains on in child and parent both after a fork. Profiling will be turned off if an update in buff would cause a memory fault.

---

read – read from file   READ (2)

```
int read(fildes, buf, nbyte)
int fildes;
char *buf;
unsigned nbyte;
```

read attempts to read nbyte bytes from the file associated with fildes into the buffer pointed to by buf.

On devices capable of seeking, the read starts at a position in the file given by the file pointer associated with fildes. Upon return from read, the file pointer is incremented by the number of bytes actually read.

Devices that are incapable of seeking always read from the current position. The value of a file pointer associated with such a file is undefined.

Upon successful completion, read returns the number of bytes actually read and placed in the buffer; this number may be less than nbyte if the file is associated with a communication line (see ioctl(2)) or if the number of bytes left in the file is less than nbyte bytes. A value of 0 is returned when an end-of-file has been reached.

If O_NDELAY is set when attempting to read from an empty pipe (or fifo), the read will return a 0. Otherwise, the read will block until data is written to the file or the file is no longer open for writing.

If O_NDELAY is set when attempting to read a file associated with a tty that has no data currently available the read will return a 0. Otherwise, the read will block until data becomes available.

read returns the number of bytes read if successful, −1 otherwise.

---

setpgrp – set process group ID   SETPGRP (2)

```
int setpgrp ()
```

setpgrp sets the process group-id of the calling process to the process-id of the calling process and returns the new process group-id.

---

setuid, setgid – set user and group-ids   SETUID (2)

```
int setuid(uid)
int uid;

int setgid(gid)
int gid;
```

   setuid (setgid) is used to set the real user-id (group-id) and effective-user-id (group-id) of the calling process.

   If the effective-user-id of the calling process is super-user, the real user-id (group-id) and effective-user-id (group-id) are set to uid (gid).

   If the effective-user-id of the calling process is not super-user, but its real user-id (group-id) is equal to uid (gid), the effective-user-id (group-id) is set to uid (gid).

   If the effective-user-id of the calling process is not super-user, but the saved set-user-id (set-group-id) from exec(2) is equal to uid (gid), the effective-user-id (group-id) is set to uid (gid).

   setuid returns 0 if successful, −1 otherwise.

---

signal – specify what to do upon receipt of a signal   SIGNAL (2)

```
#include <signal.h>

int (*signal (sig, func))( )
int sig;
void (*func)( );
```

   signal allows the calling process to choose one of three ways to handle the receipt of a specific signal. sig specifies the signal and func specifies the choice. The signals are listed in section 6.6.1.

   func is assigned one of three values: SIG_DFL, SIG_IGN, or a function address. The actions prescribed by these values are as follows:

   SIG_DFL   Terminate process upon receipt of a signal. Upon receipt of the signal sig, the receiving process is to be terminated with all of the consequences outlined in exit(2). In addition a *core image* will be made in the current working directory of the receiving process if sig is one for which an asterisk appears in the list in section 6.6.1 and the effective-user-id and the real user-id of the receiving process are equal.

   SIG_IGN   Ignore signal. The signal sig is to be ignored. (The signal SIGKILL cannot be ignored.)

   function address
             Catch signal. Upon receipt of the signal sig, the receiving process is to execute the signal-catching function pointed to by func. The signal number sig will be passed as the only argument to the signal-catching function. Additional arguments are passed to the signal-catching function for hardware-generated signals. Before entering the signal-catching function, the value of func for the caught signal

will be set to SIG_DFL unless the signal is SIGILL, SIGTRAP, or SIGPWR.

Upon return from the signal-catching function, the receiving process will resume execution at the point it was interrupted.

When a signal that is to be caught occurs during a read, a write, an open, or an ioctl system call on a slow device (like a terminal; but not a file), during a pause system call, or during a wait system call that does not return immediately due to the existence of a previously stopped or zombie process, the signal catching function will be executed and then the interrupted system call may return a −1 to the calling process with errno set to EINTR.

signal returns the previous func value for the signal sig if successful, −1 otherwise.

---

stat, fstat − get file status   STAT(2)

```
#include <sys/types.h>
#include <sys/stat.h>

int stat(name, buf)
char *name;
struct stat *buf;

int fstat(fildes, buf)
int fildes;
struct stat *buf;
```

Read, write, or execute permission of the file name is not required, but all directories listed in the pathname leading to the file must be searchable. stat obtains information about the named file.

Similarly, fstat obtains information about an open file known by the file descriptor fildes.

buf is a pointer to a stat structure into which information is placed concerning the file.

The contents of the structure pointed to by buf are defined in <sys/stat.h> and are described in chapter 6.

The access time is changed by creat(2), mknod(2), pipe(2), utime(2), and read(2).

The modification time is changed by creat(2), mknod(2), pipe(2), utime(2), and write(2).

The time of the last change in file status is changed by chmod(2), chown(2), creat(2), link(2), mknod(2), pipe(2), unlink(2), utime(2), and write(2).

stat returns 0 if successful, −1 otherwise.

---

time − get time   TIME (2)

long time(tloc)
long *tloc;

time returns the value of time in seconds since 00:00:00 GMT, January 1, 1970.

If tloc is non-zero, the return value is also stored in the location to which tloc points.

Upon successful completion, time returns the value of time. Otherwise, −1 is returned and errno is set.

---

times − get process and child process times   TIMES (2)

#include <sys/types.h>
#include <sys/times.h>

long times(buffer)
struct tms *buffer;

times fills the structure pointed to by buffer with time-accounting information.

This information comes from the calling process and each of its terminated child processes for which it has executed a wait. Times are in 60ths of a second or 100ths of a second depending on the particular processor being used.

tms_utime is the CPU time used while executing instructions in the user space of the calling process.

tms_stime is the CPU time used by the system on behalf of the calling process.

tms_cutime is the sum of the tms_utimes and tms_cutimes of the child processes.

tms_cstime is the sum of the tms_stimes and tms_cstimes of the child processes.

Upon successful completion, times returns the elapsed real time, in 60ths (100ths) of a second, since an arbitrary point in the past (e.g. system start-up time). This point does not change from one invocation of times to another. If times fails, a −1 is returned and errno is set to indicate the error.

---

umask − set and get file creation mask   UMASK (2)

int umask(cmask)
int cmask;

umask sets the process's file mode creation mask to cmask and returns the previous value of the mask. Only the low-order 9 bits of cmask and the file mode creation mask are used.

The previous value of the file mode creation mask is returned.

unlink – remove directory entry   UNLINK (2)

```
int unlink(name)
char *name;
```

unlink removes the directory entry name.

When all links to a file have been removed and no process has the file open, the space occupied by the file is freed and the file ceases to exist. If one or more processes have the file open when the last link is removed, the removal is postponed until all references to the file have been closed.

unlink returns 0 if successful, −1 otherwise.

---

wait – wait for child process to stop or terminate   WAIT (2)

```
int wait(stat_loc)
int *stat_loc;
```

```
int wait((int *)0)
```

wait suspends the calling process until one of the immediate children terminates or until a child that is being traced stops because it has hit a breakpoint. The wait system call will return prematurely if a signal is received, and if a child process stopped or terminated prior to the call on wait, return is immediate.

If stat_loc (taken as an integer) is non-zero, 16 bits of information called *status* are stored in the low-order 16 bits of the location pointed to by stat_loc. *status* can be used to differentiate between stopped and terminated child processes. If the child process terminated, *status* identifies the cause of termination and passes useful information to the parent.

- If the child process stopped, the high-order 8 bits of *status* will contain the number of the signal that caused the process to stop and the low-order 8 bits will be set equal to 0177.
- If the child process terminated due to an exit call, the low-order 8 bits of *status* will be zero and the high-order 8 bits will contain the low-order 8 bits of the argument that the child process passed to exit; see exit(2).
- If the child process terminated due to a signal, the high-order 8 bits of *status* will be zero and the low-order 8 bits will contain the number of the signal that caused the termination. In addition, if the low-order seventh bit (i.e. bit 0200) is set, a core image will have been produced; see signal(2).
- If a parent process terminates without waiting for its child processes to terminate, the parent process-id of each child process is set to 1. This means the initialization process inherits the child processes; see intro(2).

If wait returns due to the receipt of a signal, a value of −1 is returned to the calling process and errno is set to EINTR. If wait returns due to a stopped or terminated child process, the process-id of the child is returned to the calling process. Otherwise, a value of −1 is returned and errno is set to indicate the error.

write − write on a file   WRITE(2)

```
int write(fildes, buf, nbyte)
int fildes;
char *buf;
unsigned nbyte;
```

write attempts to write nbyte bytes from the buffer pointed to by buf to the file associated with the fildes.

On devices capable of seeking, the actual writing of data proceeds from the position in the file indicated by the file pointer. Upon return from write, the file pointer is incremented by the number of bytes actually written.

On devices incapable of seeking, writing always takes place starting at the current position. The value of a file pointer associated with such a device is undefined.

If the O_APPEND flag of the file status flags is set, the file pointer will be set to the end of the file prior to each write.

If a write requests that more bytes be written than there is room for (e.g. the ulimit (see ulimit(2)) or the physical end of a medium), only as many bytes as there is room for will be written. For example, suppose there is space for 20 bytes more in a file before reaching a limit. A write of 512 bytes will return 20. The next write of a non-zero number of bytes will give a failure return (except as noted below).

If the file being written is a pipe (or fifo) and the O_NDELAY flag of the file flag word is set, then write to a full pipe (or fifo) will return a count of 0. Otherwise (O_NDELAY clear), writes to a full pipe (or fifo) will block until space becomes available.

Upon successful completion the number of bytes actually written is returned. Otherwise, −1 is returned and errno is set.

Appendix 3 C Subroutines

```
#include <time.h>

char *ctime(clock)
long *clock;

struct tm *localtime(clock)
long *clock;

struct tm *gmtime(clock)
long *clock;

char *asctime(tm)
struct tm *tm;

extern long timezone;

extern int daylight;

extern char *tzname[2];

void tzset( )
```

ctime converts a long integer, pointed to by clock, representing the time in seconds since 00:00:00 GMT, January 1, 1970, and returns a pointer to a 26-character string in the following form. (All the fields have constant width.)

```
Sun Sep 16 01:03:52 1973\n\0
```

localtime corrects for the time zone and possible Daylight Saving Time; gmtime converts directly to Greenwich Mean Time (GMT), which is the time the system uses. asctime converts a structure to a 26-character string, as shown in the above example, and returns a pointer to the string.

Declarations of all the functions and externals, and the tm structure, are in the <time.h> header file. The structure declaration is:

```
struct tm { /* see ctime(3) */
        int     tm_sec;
        int     tm_min;
        int     tm_hour;
        int     tm_mday;
        int     tm_mon;
        int     tm_year;
```

```
     int      tm_wday;
     int      tm_yday;
     int      tm_isdst;
};
```

tm_isdst is non-zero if Daylight Saving Time is in effect.

The external long variable timezone contains the difference, in seconds, between GMT and local standard time (in EST, timezone is 5*60*60); the external variable daylight is non-zero if and only if the standard USA Daylight Saving Time conversion should be applied. The program knows about the peculiarities of this conversion in 1974 and 1975; if necessary, a table for these years can be extended.

If an environment variable named TZ is present, asctime uses the contents of the variable to override the default time zone. The value of TZ must be a three-letter time zone name, followed by a number representing the difference between local time and Greenwich Mean Time in hours, followed by an optional three-letter name for a daylight time zone. For example, the setting for New Jersey would be EST5EDT. The effects of setting TZ are thus to change the values of the external variables timezone and daylight; in addition, the time zone names contained in the external variable

```
char *tzname[2] = { "EST", "EDT" };
```

are set from the environment variable TZ. The function tzset sets these external variables from TZ; tzset is called by asctime and may also be called explicitly by the user.

---

fclose, fflush – close or flush a stream   FCLOSE (3S)

```
#include <stdio.h>

int fclose(stream)
FILE *stream;

int fflush(stream)
FILE *stream;
```

fclose causes any buffered data for the named stream to be written out, and the stream to be closed.

fclose is performed automatically for all open files upon calling exit(2).

fflush causes any buffered data for the named stream to be written to that file. The stream remains open.

These functions return 0 for success, and EOF if any error (such as trying to write to a file that has not been opened for writing) was detected.

ferror, feof, clearerr, fileno − stream status inquiries   FERROR (3S)

#include <stdio.h>

int ferror(stream)
FILE *stream;

int feof(stream)
FILE *stream;

void clearerrstream( )
FILE *stream;

int fileno(stream)
FILE *stream;

ferror returns non-zero when an input-output error has previously occurred reading from or writing to the named stream, otherwise zero.

feof returns non-zero when EOF has previously been detected reading the named input stream, otherwise zero.

clearerr resets the error indicator and EOF indicator to zero on the named stream.

fileno returns the integer file descriptor associated with the named stream; see open(2).

---

fopen, freopen, fdopen − open a stream   FOPEN (3S)

#include <stdio.h>

FILE *fopen(filename, type)
char *filename, *type;

FILE *freopen(filename, type, stream)
char *filename, *type;
FILE *stream;

FILE *fdopen(fildes, type)
char *type;

fopen opens the file named by filename and associates a stream with it. fopen returns a pointer used to identify the stream in subsequent operations. type is a character string having one of the following values.

r   Open for reading.
w   Create for writing.
a   Open for writing at the end of file, or create for writing.

fopen and freopen return the pointer NULL if filename cannot be accessed.

In addition, each type may be followed by a + to have the file opened for reading and writing. r+ positions the stream at the beginning of the file, w+ creates or truncates it, and a+ positions it at the end. Both reads and writes may be used on read/write streams, with the limitation that an fseek, rewind, or reading an end-of-file must be used between a read and a write or vice versa.

freopen substitutes the named file in place of the open stream. It returns the original value of stream. The original stream is closed.

freopen is typically used to attach the preopened constant names, *stdin, stdout, stderr,* to specified files.

fdopen associates a stream with a file descriptor obtained from open, dup, creat, or pipe(2). The type of the stream must agree with the mode of the open file.

---

fread, fwrite − buffered binary input/output   FREAD (3S)

#include <stdio.h>

int fread(ptr, size, nitems, stream)
char *ptr;
int size, nitems;
FILE *stream;

int fwrite(ptr, size, nitems, stream)
char *ptr;
int size, nitems;
FILE *stream;

fread reads, into a block beginning at ptr, nitems of data of the type of *ptr from the named input stream. It returns the number of items actually read.

fread and fwrite return 0 upon end-of-file or error.

If stream is *stdin* and the standard output is line buffered, then any partial output line will be flushed before any call to read(2) to satisfy the fread.

fwrite appends at most nitems of data of the type of *ptr beginning at ptr to the named output stream. It returns the number of items actually written.

size is typically sizeof(*ptr).

---

fseek, ftell, rewind − reposition a stream   FSEEK (3S)

#include <stdio.h>

int fseek(stream, offset, ptrname)
FILE *stream;
long offset;
int ptrname;

void rewind(stream)
FILE *stream;

long ftell(stream)
FILE *stream;

fseek sets the position of the next input or output operation on the stream. The new position is at the signed distance offset bytes from the beginning, the current position, or the end of the file, according as ptrname has the value 0, 1, or 2.

fseek undoes any effects of ungetc(3S).

ftell returns the current value of the offset relative to the beginning of the file associated with the named stream. It is measured in bytes and is the only foolproof way to obtain an offset for fseek.

rewind(stream) is equivalent to fseek(stream, 0L, 0).
fseek returns non-zero for improper seeks.

---

getc, getchar, fgetc, getw – get character or word from stream   GETC (3S)

#include <stdio.h>

int getc(stream)
FILE *stream;

int getchar( )

int fgetc(stream)
FILE *stream;

int getw(stream)
FILE *stream;

getc returns the next character from the named input stream.
getchar( ) is identical to getc(stdin).
fgetc behaves like getc, but is a genuine function, not a macro.
getw returns the next word (32-bit integer on a VAX 11) from the named input stream. It returns the constant EOF upon end-of-file or error, but since that is an integer value, feof and ferror(3C) should be used to check the success of getw. No special alignment in the file is assumed by getw.

These functions return EOF at end-of-file or upon read error.

A stop with the message, *Reading bad file,* means an attempt has been made to read from a stream that has not been opened for reading by fopen.

---

getenv – value for environment name   GETENV (3C)

extern char **environ;

char *getenv(name)
char *name;

getenv searches the environment list for a string of the form name=value and returns value if such a string is present, otherwise 0.

The external variable environ is an array of strings called the environment and is made available by exec(2) when a process begins. By convention these strings have the form name=value.

Further names may be placed in the environment by the export command and name=value arguments in sh(1). Arguments may also be placed in the environment at the point of an exec(2).

gets, fgets – get a string from a stream   GETS (3S)

#include <stdio.h>

char *gets(s)
char *s;

char *fgets(s, n, stream)
char *s;
int n;
FILE *stream;

gets reads a string into s from the standard input stream *stdin.* The string is terminated by a newline, which is replaced in s by a null character. gets returns its argument.

fgets reads n−1 characters (or up to a newline character, whichever comes first) from the stream into the string s. The last character read into s is followed by a null character. fgets returns its first argument.

gets and fgets return the constant pointer NULL upon end-of-file or error.

malloc, free, realloc, calloc – main memory allocator   MALLOC (3C)

char *malloc(size)
unsigned size;

free(ptr)
char *ptr;

char *realloc(ptr, size)
char *ptr;
unsigned size;

char *calloc(nelem, elsize)
unsigned nelem, elsize;

malloc and free provide a simple general-purpose memory allocation package. malloc returns a pointer to a block of at least size bytes beginning on a word boundary.

The argument to free is a pointer to a block previously allocated by malloc. This space is made available for further allocation, but its contents are left undisturbed.

Needless to say, grave disorder will result if the space assigned by malloc is overrun or if some random number is handed to free.

malloc allocates the first block of contiguous free space that is large enough found in a circular search from the last block allocated or freed, coalescing adjacent free blocks as it searches. It calls sbrk to get more memory from the system when there is no suitable space already free.

realloc changes the size of the block pointed to by ptr to size bytes and returns a pointer to the (possibly moved) block. The contents will be unchanged up to the lesser of the new and old sizes.

realloc also works if ptr points to a block freed since the last call of malloc, realloc, or calloc thus sequences of free, malloc, and realloc can exploit the search strategy of malloc to do storage compaction.

calloc allocates space for an array of nelem elements of size elsize. The space is initialized to zeros.

Each of the allocation routines returns a pointer to space suitably aligned for storage of any type of object.

malloc, realloc, and calloc return a null pointer (0) if there is no available memory or if the arena has been detectably corrupted by storing outside the bounds of a block.

When realloc returns 0, the block pointed to by ptr may be destroyed.

---

mktemp − make a unique file name   MKTEMP(3C)

```
char *mktemp(template)
char *template;
```

mktemp replaces template by a unique file name, and returns the address of the template. The template should be a file name with six trailing Xs, that will be replaced with the current process-id and a unique letter.

---

monitor − prepare execution profile   MONITOR(3C)

```
#include <mon.h>

monitor(lowpc, highpc, buffer, bufsize, nfunc)
int (*lowpc)( ), (*highpc)( );
WORD buffer[ ];
int bufsize, nfunc;
```

An executable program created by cc −p automatically includes calls for monitor with default parameters; monitor need not be called explicitly except to gain fine control over profiling.

monitor is an interface to profil(2). lowpc and highpc are the addresses of two functions; buffer is the address of a (user supplied) array of bufsize short integers. monitor arranges to record a histogram of periodically sampled values of the program counter, and of counts of calls of certain functions, in the buffer. The lowest address sampled is that of lowpc and the highest is just below highpc. At most nfunc call counts can be kept; only calls of functions compiled with the profiling option −p of cc(1) are recorded. For the results to be significant, especially where there are small, heavily used routines, it is suggested that the buffer be no more than a few times smaller than the range of locations sampled.

---

perror, errno, sys_errlist, sys_nerr − system error messages   PERROR(3C)

```
void perror(s)
char *s;

extern int errno;
extern int sys_nerr;
extern char *sys_errlist[ ];
```

perror produces a short error message on the standard error file describing the last error encountered during a call to the system from a C program. First the argument string s is printed, then a :, then the message and a newline. Most usefully, the argument string is the name of the program that incurred the error. The error number is taken from the external variable errno which is set when errors occur but not cleared when non-erroneous calls are made.

To simplify variant formatting of messages, the vector of message strings sys_errlist is provided; errno can be used as an index in this table to get the message string without the newline. sys_nerr is the number of messages provided for in the table; it should be checked because new error codes may be added to the system before they are added to the table.

---

popen, pclose − initiate input-output to/from a process   POPEN (3S)

#include <stdio.h>

FILE *popen(command, type)
char *command, *type;

int pclose(stream)
FILE *stream;

The arguments to popen are pointers to null-terminated strings containing respectively a shell command line and an input-output mode, either r for reading or w for writing. It creates a pipe between the calling process and the command to be executed. The value returned is a stream pointer that can be used (as appropriate) to write to the standard input of the command or read from its standard output.

A stream opened by popen should be closed by pclose, that waits for the associated process to terminate and returns the exit status of the command.

Because open files are shared, a type r command may be used as an input filter, and a type w as an output filter.

popen returns NULL if files or processes cannot be created, or the shell cannot be accessed.

pclose returns −1 if stream is not obtained via popen.

---

printf, fprintf, sprintf − formatted output conversion   PRINTF (3S)

#include <stdio.h>

int printf(format [, arg] ...)
char *format;

int fprintf(stream, format [, arg] ...)
FILE *stream;
char *format;

int sprintf(s, format [, arg] ...)
char *s, format;

printf places output on the standard output stream stdout. fprintf places output on the named output stream. sprintf places output in the string s, followed by the null character.

Each of these functions converts, formats, and prints its second and subsequent arguments under control of the first argument. The first argument is a character string that contains two types of objects: plain characters, that are copied to the output stream, and conversion specifications, each of which causes conversion and printing of the next successive arg printf.

Each conversion specification is introduced by the character % followed by one of the following.

- Zero or more flags, which modify the meaning of the conversion specification.
- An optional digit string specifies a field width; if the converted value has fewer characters than the field width it will be blank-padded on the left (or right, if the left adjustment indicator has been given) to make up the field width; if the field width begins with a zero, zero-padding will be used instead of blank-padding.
- An optional . serves to separate the field width from the next digit string.
- An optional digit string, precision, specifies the minimum number of digits to appear for the d, o, u, x, or X conversions, the number of digits to appear after the decimal point, for e and f conversion, or the maximum number of characters to be printed from a string.
- The letter l specifies that a following d, o, u, or x corresponds to a long integer arg.
- A character that indicates the type of conversion to be applied.

A field width or precision may be * instead of a digit string. In this case an integer arg supplies the field width or precision. The flag characters and their meanings are as follows:

-    The result of the conversion will be left-justified within the field.

+   The result of a signed conversion will always begin with a sign (+ or −).

blank   If the first character of a signed conversion is not a sign, a blank will be prefixed to the result. This implies that if the blank and + flags both appear, the blank will be ignored.

\#   This flag specifies that the value is to be converted to an alternate form. For c, d, s, and u conversions, the flag has no effect. For o conversion, it increases the precision to force the first digit of the result to be a zero. For x or X conversion, a non-zero result will have 0x or 0X prefixed to it. For e, E, f, g, and G conversions, the result will always contain a decimal point, even if no digits follow the point. For g and G conversions, trailing zeros will not be removed from the result.

The conversion characters and their meanings are as follows. In no case does a non-existent or small field width cause truncation of a field; padding takes place only if the specified field width exceeds the actual width. Characters generated by printf are printed by putc(3S).

douxX   The integer arg is converted to signed decimal, unsigned octal, unsigned decimal, or hexadecimal notation (x and X) respectively. The letters abcdef and ABCDEF are used for (x and X) respectively.

f   The float or double arg is converted to decimal notation in the style [–]*ddd.ddd* where the number of ds after the decimal point is equal to the precision specification for the argument. If the precision is missing, six digits are given; if the precision is explicitly 0, no digits and no decimal point are printed.

e,E   The float or double arg is converted in the style [–]*d.ddd*e±*dd* where there is one digit before the decimal point and the number after is equal to the precision specification for the argument; when the precision is missing, six digits are produced. The E format code will produce a number with E instead of e introducing the exponent.

g,G   The float or double arg is printed in style f or e (or in style E in the case of a G format code), whichever gives full precision in minimum space.

c   The character arg is printed.

s   arg is taken to be a string and characters from the string are printed until a null character or until the number of characters indicated by the precision specification is reached; however if the precision is 0, or missing, all characters up to a null are printed.

%   Print a %; no argument is converted.

---

putc, putchar, fputc, putw – put character or word on a stream   PUTC (3S)

#include <stdio.h>

int putc(c, stream)
int c;
FILE *stream;

putchar(c)
int c;

int fputc(c, stream)
int c;
FILE *stream;

int putw(w, stream)
int w;
FILE *stream;

putc writes the character c to the named output stream at the position where the file pointer, if defined, is pointing. It returns the character written.

putchar(c) is defined as putc(c, stdout).

fputc behaves like putc, but is a genuine function rather than a macro.

putw writes an int sized word w to the output stream at the position where the file pointer, if defined, is pointing. It returns the word written. putw neither assumes nor causes special alignment in the file.

The standard stream stdout is normally buffered if and only if the output does not refer to a terminal; this default may be changed by setbuf(3S). The standard stream stderr is by default unbuffered unconditionally, but use of freopen will cause it to become buffered; setbuf, again, will set the state to whatever is desired. When an output stream is unbuffered information appears on the destination file or terminal as soon as written; when it is buffered characters are saved up and written as a block. fflush may be used to force the block out before it has been filled.

These functions return the constant EOF upon error. Since this is an integer, ferror(3C) should be used to detect putw errors.

---

puts, fputs − put a string on a stream   PUTS (3S)

#include <stdio.h>

int puts(s)
char *s;

int fputs(s, stream)
char *s;
FILE *stream;

puts copies the null-terminated string s to the standard output stream, stdout, and appends a newline.

fputs copies the null-terminated string s to the named output stream.

Neither routine copies the terminal null character.

---

scanf, fscanf, sscanf − formatted input conversion   SCANF (3S)

#include <stdio.h>

int scanf(format [, pointer] ...)
char *format;

int fscanf(stream, format [, pointer] ...)
FILE *stream;
char *format;

int sscanf(s, format [, pointer] ...)
char *s, *format;

scanf reads from the standard input stream stdin. fscanf reads from the named input stream. sscanf reads from the character string s. Each function reads characters, interprets them according to a format, and stores the results in its arguments. Each expects as arguments a control string format, described below, and a set of pointer arguments indicating where the converted input should be stored.

The control string may contain conversion specifications, that are used to direct interpretation of input sequences. The control string may contain:

- spaces, tabs, or newlines, that match optional white space in the input.
- An ordinary character (not %) that must match the next character of the input stream.
- Conversion specifications, consisting of the character %, an optional assignment suppressing character *, an optional numerical maximum field width, and a conversion character.

A conversion specification directs the conversion of the next input field; the result is placed in the variable pointed to by the corresponding argument, unless assignment suppression was indicated by *. An input field is defined as a string of non-blank characters; it extends to the next inappropriate character or until the field width, if specified, is exhausted.

The conversion character indicates the interpretation of the input field; the corresponding pointer argument must usually be of a restricted type. The following conversion characters are legal:

%   A single % is expected in the input at this point; no assignment is done.

d   A decimal integer is expected; the corresponding argument should be an integer pointer.

u   An unsigned decimal integer is expected; the corresponding argument should be an unsigned integer pointer.

o   An octal integer is expected; the corresponding argument should be an integer pointer.

x   A hexadecimal integer is expected; the corresponding argument should be an integer pointer.

s   A character string is expected; the corresponding argument should be a character pointer pointing to an array of characters large enough to accept the string and the terminating null character that will be added. The input field is terminated by a space or a newline.

c   A character is expected; the corresponding argument should be a character pointer. The normal skipping over space characters is suppressed in this case; to read the next non-blank character, try %1s. If a field width is given, the corresponding argument should refer to a character array, and the indicated number of characters is read.

e, f, g   A floating point number is expected; the next field is converted accordingly and stored through the corresponding argument, that should be a pointer to a float. The input format for floating point numbers is an optionally signed string of digits possibly containing a decimal point, followed by an optional exponent field consisting of an E or e followed by an optionally signed integer.

[Introduce a string not to be delimited by space characters. The left bracket is followed by a set of characters and a right bracket; the characters between the brackets define a set of characters making up the string. If the first character is not ^, the input field is all characters until the first character not in the set between the brackets; if the first character after the left bracket is ^, the input field is all characters until the first character that is in the remaining set of characters between the brackets. The corresponding argument must point to a character array.

The conversion characters d, o, u, and x may be capitalized or preceded by l to indicate that a pointer to long rather than to int is in the argument list. Similarly, the conversion characters e, f, and g may be capitalized or preceded by the letter l to indicate a pointer to double rather than to float. The conversion characters d, o, u, and x may be preceded by h to indicate a pointer to short rather than to int.

The scanf functions return the number of successfully matched and assigned input items. This can be used to decide how many input items were found. The constant EOF is returned upon end of input; note that this is different from 0, that means that no conversion was done; if conversion was intended, it was frustrated by an inappropriate character in the input.

The scanf functions return EOF on end of input, and a short count for missing or illegal data items.

---

setbuf, setvbuf − assign buffering to a stream   SETBUF (3S)

#include <stdio.h>

void setbuf(stream, buf)
FILE *stream;
char *buf;

int setvbuf(stream, buf, type, size)
FILE *stream;
char *buf;
int type, size;

setbuf may be used after a stream has been opened but before it is read or written. It causes the array pointed to by buf to be used instead of an automatically allocated buffer. If buf is the NULL pointer input-output will be completely unbuffered.

A constant BUFSIZ, defined in the <stdio.h> header file, tells how big an array is needed:

    char buf[BUFSIZ];

setvbuf may be used after a stream has been opened but before it is read or written. type determines how stream will be buffered. Legal values for type are as follows:

    _IOFBF   Input-output is fully buffered.
    _IOLBF   Output is line buffered.
    _IONBF   Input-output is completely unbuffered.

If buf is not the NULL pointer, the array it points to will be used for buffering, instead of an automatically allocated buffer. size specifies the size of the buffer to be used. The constant BUFSIZ in <stdio.h> is suggested as a good buffer size. If input-output is unbuffered, buf and size are ignored.

By default, output to a terminal is line buffered and all other input-output is fully buffered.

---

setjmp, longjmp − non-local goto   SETJMP (3C)

#include <setjmp.h>

int setjmp(env)
jmp_buf env;

void longjmp(env, val)
jmp_buf .env;
int val;

These routines are useful for dealing with errors and interrupts.

setjmp saves its stack environment in env for later use by longjmp. It returns value 0.

longjmp restores the environment saved by the last call of setjmp. It then returns in such a way that execution continues as if the call of setjmp had just returned the value val to the function that invoked setjmp, which must not itself have returned in the interim. All accessible external variables have values as of the time longjmp was called.

---

stdio – standard buffered input-output package   STDIO (3S)

#include <stdio.h>

FILE *stdin;
FILE *stdout;
FILE *stderr;

The standard input-output library is described in chapter 5.

---

strcat, strncat, strcmp, strncmp, strcpy, strncpy, strlen,   STRING (3C)
strchr, strrchr, strpbrk, strspn, strcspn, strtok

#include <string.h>

/* argument declarations applicable in definitions below
  char *s, *s1, *s1; int n, c;
  */

char *strcat(s1, s2)

char *strncat(s1, s2, n)

int strcmp(s1, s2)

int strncmp(s1, s2, n)

char *strcpy(s1, s2)

char *strncpy(s1, s2, n)

int strlen(s)

char *strchr(s, c)

char *strrchr(s, c)

char *strpbrk(s1, s2)

int strspn(s1, s2)

int strcspn(s1, s2)

char *strtok(s1, s2)

These functions operate on null-terminated strings. They do not check for overflow of any receiving string.

strcat appends a copy of string s2 to the end of string s1. strncat copies at most n characters. Both return a pointer to the null-terminated result.

strcmp compares its arguments and returns an integer greater than, equal to, or less than 0, according as s1 is lexicographically greater than, equal to, or less than s2. strncmp makes the same comparison but with at most n characters.

strcpy copies string s2 to s1, stopping after the null character has been moved. strncpy copies exactly n characters, truncating s2 or adding null characters to s1 if necessary. The target may not be null-terminated if the length of s2 is n or more. Both return s1.

strlen returns the number of non-null characters in s.

strchr (strrchr) returns a pointer to the first (last) occurrence of character c in string s, or a NULL pointer if c does not occur in the string. The null character terminating a string is considered to be part of the string.

strpbrk returns a pointer to the first occurrence in string s1 of any character from string s2, or a NULL pointer if no character from s2 exists in s1.

strspn (strcspn) returns the length of the initial segment of string s1 which consists entirely of characters from (not from) string s2.

strtok considers the string s1 to consist of a sequence of zero or more text tokens separated by spans of one or more characters from the separator string s2. The first call (with pointer s1 specified) returns a pointer to the first character of the first token, and will have written a null character into s1 immediately following the returned token. The function keeps track of its position in the string between separate calls, so that subsequent calls (which must be made with the first argument a NULL pointer) will work through the string s1 immediately following that token. In this way subsequent calls will work through the string s1 until no tokens remain. The separator string s2 may be different from call to call. When no token remains in s1, a NULL pointer is returned.

---

ungetc – push character back into input stream   UNGETC (3S)

#include <stdio.h>

int ungetc(c, stream)
int c;
FILE *stream;

ungetc pushes the character c back on an input stream. That character will be returned by the next getc call on that stream. ungetc returns c.

One character of pushback is guaranteed provided something has been read from the stream and the stream is buffered. Attempts to push EOF are rejected.

fseek(3S) erases all memory of pushed back characters.

ungetc returns EOF if the character cannot be pushed back.

Appendix 4   adb **Requests**

Formatted printing

?_format_	Print from *a.out* file according to *format*.
/ *format*	Print from *core* file according to *format*.
= *format*	Print the value of *dot*.
?w expr	Write expression into *a.out* file.
/w expr	Write expression into *core* file.
?l expr	Locate expression in *a.out* file.

Breakpoint and program control

:b	Set a breakpoint at *dot*.
:c	Continue running program.
:d	Delete breakpoint.
:k	Kill the program being debugged.
:r	Run *a.out* file under adb control.
:s	Run the program a single step at a time.

Printing

$b	Print current breakpoints.
$c	C stack trace.
$e	Print external variables.
$f	Print floating registers.
$m	Print adb segment maps.
$q	Exit from adb.
$r	Print the general registers.
$s	Specify offset for symbol match.
$v	Print adb variables.
$w	Set output line width.

Miscellaneous

!	Call *shell* to read rest of line.
>_name_	Assign dot to variable or register *name*.

Format summary

a	The value of dot.
b	One byte in octal.
c	One byte as a character.
d	One word in decimal.

f	Two words in floating point.
i	Machine instruction.
o	One word in octal.
n	Print a newline.
r	Print a space.
s	A null-terminated character string.
*n***t**	Move to next n-space tab.
u	One word as unsigned integer.
x	Hexadecimal.
Y	Date.
^	Backup dot.
"..."	Print string.

Expression components

decimal integer	E.g. 256
octal integer	E.g. 0277
hexadecimal integer	E.g. #ff
symbols	E.g. flag _main main.argc
variables	E.g. <b
registers	E.g. <pc <r0
(expression)	Expression grouping.

Binary operators

These operators group from left to right and there is no operator precedence.

+	Add.
−	Subtract.
∗	Multiply.
%	Integer division.
&	Bitwise and.
|	Bitwise or.
#	Round up to the next multiple.

Unary operators

~	Not – logical complement.
∗	Contents of location in core file.
@	Contents of location in a.out file.
−	Integer negate.

Appendix 5   ed **Requests**

^	Match the start of the line.
$	Match the end of the line.
\c	The character c is not treated as special.

Addresses

.	The current line.
n	The n-th line.
$	The last line of the document.
$'x$	Addresses the line marked with an x.
$/e/$	The next line containing e.
$?e?$	The previous line containing e.
$a+n$	Addresses line $\pm n$.
$a\pm$	$a\pm 1$.

Appendix 6   sh **Requests**

341

Syntax

item:	*word*
	input-output
	name = value
simple-command:	*item*
	simple-command item
command:	*simple-command*
	(*command-list*)
	{ *command-list* }
	for *name* do *command-list* done
	for *name* in *word* . . . do *command-list* done
	while *command-list* do *command-list* done
	until *command-list* do *command-list* done
	case *word* in *case-part* . . . esac
	if *command-list* then *command-list else-part* fi
	function-definition
pipeline:	*command*
	pipeline | *command*
andor:	*pipeline*
	andor && *pipeline*
	andor | | *pipeline*
command-list:	*andor*
	command-list ;
	command-list &
	command-list ; *andor*
	command-list & *andor*
input-output:	> *file*
	< *file*
	≫ *word*
	≪ *word*
file:	*word*
	& *digit*
	& −
case-part:	*pattern*) *command-list* ;;
pattern:	*word*
	pattern | *word*

else-part:	elif *command-list* then *command-list else-part*
	else *command-list*
	empty
function-definition:	*name* ( ) *command*
empty:	
word:	a sequence of non-blank characters
name:	a sequence of letters, digits or underscores
	starting with a letter
digit:	0 1 2 3 4 5 6 7 8 9

Syntactic characters

|	Pipe symbol.
&&	'andf' symbol.
||	'orf' symbol.
;	Command separator.
;;	Case delimiter.
&	Background commands.
( )	Command grouping.
<	Input redirection.
≪	Input from a here document.
>	Output creation.
≫	Output append.

Patterns

*	Match any character(s) including none.
?	Match any single character.
[...]	Match any of the enclosed characters.

Substitution

${...}	Substitute shell variable.
`...`	Substitute command output.

Quoting conventions

\	Quote the next character.
'...'	Quote the enclosed characters except for '.
"..."	Quote the enclosed characters except for $ ` \ ".

Reserved words

if	case	do	done	elif	else	esac	fi
for	in	then	until	while	{	}	

Appendix 7 troff **Requests**

In the following summary certain abbreviations are used as follows.

F	A font name (see the .ft request).
M	A numerical expression.
N	A numerical expression.
R	A one or two character register name.

.ad *c*	Adjust output lines with mode *c*.
.af *R c*	Assign format to register *R* (*c*=**1, i, I, a, A**).
.am *xx yy*	Append to a macro.
.as *xx string*	Append *string* to string *xx*.
.bd *F N*	Embolden font *F* by *N*−1 units.
.bd S *F N*	Embolden Special Font when current font is *F*.
.bp ±*N*	Eject current page; next page number *N*.
.br	Break.
.c2 *c*	Set nobreak control character to *c*.
.cc *c*	Set control character to *c*.
.ce *N*	Center following *N* input text lines.
.ch *xx N*	Change trap location.
.cs *F N M*	Constant character space (width) mode (font *F*).
.cu *N*	Continuous underline in nroff; like **ul** in troff.
.da *xx*	Divert and append to macro *xx*.
.de *xx yy*	Define or redefine macro *xx;* end at call of *yy*.
.di *xx*	Divert output to macro *xx*.
.ds *xx string*	Define a string *xx* containing *string*.
.dt *N xx*	Set the diversion trap.
.ec *c*	Set escape character.
.el *anything*	Else part of if-else.
.em *xx*	End macro is *xx*.
.eo	Turn off escape character mechanism.
.ev *N*	Environment switched (*push down*).
.ex	Exit from nroff/troff.
.fc *a b*	Set field delimiter *a* and pad character *b*.
.fi	Fill output lines.
.fl	Flush output buffer.
.fp *N F*	Font named *F* mounted on physical position 1≤*N*≤4.
.ft *F*	Change to font *F* = *x*, *xx*, or 1–4. Also \f*x*, \f(*xx*, \f*N*.
.hc *c*	Hyphenation indicator character *c*.
.hw *word1* ...	Exception words.
.hy *N*	Hyphenate; *N* = mode.

.ie *c anything*	If portion of if-else; has same forms as **if**.
.if *N anything*	If expression *N* > 0, accept *anything*.
.if *´string1 ´string2 ´ anything*	
	If *string1* identical to *string2*, accept *anything*.
.if *c anything*	If condition *c* true, accept *anything* as input, for multi-line use \{*anything*\}.
.if *!N anything*	If expression *N* ≤ 0, accept *anything*.
.if *! ´string1 ´string2 ´ anything*	
	If *string1* not identical to *string2*, accept *anything*.
.if *!c anything*	If condition *c* false, accept *anything*.
.ig *yy*	Ignore text till call of *yy*.
.in *±N*	Indent.
.it *N xx*	Set an input-line count trap.
.lc *c*	Leader repetition character.
.lg *N*	Ligature mode on if *N*>0.
.ll *±N*	Set line length.
.ls *N*	Output *N*−1 *V*s after each text output line.
.lt *±N*	Length of title.
.mc *c N*	Set margin character *c* and separation *N*.
.mk *R*	Mark current vertical place in register *R*.
.na	No output line adjusting.
.ne *N*	Need *N* vertical space (*V* = vertical spacing).
.nf	No filling or adjusting of output lines.
.nh	No hyphenation.
.nm *±N M S I*	Number mode on or off, set parameters.
.nn *N*	Do not number next *N* lines.
.nr *R ±N M*	Define and set number register *R*; auto-increment by *M*.
.ns	Turn no-space mode on.
.nx *filename*	Next file.
.os	Output saved vertical distance.
.pc *c*	Page number character.
.pi *program*	Pipe output to *program* (nroff only).
.pl *±N*	Page length.
.pm *t*	Print macro names and sizes; if *t* present, print only total of sizes.
.pn *±N*	Next page number *N*.
.po *±N*	Page offset.
.ps *±N*	Point size; also \s*±N*.
.rd *prompt*	Read insertion.
.rm *xx*	Remove request, macro, or string.
.rn *xx yy*	Rename request, macro, or string *xx* to *yy*.
.rr *R*	Remove register *R*.
.rs	Restore spacing; turn no-space mode off.
.rt *±N*	Return *(upward only)* to marked vertical place.
.so *filename*	Switch source file *(push down)*.
.sp *N*	Space vertical distance *N in either direction*.
.ss *N*	Space-character size set to *N*/36 em.
.sv *N*	Save vertical distance *N*.
.ta *Nt ...*	Tab settings; *left* type, unless *t*=**R**(right), **C**(centered).
.tc *c*	Tab repetition character.
.ti *±N*	Temporary indent.

.tl *'left 'center 'right '*

        Three part title.

.tm *string*   Print *string* on terminal (UNIX standard message output).

.tr *abcd....*   Translate *a* to *b*, *c* to *d*, . . . on output.

.uf *F*   Underline font set to *F* (to be switched to by **ul**).

.ul *N*   Underline (italicize in troff) *N* input lines.

.vs *N*   Vertical base line spacing (*V*).

.wh *N xx*   Set location trap; negative is from page bottom.

Escape sequences, functions and characters

\\	\ (to prevent or delay the interpretation of \).
\e	Printable version of the *current* escape character.
\'	´ (acute accent); equivalent to \(**aa**.
\`	` (grave accent); equivalent to \(**ga**.
\-	− Minus sign in the *current* font.
\.	Period (dot) (see **de**).
\(space)	Unpaddable space-size space character.
\0	Digit width space.
\\|	1/6 em narrow space character (zero width in nroff).
\^	1/12 em half-narrow space character (zero width in nroff).
\&	Non-printing, zero width character.
\!	Transparent line indicator.
\"	Beginning of comment.
\$*N*	Interpolate argument 1≤*N*≤9.
\%	Default optional hyphenation character.
\(*xx*	Character named *xx*.
*x, *(*xx*	Interpolate string *x* or *xx*.
\a	Non-interpreted leader character.
\b *'abc... '*	Bracket building function.
\c	Interrupt text processing.
\d	Forward (down) 1/2 em vertical motion (1/2 line in nroff).
\f*x*,\f(*xx*,\f*N*	Change to font named *x* or *xx*, or position *N*.
\h *'N '*	Local horizontal motion; move right *N (negative left)*.
\k*x*	Mark horizontal *input* place in register *x*.
\l *'Nc '*	Horizontal line drawing function (optionally with *c*).
\L *'Nc '*	Vertical line drawing function (optionally with *c*).
\n*x*,\n(*xx*	Interpolate number register *x* or *xx*.
\o *'abc... '*	Overstrike characters *a, b, c, ...*
\p	Break and spread output line.
\r	Reverse 1 em vertical motion (reverse line in nroff).
\s*N*, \s±*N*	Point-size change function.
\t	Non-interpreted horizontal tab.
\u	Reverse (up) 1/2 em vertical motion (1/2 line in nroff).
\v *'N '*	Local vertical motion; move down *N (negative up)*.
\w *'string '*	Interpolate width of *string*.
\x *'N '*	Extra line-space function *(negative before, positive after)*.
\z*c*	Print *c* with zero width (without spacing).
\{	Begin conditional input.
\}	End conditional input.
\(newline)	Concealed (ignored) newline.

\X   X, any character *not* listed above.

Predefined general number registers

%	Current page number.
ct	Character type (set by *width* function).
dl	Width (maximum) of last completed diversion.
dn	Height (vertical size) of last completed diversion.
dw	Current day of the week (1–7).
dy	Current day of the month (1–31).
hp	Current horizontal place on *input* line.
ln	Output line number.
mo	Current month (1–12).
nl	Vertical position of last printed text base-line.
sb	Depth of string below base line (generated by *width* function).
st	Height of string above base line (generated by *width* function).
yr	Last two digits of current year.

Predefined read-only number registers

.$	Number of arguments available at the current macro level.
.A	Set to 1 in troff, if −a option used; always 1 in nroff.
.H	Available horizontal resolution in basic units.
.T	Set to 1 in nroff, if −T option used; always 0 in troff.
.V	Available vertical resolution in basic units.
.a	Post-line extra line-space most recently utilized using \x′N ′.
.c	Number of *lines* read from current input file.
.d	Current vertical place in current diversion; equal to **nl**, if no diversion.
.f	Current font as physical quadrant (1–4).
.h	Text base-line high-water mark on current page or diversion.
.i	Current indent.
.l	Current line length.
.n	Length of text portion on previous output line.
.o	Current page offset.
.p	Current page length.
.s	Current point size.
.t	Distance to the next trap.
.u	Equal to 1 in fill mode and 0 in nofill mode.
.v	Current vertical line spacing.
.w	Width of previous character.
.x	Reserved version-dependent register.
.y	Reserved version-dependent register.
.z	Name of current diversion.

Special characters

'	´		μ	\(*m		≈	\(~=
'	`		ν	\(*n		~	\(ap
—	\(em		ξ	\(*c		≠	\(!=
-	–		ο	\(*o		→	\(->
-	\(hy		π	\(*p		←	\(<-
–	\-		ρ	\(*r		↑	\(ua
•	\(bu		σ	\(*s		↓	\(da
□	\(sq		ς	\(ts		×	\(mu
_	\(ru		τ	\(*t		÷	\(di
¼	\(14		υ	\(*u		±	\(+-
½	\(12		φ	\(*f		∪	\(cu
¾	\(34		χ	\(*x		∩	\(ca
fi	\(fi		ψ	\(*q		⊂	\(sb
fl	\(fl		ω	\(*w		⊃	\(sp
ff	\(ff		Α	\(*A		⊆	\(ib
ffi	\(Fi		Β	\(*B		⊇	\(ip
ffl	\(Fl		Γ	\(*G		∞	\(if
°	\(de		Δ	\(*D		∂	\(pd
†	\(dg		Ε	\(*E		∇	\(gr
´	\(fm		Ζ	\(*Z		¬	\(no
¢	\(ct		Η	\(*Y		∫	\(is
®	\(rg		Θ	\(*H		∝	\(pt
©	\(co		Ι	\(*I		∅	\(es
+	\(pl		Κ	\(*K		∈	\(mo
−	\(mi		Λ	\(*L		│	\(br
=	\(eq		Μ	\(*M		‡	\(dd
*	\(**		Ν	\(*N		⇒	\(rh
§	\(sc		Ξ	\(*C		⇐	\(lh
´	\(aa		Ο	\(*O		♥	\(bs
`	\(ga		Π	\(*P		│	\(or
	\(ul		Ρ	\(*R		○	\(ci
/	\(sl		Σ	\(*S		⌈	\(lt
α	\(*a		Τ	\(*T		⌊	\(lb
β	\(*b		Υ	\(*U		⌉	\(rt
γ	\(*g		Φ	\(*F		⌋	\(rb
δ	\(*d		Χ	\(*X		{	\(lk
ε	\(*e		Ψ	\(*Q		}	\(rk
ζ	\(*z		Ω	\(*W		│	\(bv
η	\(*y		√	\(sr		⌊	\(lf
θ	\(*h			\(rn		⌋	\(rf
ι	\(*i		≥	\(>=		⌈	\(lc
κ	\(*k		≤	\(<=		⌉	\(rc
λ	\(*l		≡	\(==			

Appendix 8 vi **Requests**

Simple requests

^D	Scroll the window forwards.
^U	Scroll the window backwards.
^F	Move forward a page.
^B	Move backward a page.
return	Move the cursor down.
—	Move the cursor up.
space	Move the cursor right.
backspace	Move the cursor left.
dd	Delete the current line.
i	Insert text before the current character.
o	Insert text after the current line.
p	Put back deleted or yanked text.
x	Delete the current character.
Y	Yank lines into a buffer.
:w *file*	Write out the changes to *file*.
:q	Quit. :q! bypasses checking.
del	Abandon the current request.

Screen and cursor control

H	Move cursor to the home (first) line of the screen.
L	Move cursor to the last line of the screen.
M	Move cursor to the middle of the screen.
hjkl	Move the cursor left, down, up or right respectively.
wbe	Move the cursor forward, back, or to the end of a word.
/.../	Search forwards for the pattern ....
?...?	Search backwards for the pattern ....
z.	Center the screen at the current line.
z cr	Redraw the screen at the current line; cr denotes return.
z *n*.	Use an *n* line window centered on the screen.
%	Move to the next or previous balanced (,), {, or }.
^E	Display one more line at the bottom of the screen.
^L	Redraw the screen.
^Y	Display one more line at the top of the screen.
0	Move the cursor to the start of the line.

Editing requests

A...	Append to the end of the current line (ends with esc).
C...	Change the rest of the line (ends with esc).
D	Delete the rest of the line.
I...	Insert at the beginning of the current line (ends with esc).
J	Join the current line and the next line.
X	Delete the character before the cursor.
cw...	Change the current word (ends with esc).
rx	Replace the current character with x.
~	Change the case (upper/lower) of the current character.
&	Repeat the last :s request.

Using ed requests

ed requests may be used from vi by preceding them with a : .

:sh	Execute a shell.
:!cmd	Execute cmd and return to vi.
:r file	Read file.
:s...	Substitute one string for another.
:g...	Globally search for a string.

Objects

Objects are specified as follows:

c	A single character.
w	The next alphanumeric word.
W	The next non-blank word.
H	The home line (top) of the screen. 3H is 3 lines from the top of the screen.
G	The end of the document.
L	The last line on the screen. 3L is 3 lines from the bottom of the screen.
/.../	The next line containing the pattern ....
)	The end of the current sentence. A sentence ends with a blank line, or one of the characters . ! ? followed by a blank line or two spaces.
(	The start of the current sentence.
}	The end of the current paragraph. A paragraph is defined as ending with a blank line or one of the nroff requests .bp, .IP, .LP, .PP, .QP, .LI, or .P.
{	The start of the current paragraph.
]]	The end of the current section; defined as ending with one of the nroff macros .NH, .SH, .HU, or .H
[[	The start of the current section.

The following requests take one of the objects listed above:

cx...	Change up to and including x with material terminated by an esc.
dx	Delete up to and including x.
yx	Yank the object x for use by a subsequent p or P request.

>*x*   Indent by 8 spaces up to and including the line containing *x*.

<*x*   Remove an indent of 8 spaces up to and including the line containing *x*.

!*x cmd*   The text of the object specified is passed as the standard input to cmd. The command is executed and its standard output replaces the object text.

Counts

A number preceding a request is a repeat count with the following exceptions.

new window size	[[	]]	:	/	?	
scroll amount	^D	^U				
line or column number	z	G	|			

Setting options

Each option has a name and is set by one of the forms

:set *option-name*

:set *option-name* = *value*

and is unset by

:set no *option-name*

The options are described below with the abbreviation, if any, in parentheses.

autoindent(ai)	Supply program indentation automatically.
autowrite(aw)	Automatic write before :n and ! .
ignorecase(ic)	Ignore upper/lower case when searching.
list	Tabs print as ^I.
number(nu)	Lines are displayed prefixed by numbers.
paragraphs(para)	The names of nroff macros that start paragraphs for the } and { requests. Initially set to IPLPPPQPbpP LI.
redraw(re)	Simulate a smart terminal.
sections(sect)	The name of macros that start sections for the [[and]] requests. Initially set to NHSHH HU.
term	The name of the terminal type being used.

Appendix 9   A Macro Library

```
. .                     \" The macro library described in chapter 7 .
. .
. .                     \" The first few requests set registers and traps
                        \" for general use .   Later requests are grouped by
. .                     \" function and are described in section 7 . 1 . 4 .
. .                     \" ===============================
. .
. .                     \" default ligatures
. .
. lg 0
. .                     \" double spacing for nroff or drafts
. if n . ls 2
. .                     \" vertical line spacing – publisher's style
. ps 10
. vs 12p
. .                     \" line and title lengths
. ll 4 . 65i
. lt 4 . 65i
. .                     \" rs register for current indentation
. nr rs 0
. in \n(rs
. .                     \" pd register for inter–paragraph vertical gap
. if n . nr pd 1
. if t . nr pd . 4
. .                     \" register hl for half line spacing
. if n . nr hl 1v
. if t . nr hl . 5v
. .                     \" register sd for section heading line spacing flag
. nr sd 1
. .                     \" ip register for indented paragraphs
. nr ip 2
. .                     \" fn register for figure numbering
. nr fn 0 1
. .                     \" set traps for page top and bottom
. .                     \" =======================
. .
. .                     \" top of page trap
. wh 0 aa
. .                     \" end of page trap
. if n . wh –5 zz
. if t . wh 9i zz
```

```
. .                     \" top of page macro
. de aa
. ev 1
. lt 7i
. tl ´——´´——´
. ll 4 . 65i
. lt 4 . 65i
´sp 5
. ps 8
. ft R
. if e . tl ´%\h´2m´The UNIX System´´\\*(sh´
. if o . tl ´\\*(sh´´\\*(ct\h´2m´%´
. ev
´sp
. mk
. .
. .                     \" end of page macro
. de zz
´sp
. tl ´´\\*(pn´´
\\. ds pn
´bp
. .
. .                     \" set end of file macro
. em ee
. .                     \" end of file macro
. de ee
. af % 1
. tm LAST \\n%
. .
. .                     \" two column output for index
. de 2c
. ie \\n(sw \{
. nr sw 0
. in 0
. bp
. ns \}
. el \{
. nr sw 1
. rt
. in | 3i \}
. .
. .
. .                     \" The requests seen by a user of the library follow
. .                     \" ==============================
. .
. de CH              \" chapter heading  . CH 1 "Introduction"
. }H "Chapter \\$1" "\\$2"
```

```
\\ . ds sh \\$1
. .
. de AH            \" appendix heading        . AH 1 "Commands"
.}H "Appendix \\$1" "\\$2"
. .
. de }H           \" internal macro for chapter and appendix headings
. tm ======== .}H "\\$1" "\\$2" \\n%
. sp 7
\\ . ds cf \\$1
\\ . ds ct \\$2
\\ . ds pn \\n%
. ft H
. ps 24
. sp 24p
. ce 2
\\$1
. sp 2
\\$2
. sp 4
. ft
. ps
. mk
. .
. de SH           \" section heading  . SH 1 . 1 "History"
. tm ======== . SH "\\$1" "\\$2" \\n%
. if n  . sp 2
\\ . ds sh \\$1
. if t  . sp 15p
. ne 2
. ps +2
. ft HB
. in \\n(rs
\\$1\\ \\ \\$2
. ps −2
. ft R
. if n  . sp
. if t  . sp 6p
. NS
. .
. de SS           \" sub section      . SS 6 . 2 . 1 "Command names"
. tm ======== . SS "\\$1" "\\$2" \\n%
. sp \\n(sd
\\ . ds sh \\$1
. ne 3
. ft HB
. in \\n(rs
\\$1\\ \\ \\$2
. ft R
```

```
. sp 3p
. NS
. .
. de MS            \" minor section       . MS "Use of backslash"
. sp \\n(sd
. ne 2
. ft HI
. in \\n(rs
\\$1
. ft R
. sp 3p
. NS
. .
. de NS            \" turn off line space after heading
. it 1 on          \" turn on line spacing unless another heading
. nr sd 0
. .
. de on
. nr sd 1
. .
. de LP            \" blocked paragraph start    . LP
. sp \\n(pd
. in \\n(rs
. ta 2m
. .
. de PP            \" normal paragraph start     . PP
. LP
. ti +2m
. .
. .               \"                                          . IP "(a)" 12
. de IP            \" indented paragraph with hanging text
. MP "\\fR\\$1\\fP" "\\$2"
. .
. de BU            \" bulletted paragraph        . BU
. MP "\\fR\(bu\\fP" "4"
. .
. .               \"                                          . MP "main( )" 12
. de MP            \" indented para with hanging program text
. sp \\n(pd
. ie \\$2 . nr xi \\$2−\\n(ip
. el . nr xi 4
. in \\n(rs+\\n(xi+\\n(ip
. ta \\n(xi
. ti −\\n(xi
. ft H
\&\\$1\t\c
\. if \\w´\\$1´u−\\n(xim . br
. ft R
```

```
. .
. de XV
. nr hl + . 1v

. .
. de VX
. nr hl − . 1v

. .
. de HL            \" half line spacing  . HL
. sp \\n(hlu
. .

. .
. .                \" Displays and blocked program text
. .                \" =====================
. .
. de DS            \" display start            . DS
'in +2m
'ta 4m 8m 12m 16m 20m 24m 28m 32m
. HL
'nf
'ne \\$1

. .
. de DE            \" end display              . DE
. HL
. fi
. in −2m
. ft R

. .
. de TS            \" tbl start                . TS
. HL
. DS

. .
. de TE            \" tbl end         . TE
. DE
. HL

. .
. de EX            \" start of example  . EX 24
. ft H
. fl
. ss 20
'DS \\$1

. .
. de XE            \" end example              . XE
. DE
. ss 12
. ft R

. .
. de RS            \" relative section start   . RS
. nr rs +2
```

```
. .
. de RE          \" relative section end      . RE
. nr rs −2
. .
. de RU          \" horizontal rule           . RU
. br
\l´4 . 65i−4´
. .
. de FX          \" figure in the text  . FX 24
´EX \\$1
´RU
. .
. de XF          \" end of figure in text     . XF
´RU
. XE
. .
. de FG          \" inclusion of figure       . FG lock . c 13
. FX \\$2
. so figs/\\$1
. XF
. .
. de FC          \" caption of a figure       . FC 6 . 3 "Create a lock file"
. ft B
. ce
Figure \\$1\ \ \\$2
. ft R
. sp
. NS
. .
. de CN          \" command text              . CN "ls"
\&\fH\\$1\fR
. .
. de DN          \" definition in text        . DN "mode"
\&\fI\\$1\fR
. .
. de SN          \" symbol (character) name in text     . SN "NEWLINE"
\&\fH\\$1\fR
. .
. de HI          \" sub section heading font   . HI "heading"
\&\f(HI\\$1\fP
. .
. de IX          \" index macro
. tm \\$1 \\$2 \\$3 \\$4 \\$5 \\$6 \\$7    \\n%
. .
. de CX          \" commutative index
. IX "\\$1," "\\$2"
. IX "\\$2," "\\$1"
. .
```

```
. .                       \" String definitions
. .                       \" ==========
. if \n(mo-0 . ds MO January
. if \n(mo-1 . ds MO February
. if \n(mo-2 . ds MO March
. if \n(mo-3 . ds MO April
. if \n(mo-4 . ds MO May
. if \n(mo-5 . ds MO June
. if \n(mo-6 . ds MO July
. if \n(mo-7 . ds MO August
. if \n(mo-8 . ds MO September
. if \n(mo-9 . ds MO October
. if \n(mo-10 . ds MO November
. if \n(mo-11 . ds MO December
. .                                   \" D        .
. ds D \& .
. .                                   \" DD       . .
. ds DD . \| .
. .                                   \" ZZ       . . .
. ds ZZ \& . \| . \| .
. .                                   \" ST       *
. ds ST \s+1\(**\s-1
. .                                   \" VT       |
. ds VT \ | \(or\ |
. .                                   \" AP       ≫
. ds AP >\h´- . 2m´>
. .                                   \" HE       ≪
. ds HE <\h´- . 2m´<
. .                                   \" TW       ~
. ds TW \v´ . 6m´\s+4~\s0\v´- . 6m´
. .                                   \" CT       ^
. ds CT \v´ . 6m´\s+4^\s0\v´- . 6m´
. .                                   \" AT       @
. ds AT \v´- . 2m´@\v´ . 2m´
. .                                   \" T        circled T for tab
. .
. ds T \ | \h´ . 5n´\v´- . 2n´\s7\zT\s0\s12\v´ . 2n´\h´- . 5n´\(ci\ | \s0
. .
. .                                   \" subscripts
. ds 0 \v´ . 25m´\s-40\s0\v´- . 25m´
. ds 1 \v´ . 25m´\s-41\s0\v´- . 25m´
. ds 2 \v´ . 25m´\s-42\s0\v´- . 25m´
. ds 3 \v´ . 25m´\s-43\s0\v´- . 25m´
. ds n \v´ . 25m´\s-4n\s0\v´- . 25m´
```

Appendix 10 The ASCII Character Set

Octal values							
000 nul	001 soh	002 stx	003 etx	004 eot	005 enq	006 ack	007 bel
010 bs	011 ht	012 nl	013 vt	014 np	015 cr	016 so	017 si
020 dle	021 dc1	022 dc2	023 dc3	024 dc4	025 nak	026 syn	027 etb
030 can	031 em	032 sub	033 esc	034 fs	035 gs	036 rs	037 us
040 sp	041 !	042 "	043 #	044 $	045 %	046 &	047 ´
050 (	051)	052 *	053 +	054 ,	055 –	056 .	057 /
060 0	061 1	062 2	063 3	064 4	065 5	066 6	067 7
070 8	071 9	072 :	073 ;	074 <	075 =	076 >	077 ?
100 @	101 A	102 B	103 C	104 D	105 E	106 F	107 G
110 H	111 I	112 J	113 K	114 L	115 M	116 N	117 O
120 P	121 Q	122 R	123 S	124 T	125 U	126 V	127 W
130 X	131 Y	132 Z	133 [	134	135]	136 ^	137 _
140 `	141 a	142 b	143 c	144 d	145 e	146 f	147 g
150 h	151 i	152 j	153 k	154 l	155 m	156 n	157 o
160 p	161 q	162 r	163 s	164 t	165 u	166 v	167 w
170 x	171 y	172 z	173 {	174		175 }	176 ~	177 del

Hexadecimal							
00 nul	01 soh	02 stx	03 etx	04 eot	05 enq	06 ack	07 bel
08 bs	09 ht	0a nl	0b vt	0c np	0d cr	0e so	0f si
10 dle	11 dc1	12 dc2	13 dc3	14 dc4	15 nak	16 syn	17 etb
18 can	19 em	1a sub	1b esc	1c fs	1d gs	1e rs	1f us
20 sp	21 !	22 "	23 #	24 $	25 %	26 &	27 ´
28 (	29)	2a *	2b +	2c ,	2d –	2e .	2f /
30 0	31 1	32 2	33 3	34 4	35 5	36 6	37 7
38 8	39 9	3a :	3b ;	3c <	3d =	3e >	3f ?
40 @	41 A	42 B	43 C	44 D	45 E	46 F	47 G
48 H	49 I	4a J	4b K	4c L	4d M	4e N	4f O
50 P	51 Q	52 R	53 S	54 T	55 U	56 V	57 W
58 X	59 Y	5a Z	5b [	5c	5d]	5e ^	5f _
60 `	61 a	62 b	63 c	64 d	65 e	66 f	67 g
68 h	69 i	6a j	6b k	6c l	6d m	6e n	6f o
70 p	71 q	72 r	73 s	74 t	75 u	76 v	77 w
78 x	79 y	7a z	7b {	7c		7d }	7e ~	7f del

Bibliography

Aho, A. V., Ullman, J. D. 1977. *Principles of Compiler Design.* Addison Wesley: Reading, Mass.

Book, R. V. (Ed.). 1980. *Formal Language Theory. Perspectives and Open Problems.* 325-44. Academic Press: New York.

Bourne, S. R. 1978. "UNIX Time-Sharing System: The UNIX Shell". *Bell Sys. Tech. J.* **57(6)** 1971-90.

Crisman, P. A. (Ed.). 1965. *The Compatible Time-Sharing System.* M.I.T. Press: Cambridge, Mass.

Deutsch, L. P., Lampson, B. W. 1965. *SDS$_n$ 930 time-sharing system preliminary reference manual.* Doc. 30.10.10, Project GENIE$_n$. Univ. Cal. at Berkeley.

Deutsch, L. P., Lampson, B. W. 1967. "An online editor," *Comm. Assoc. Comp. Mach.* **10(12)**, 793-9, 803.

Dolotta, T. A., Mashey, J. R. 1976. "An Introduction to the Programmer's Workbench," *Proc. 2nd Int. Conf. on Software Engineering.* 164-8.

Dolotta, T. A., Haight, R. C., Mashey, J. R. 1978. "UNIX Time-Sharing System: The Programmer's Workbench," *Bell Sys. Tech. J.* **57(6)** 2177-2200.

Feiertag, R. J., Organick, E. I. 1971. "The Multics input-output system" *Proc. Third Symposium on Operating Systems Principles.* 35-41.

Hartley, D. F. (Ed.). 1968. *The Cambridge Multiple Access System – Users Reference Manual.* University Mathematical Laboratory: Cambridge, England.

Johnson, S. C. 1975. "Yacc — Yet Another Compiler-Compiler. Comp. Sci. Tech. Rep. No. 32." Bell Laboratories: Murray Hill, New Jersey.

Johnson, S. C. 1978. "Lint, a C Program Checker. Comp. Sci. Tech. Rep. No. 65." Bell Laboratories: Murray Hill, New Jersey.

Johnson, S. C., Ritchie, D. M. 1978. "UNIX Time-Sharing System: Portability of C Programs and the UNIX System," *Bell Sys. Tech. J.* **57(6)** 2021-2048.

Kernighan, B. W., Cherry, L. L. 1977. "A System for Typesetting Mathematics," *Comm. Assoc. Comp. Mach.* **18** 151-7

Kernighan, B. W., Ritchie, D. M. 1978. *The C Programming Language.* Prentice-Hall: Englewood Cliffs, New Jersey.

Kernighan, B. W., Lesk, M. E., Ossanna, J. F. 1978. "UNIX Time-Sharing System: Document Preparation," *Bell Sys. Tech. J.* **57(6)** 2115-35.

Kevorkian, D. E. (Ed.). 1985. *System V Interface Definition.* AT&T Technologies.

Lesk, M. E. 1975. "Lex — A Lexical Analyzer Generator. Comp. Sci. Tech. Rep. No. 39." Bell Laboratories: Murray Hill, New Jersey.

Lesk, M. E. 1977. "Typing Documents on UNIX and GCOS: The –ms Macros for Troff." Bell Laboratories: Murray Hill, New Jersey.

Lycklama, H., 1978. "UNIX Time-Sharing System: UNIX on a Microprocessor," *Bell Sys. Tech. J.* **57(6)** 2087-2101.

McMahon, L. E., Cherry, L. L., Morris, R. 1978. "UNIX Time-Sharing System: Statistical Text Processing," *Bell Sys. Tech. J.* **57(6)** 2137-54.

Ossanna, J. F. 1976. "NROFF/TROFF User's Manual. Comp. Sci. Tech. Rep. No. 54." Bell Laboratories: Murray Hill, New Jersey.

Richards, M. 1969. "BCPL: A Tool for Compiler Writing and Systems Programming," *Proc. AFIPS SJCC.* **34**

Ritchie, D. M., Johnson, S. C., Lesk, M. E., Kernighan, B. W. 1978. "UNIX Time-Sharing System: The C Programming Language," *Bell Sys. Tech. J.* **57(6)**, 1991-2019

Ritchie, D. M. 1978. "UNIX Time-Sharing System: A Retrospective," *Bell Sys. Tech. J.* **57(6)** 1947-69.

Ritchie, D. M., Thompson, K. 1978. "The UNIX Time-Sharing System," *Bell Sys. Tech. J.* **57(6)** 1905-29.

Ritchie, D. M. 1980. *The Evolution of the Unix Time-sharing System.* Language Design and Programming Methodology: Lecture Notes in Computer Science 79, 25-35, Springer-Verlag: New York.

Thompson, K. 1975. *The UNIX Command Language. Structured Programming—Infotech State of the Art Report* 375-384. Nicholson House, Maidenhead, Berkshire, England: Infotech International Ltd.

Thompson, K., Ritchie, D. M. 1975. *UNIX Programmer's Manual. Sixth Edition.* Bell Laboratories: Murray Hill, New Jersey.

Thompson, K. 1978. "UNIX Time-Sharing System: UNIX Implementation," *Bell Sys. Tech. J.* **57(6)** 1931-46.

Thompson, K., Ritchie, D. M. 1978. *UNIX Programmer's Manual. Seventh Edition.* Bell Laboratories: Murray Hill, New Jersey.

UNIX System V Programming Guide, Release 2.0. April 1984. AT&T Technologies.

UNIX System V Support Tools Guide, Release 2.0. April 1984. AT&T Technologies.

UNIX System V Programmer Reference Manual DEC Processors, Release 2.0. April 1984. AT&T Technologies.

Index